BUGLES AND
A TIGER

Also by John Masters

THE ROAD PAST MANDALAY

BUGLES AND A TIGER

My Life in the Gurkhas

JOHN MASTERS

WEIDENFELD & NICOLSON

A W&N PAPERBACK

First published in 1956
by Michael Joseph
This paperback edition published in 2002
by Weidenfeld & Nicolson,
an imprint of Orion Books Ltd,
Carmelite House, 50 Victoria Embankment,
London EC4Y 0DZ

An Hachette UK company

3 5 7 9 10 8 6 4

Reissued 2012

Copyright © The Estate of John Masters 1956

British Library Cataloguing-in-Publication Data.
A catalogue record for this book is available
from the British Library.

ISBN 978-0-3043-6156-4

Printed and bound in by CPI Group (UK) Ltd,
Croydon, CR0 4YY

The Orion Publishing Group's policy is to use papers
that are natural, renewable and recyclable products and
made from wood grown in sustainable forests. The logging
and manufacturing processes are expected to conform to
the environmental regulations of the country of origin.

www.orionbooks.co.uk

DEDICATION

. . . my thoughts return to you who were my comrades, the stubborn and indomitable peasants of Nepal. Once more I hear the laughter with which you greeted every hardship. Once more I see you in your bivouacs or about your camp fires, on forced march or in the trenches, now shivering with wet and cold, now scorched by a pitiless and burning sun. Uncomplaining you endure hunger and thirst and wounds; and at the last your unwavering lines disappear into the smoke and wrath of battle. Bravest of the brave, most generous of the generous . . .

From the Foreword to *A Comparative and Etymological Dictionary of the Nepali Language* by R. L. Turner

FOREWORD

This is a factual story, but not a history. Please do not
pounce on me with scorn if it turns out there were seven,
not eight, platoons of Tochi Scouts on the Iblanke that
night of May 11th–12th, 1937. For the purpose of this
book, it does not matter. That purpose is to tell the story
of how a schoolboy became a professional soldier of the old
Indian Army. This is also the tale of a race against time,
for the Second World War is beginning as this story ends.

In the course of the story I hope to have given an idea of
what India was like in those last twilit days of the Indian
Empire, and something more than a tourist's view of some
of the people who lived there.

The drawings at the beginnings of the chapters, by Lieutenant-Colonel C. G. Borrowman, are reproduced from *A History of the 4th Prince of Wales's Own Gurkha Rifles* by permission of the Trustees of the 4th Gurkha Rifles Private Fund.

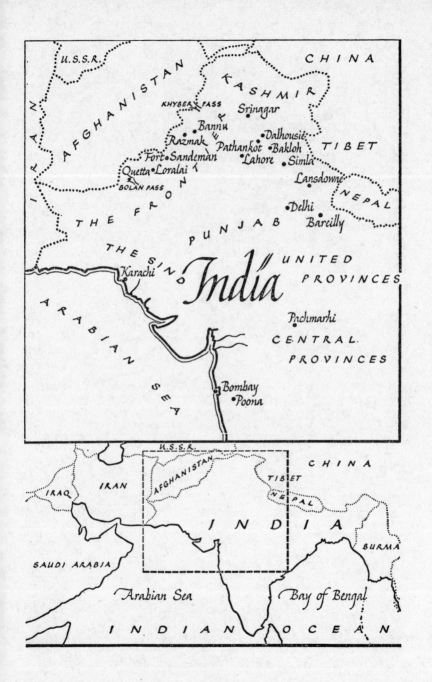

CHAPTER ONE

AT five o'clock on February 24th, 1935, snow was falling in thick flurries. The snow blew gustily across the middle air so that I could not always see the men and horses and mules and guns tramping into the hollow eight hundred feet below. Nor could they see me.

Now if the Pathan tribesmen of this part of the North-West Frontier of India decided to attack our little hill-top, their running knifemen could be in among us and out again before I could get a message down to the howitzers and machine-guns that stood ready to support me. The gunners down there were nearly as cold and miserable as I was. On the way up I had passed them, hunched round their guns, blowing on their fingernails and cursing steadily. The barrels pointed just to right, left, and over my position.

In the thick holly-oak scrub on my hill-top I could hardly see the men of my platoon either. We had levered big stones out of the soil with frozen hands, and built a *sangar*, a circular chest-high bullet-proof wall. We had cut tough and spiny branches with bayonets and cleared a field of vision. Conditions might have been worse, but I don't know how.

My father had told me about the Frontier, and I had expected this winter cold and sleet. So had some of the soldiers, but I could almost feel around me the peevish disillusionment of the younger men. Their Hollywood-inspired visions of Maharajahs, snake-charmers, and sinuous dancers had long faded, but they still had an ineradicable feeling that India ought to be hot—ceaselessly, blindingly hot. Private Welman picked up a handful of snow and stared at it resentfully. It was real; the temperature was eighteen degrees above zero.

In the morning it had been fine but cloudy. The sun shone between light showers, the air felt unnaturally balmy for our height of six thousand feet above sea level, and the soldiers sang as they marched along the hard road. When we turned right up the Sre Mela Valley the showers became heavier, colder, and more frequent. Soon we were soaked through everything we wore—dark brown woollen shirts under coarse jerseys, knee-length shorts of khaki drill, long, footless stockings called hosetops, woollen socks, short puttees, nailed boots. In the infantry we did not wear raincoats or capes because they make it difficult to handle weapons, and in Waziristan men who were not always and instantly ready to fight for their lives were unlikely to reach old age.

About two o'clock the rain changed to a merciless sleet; a bitter north wind drove up the valley, and our clothes froze on us into wet boards. It began to snow.

I had found this bad enough, but still not actually intolerable. When a man is expending physical energy in moving, when he is just twenty, when the lonely stars of a second lieutenant still feel warm on his shoulders, any discomfort but the worst seems trivial.

But now, on our hill, we had it—the very worst. When I had forded the bleak Sre Mela torrent for the fifteenth and last time and stepped out at the head of my platoon into the hollow where the brigade was going to camp, I had said to myself, 'Here we are at last.' All our minds were one, all wrapped luxuriously in the same dreams—dry clothes, a fire, food, hot drinks. But my company commander was waiting there at the far bank of the stream. He had ordered me to take the platoon at once up to the peak he pointed out, build a *sangar*, clear the scrub, and guard the hill-top till relieved. He did not know when that would be.

The evening advanced; the wind slashed deeper. One officer, one sergeant, three corporals, four lance-corporals and sixteen private soldiers of No. 7 Platoon, B Company, 1st Battalion, the Duke of Cornwall's Light Infantry grew more paralysed with misery. The soldiers did not talk much. We had had nothing to eat since an early breakfast, and I had forbidden them to touch their emergency rations in case we had to stay up there all night. Gnawing hunger blended now with frozen clothes, aching hands, and stabbing winds to form the very pattern of utter dejection.

Private Welman, a small man with a battered face, muttered, 'I feels like ten men . . .'

The cold had deranged my sense of humour. I turned to snap at him to be quiet. He went on with a broad and snow-swept smile. 'Yessir! Nine dead and one in 'ospital.'

There was no sunset, but as the greyness darkened to blackness the relieving platoon struggled up the steep hill. I hurriedly explained the position to its commander—the arcs of fire, the danger spots, all dim in the driving snow—and quickly took my men down the hill into camp. There was some relief now. At least I could thank God that it was not we who were to spend the night unsheltered on that dreadful summit.

In the hollow the constant movement of men and animals had churned the ground into mud six to twelve inches deep. The brigade was travelling light. There were few tents, and those only for special purposes such as hospitals, cookhouses, and messes. Many mules had stumbled in the fords, and most of the greatcoats and blankets were cold and soggy. But we were infantrymen, after all, and somehow we had lit fires, and all about the sparks towered up against the falling snow. As we officers finished seeing to our companies and platoons, we gathered round the leaping blaze outside

13

the mess tent. My spare set of clothes was in my pack and fairly dry. Garment by garment, I stripped naked in the snow, the wet greatcoat draped over my shoulders, and put on the dry clothes, and then stood in front of the fire to toast the wet ones. Clouds of steam rose, and the smell of burning as some impatient officer burned a hole in his trousers or shirt. Moderately warm and dry at last, we crowded into the mess tent, huddled round the rickety ridge-pole, and waited like so many starving rooks for food.

When an Indian cook, a *khansamah*, is given modern equipment, comfort, and an ordered routine of meals, his performance varies from good to poisonous. But set him down in a howling wilderness of rock and thorn, in the open, hunched over a tiny fire built between two stones, with rain or snow falling, and he comes up with a miracle as surprising as, and far more satisfying than, the rope trick.

It was so this night. After a bowl of hot corned-beef stew followed by suet pudding and treacle, I felt almost human again and went paddling out to find my bed. The thin beam of my flashlight shone on mud and snow and more mud—and, spread out there in the middle of nothingness, one shiny wet groundsheet, one sopping blanket. That was it—my bed. After a long look and a hard try, I decided I could not face it and went off to find someone ready to talk all night.

A small fire hissed in the snow twenty yards off, and by its light I saw the lean and perky little company sergeant-major sitting on an ammunition box. Files of men shuffled past in silhouette between the fire and me; each man paused, held out a mug, lifted it, jerked his head, shuffled on. The sergeant-major was issuing the rum ration. I went over to join him. He had plenty of service. He knew everything. He muttered, 'Lot of men in this company are teetotallers. Had a talk with the brigade supply sergeant, pal of mine. Won some extra bottles.' He took a swig from the jorum of red-hot sweet cocoa beside him and offered me his mug.

The last of the company filed away, smacking their lips.

The sergeant-major said, 'See those last four men? This is their third time round. Now it's our turn.' He invited me to share his ammunition box.

The snow piled more thickly on the ludicrous sola topis we both wore—because we were in that very hot country, India. Rum, cocoa, and anecdotes passed from the sergeant-major to me to the quartermaster-sergeant, who had come to join us. I told them about the Royal Military College; the sergeant-major told us about Chelsea, where his home was. Officers, N.C.O.s, and soldiers passed, the hours passed, and suddenly there was no more rum.

I went back to my 'bed.' It looked very cosy now. Like every other soldier there that night, I lay down fully dressed —boots, socks, greatcoat, and all—on a groundsheet in the mud, rolled myself into a wet blanket, my nose sticking out of a woollen balaclava hat, and went to sleep. In the morning I awoke with clean new snow inches thick on my blanket and had to scrabble about in the snow to find my topi.

I had little idea at that time why we were all there on the edge of the Sham Plain in central Waziristan. A 'column' had been ordered, and off we went, half fearing and half hoping that someone would shoot at us. Doubtless the general knew why a column had to go to the Sham Plain, but he had not told me. Doubtless someone knew why the tall, loosely knit men of these hills, the Pathans, were said to be always eager to shoot at us but I did not. I was a new, shiny, but altogether insignificant cog in an enormously mysterious machine called the Government of India. The machine was churning up a barren piece of earth in a snowstorm. I was not comfortable.

But there was a purpose behind our exercise, and I decided to find out what it was. I'd never become a good officer if I just lived in the present and obeyed orders. As my life was to revolve around the Frontier for the next five years, I had better describe it and tell you something of what I now began to learn.

As the conquering British, more than a hundred years

ago, moved diagonally north-westward across India from their original trading-posts in Surat, Calcutta, and Madras, they eventually reached the mountains that separate the sub-continent from Afghanistan. These mountains extend four hundred miles from the Khyber Pass in the north to the Bolan Pass in the deserts of Baluchistan to the south. They are raw and bare, and a proudly independent people live in them. These people, Semitic in origin, Moslem in religion, Pushtu in speech, are the Pathans. (The name is pronounced 'P'tahn,' except by British soldiers, who use 'Paythan.')

The Pathans, subdivided into various tribes, live astride the Indo-Afghan border, which runs roughly down the middle of the mountain chain. Not only do different members of the same tribe live on opposite sides of the international boundary, but the same family or sub-tribe may own winter fields on the Indian side and summer grazing on the Afghan side. In all historical time the Pathans have kept themselves alive by a combination of nomad life, half-hearted tillage of the barren earth, armed raids into the settled farmlands of the plains, and levying tolls on the commercial traffic that must use the few routes through their hills. The principal routes are via the Kabul River, the Khyber Pass, the Kurram River, the Tochi River, the Gomal River, and the Bolan Pass.

Well armed, owning no king or central authority, loosely organized into soviets of tribes, sub-tribes, and families, fanatically adhering to the Moslem law, addicted to blood feuds and vendettas, the Pathans gave the oncoming British serious pause. And in addition the Indian and Afghan Governments could not for a long time agree on the inter-national boundary and thus make it possible even to define responsibilities.

There seemed to be two possible solutions to this night-mare problem. The Government of India could push its powers right up to some putative boundary, disarm the tribesmen on its own side, and introduce full-scale admini-stration as it was known throughout the rest of India—the law, the lawyers, the taxes, the police, and the rest, all entirely alien to Pathan tradition and spirit.

This solution would have left the tribesmen on the Indian side of the boundary at the mercy of their still armed cousins across the Afghan border; the Afghan Government has not for centuries been strong enough to disarm its tribes even if it wanted to. The Government of India would thus have had to keep a large army in this inhospitable border country, first to keep order among its Pathans and, second, to protect those same Pathans against the Afghans. The task of disarming the tribes might have cost about twenty thousand lives and taken ten years of all-out campaigning.

The second possible solution was for the Government of India to wash its hands of the whole area, retire to the settled agricultural line of the River Indus, and let the tribesmen rule themselves according to their old traditions. But the tribes could not exist without their periodic raids into the farmlands, so this solution would have led, again, to a large standing army and annual punitive operations. It would also have left in the unreliable hands of the tribes those few and vital passes through which 'A Foreign Power' —which meant Russia—must advance if it was to attack India.

Since the Government of India was, until 1947, entirely controlled by the British it is hardly necessary to say that a third or compromise solution was adopted. The Government actually administered the country as far as a line known as the Administrative Border. West of this, in a belt varying from ten to a hundred miles in width, was Tribal Territory. Here the Pathans could govern themselves as they pleased, provided they did not raid into Afghanistan or into the settled Indian districts.

To enable punishment to be meted out quickly if the Pathans broke the rules, and to hold the strategic passes, the Government built forts and stationed soldiers at a few places of particular importance inside Tribal Territory. It also built roads linking the forts and decreed that *Pax Britannica* should apply on the roads and for a hundred yards on each side of them. A man with a blood feud on his head would build a tunnel from his house to the road so that he could take the air there in safety under the eyes of his armed enemy, and when he had had enough fresh air he would crawl back down the tunnel to his fortress-house.

Finally, the glint of steel was tactfully hidden behind the glitter of gold. The Government gave the tribal heads large annual allowances, but these could be withheld at the discretion of the resident British political officers, and were dependent on the good behaviour of the tribe.

The Government also tried to remove the conditions that made the Pathan such an awkward element in the Indian pattern. Its efforts never met with much success. Consent is part of democracy, and it was neither easy nor, perhaps, right to force the Pathans to attend school, give up vendettas, and become peaceful farmers, when the old bloodthirsty ways constituted for them life, liberty, and the pursuit of happiness. The Pathans preferred to keep to the ancient traditions and take the consequences; that is, to be left in peace—to fight.

Razmak, whence we had marched out on this column a few days earlier, was the largest of the garrisons in Tribal Territory. Here, on a plateau six thousand five hundred feet above sea level, secluded behind a triple circle of barbed wire and arc lights, had sprung up an unnatural town with a population of ten thousand men and three thousand mules. It bristled with guns, armoured cars, and all the panoply of war; but its inhabitants spent their time waiting for something to happen.

The political officers would have liked us to stay behind our barbed wire for ever. All Pathans are at all times in need of rifles and ammunition to carry on their private wars and blood feuds. The temptation to steal them from us was great, and the easiest way to get a soldier's rifle was to shoot the soldier when he was on training manoeuvres. On the other hand, the generals knew that the soldiers would go mad if they were cooped up for two years on end in this monastic wilderness. They therefore insisted that we be allowed to take periodic walks through the countryside to admire the views, smell the rare flowers, and keep fit.

Another compromise was reached. Once every two or three months the politicals thought hard, and went on thinking until they had thought of a headman whom they suspected of intrigue or harbouring outlaws or hatching embarrassments to the Afghan Government, and in whose back yard a display of force might therefore be salutary. Then we got ready. Leaving two of its six battalions in Razmak to guard the fort, the brigade gathered its guns and paraphernalia and marched out of the main gate to spend a week or ten days stamping noisily around in the suspected headman's section of country. Then it marched home again. This excursion was called a column because it usually was just that—a double string of men and animals defiling down the narrow valleys and stony passes.

In reasonable weather columns were healthful and rather romantic. We burst out of imprisonment and rampaged up and down the mountains, playing at being scouts and soldiers, but there was always the sense-sharpening chance of a sudden storm of bullets, a rush of knifemen, a bloody hand-to-hand struggle. It was a game—but we never pulled the trigger on one another, as we would have done in similar mock battles in England, because here every weapon was loaded with ball.

At evening, the day's march done and the stone wall built, we sat, sweat-stained, around the cookers and smoked and drank strong tea. At night as we made our rounds of duty the stars gleamed on the bayonets of the silent sentries along the wall. At dawn we awoke to the shrill, sweet call of the mountain artillery trumpets blowing a long reveille. The call seemed to last a golden age while I huddled deeper into my blanket and embraced my returning senses.

At the time of this February column I had been with the Duke of Cornwall's Light Infantry for over four months. Two months before that I had been a cadet at Sandhurst. I was floundering about still, like a blind puppy, in a new life and a forgotten country, and was not at all used to being an

19

officer, though the days were past when I had stood help-lessly facing my first command, overcome with self-con-sciousness, while the amazed soldiers laughed openly at me. I had found that I could not open my mouth to give an order, not even 'Dismiss.' The soldiers said loudly to one another, 'Cor, look at 'im,' and, ' 'E's a funny-looking little officer, innee?' From behind the rear rank, Sergeant Broad-hurst snapped at them until they, secretly as embarrassed as I, fell silent. I pulled myself together at last, with an enormous effort of will, and gave the command 'Attention!' Then I told them what they didn't need telling—that I was very new. I asked them to help me not to make an ass of myself again, and dismissed them.

For a few hours after that I had longed to be on the staff instead of with a regiment. The staff dealt with paper and problems, not people—I thought. Paper would not laugh at me. Problems would not snicker at me. The platoon was a good one, though, and on the whole the men had nothing against me. I did not disgrace myself again in that way, and they never, by word or look, reminded me of the incident.

Sergeant Broadhurst, in particular, stood by me at an-other moment that still causes me the most acute shame whenever I look back on it. First parade—physical training —was ordered that day for seven a.m. When I arrived at a few minutes before seven, I found the platoon assembled and ready to go. It was cold, and in the ranks the men were shivering and dancing up and down to keep warm. I was only the second-in-command of the platoon at that time, under instruction from a senior lieutenant, who was the commander. Punctually at seven I said to Broadhurst, 'March off, Sergeant. To the aerodrome, at the double.'

Broadhurst asked doubtfully whether we hadn't better wait for the platoon commander, who had not turned up. Unversed in the ways of the army, I said, 'No, march off. The men are cold.' We doubled off.

Three or four minutes later the platoon commander, who had about fourteen years of service, appeared. He was in a towering rage. He rushed straight up to Broadhurst and asked him furiously what the bloody hell he meant by marching off without his, the lieutenant's, permission.

Broadhurst said, 'I'm sorry, sir.'

My feet wouldn't move. My mouth wouldn't open. I made a gigantic effort and said, 'Sir——' But the lieutenant had given Broadhurst a final blast and taken command. I looked at Broadhurst, but he was busy. After parade I apologized to him, but I never explained to the lieutenant. Broadhurst told me the incident wasn't worth worrying about.

Does this seem a small crime to remember all one's life? I don't think so. It was the worst thing that I ever did in the army, because in it I showed cowardice and disloyalty. The only excuses I could find for myself were that it happened quickly and that I was very young. It had a result, though. I had been frightened of the lieutenant, frightened of being reprimanded, frightened of failure even in the smallest endeavour. I discovered now that being ashamed of yourself is worse than any fear. Duty, orders, loyalty, obedience—all things boiled down to one simple idea: whatever the consequences, a man must act so that he can live with himself.

But I can live with the memory of my first day in the awe-inspiring and gloomy splendour of an officers' mess. It was in Bareilly, and I was still nineteen. I sat down to tea at the polished table and cautiously admired a large fruit cake in front of me. After licking my lips for five minutes, I screwed up my courage and asked the captain next to me whether I might be allowed to have some cake. He turned, looked at me with an indescribable expression of scorn and astonishment, and said coldly, 'Yes. That's a mess cake. You're not at your prep school now.'

Christmas came. I had ceased to be nineteen, and on Christmas Day it was my turn to be orderly officer. On this day my duties included following the colonel, the second-in-command, and the adjutant round every mess hall in the battalion—seven of them—and, in each mess, drinking

21

toasts from half-tumblers of whisky thinly diluted with fizzy lemonade. The British soldiers, far from home and families, tried to forget their exile in a riot of snowballing, singing, and drinking. The sergeants waited on them at table.

After a couple of hours our bedraggled and hardly conscious convoy reached the officers' mess and sat down, without hunger, before an enormous Christmas dinner. The lieutenant at the head of the table suddenly remembered that this day was traditionally a topsy-turvy one for rank and discipline. He picked a leg of turkey off his plate and flung it accurately at the officer sitting at the other end, who happened to be a senior major. The colonel smiled, but after all he was no longer in his twenties. He collected the majors with his eye and left us. As the field officers crept silently out the air grew thick with flying potatoes, pudding, turkey, gravy, and oranges.

I watched in amazement. If we had behaved like this at the Royal Military College we would have been rusticated on the spot and told we were quite unfit to be officers. Apparently when one actually became an officer the rules were different. Amazement gave place to loneliness and a despair born of all those toasts, for I was not at all used to drinking. I have tried so hard to be an officer, I thought tearfully. I want so much to be treated as one of this family. But no one is throwing anything at *me*. They haven't forgiven me about the cake yet.

Then—oh, ecstasy!—hard fingers were rubbing brandy butter into my hair and stuffing Christmas pudding into my ears. I was forgiven, accepted! I flung myself with abandon into the riot, and the steaming rum punch flew faster round the table, and the snow fell thicker outside the windows.

When all our fiendish energy had at last been spent, and we were preparing to go and clean ourselves, someone heard a faint muttering from the floor. We knelt and looked under the wide table. We saw two doctors, both medical majors, lying comfortably on their sides, their heads pillowed on cushions. A bottle of brandy stood between them and they were arguing in an involved way about horse-breeding, for they were, of course, like most army doctors, Irishmen. They must have been there for hours and no one knew how or when they had arrived. We sent another bottle of brandy down to them, with the compliments of the regiment, and trooped out into the snow.

I looked on this regiment with mixed feelings. I was in it but not of it, for I was attached to it only for this first year of my service. It was older than any regiment of the Indian Army and carried its traditional glories easily and without offensive snobbery. Some British regiments treated their attached Indian Army subalterns like dirt. One even made them sit at a separate table in mess. (Those poor fellows spent a miserable year, but obtained revenge the night the regiment had the local general as a guest of honour. The general, seated at the colonel's right at the main table, asked in a whisper who the young men in exile were. The colonel said, 'Oh, those are Indian Army people.' The general said, 'What a coincidence! So am I!' and joined them.)

These references to the 'British Army' and the 'Indian Army' need explanation, for the difference between the two was a fundamental factor in the social and military life of imperial India. There were two distinct bodies of armed soldiers in India at that time: first, large detachments of the British Army; and second, the whole of the Indian Army. Of the British Army there were some forty-eight battalions of infantry, four regiments of cavalry, and a host of artillery. These were British throughout. The Indian Army was about three times the size of the British forces in the country; soldiers and N.C.O.s were Indians, while the officer corps, still mainly British, was gradually being nationalized by the commissioning of Indians. The whole establishment, British and Indian together, was known as the Army in India, and was ruled by a commander-in-chief selected alternately from the British and Indian Armies. The country's military problems were roughly but not fixedly apportioned between the two elements, so

23

that the good-humoured and impartial British soldier was used to keep the peace against race riots, religious disorders, and political uprisings, while the hardy and frugal Indian soldier defended the frontiers. Both armies also trained for major war.

The 1st Battalion of the Duke of Cornwall's Light Infantry was, in the year I spent with it, serving as one of the few British battalions on the North-West Frontier. That was why I had applied to do my attachment with this battalion, for I hoped, nervously, to hear shots fired in anger, and I wanted the opportunity to meet various regiments of the Indian Army and decide which to apply for. The former wish was not gratified. No one started a battle throughout my year in Razmak. As to the latter, I made up my mind within a few weeks. In Razmak we had Rajputana Rifles and Punjabis and Dogras, and on column I had seen Sikhs and Mahratta Light Infantry; but from the beginning, whatever I was supposed to be doing with my platoon of Englishmen, at least half of me was engaged in watching the slant-eyed men of the two Gurkha Rifle battalions then in Razmak. They were small and cheerful and they had the air of so many gambolling bull-pups— ugly, independent, good-humoured. I was determined to go to Gurkhas.

Meanwhile the Duke of Cornwall's Light Infantry laboured to teach me the basic techniques of my profession and something of the intangibles which, they seemed to believe, held men together in time of stress, whatever those men's colour or creed. I played football and ran cross-country with my platoon. I inspected its smelly feet and noisome socks and sat up late listening to its involved stories of domestic betrayal. I congratulated it, admonished it, put it under arrest, and admired its snapshots. With it I patrolled the walls behind the arc lights and the barbed wire. I went on columns with it and with it joined in the universal speculation—was there a woman in Razmak?

There was not supposed to be, since only tribal women were allowed west of Bannu, seventy-three miles down the road, and no female at all was allowed inside the fort. There was nevertheless an obstinate tradition that the Indian postmaster of Razmak had his daughter with him, disguised as a boy. We spent a lot of time examining the environs of the post office, but no one ever saw 'her.' We knew that a more definite attempt to break into our sanctuary had ended in failure. That was when a globe-trotting peeress had cut off her hair, dressed herself in trousers and a sheepskin coat, and driven out of Bannu in a snowstorm to try to reach Razmak. She was discovered nineteen miles short of her goal, at Dosalli, and Razmak's monasticity was preserved.

I found to my surprise that the Duke of Cornwall's Light Infantry thought rifles were for firing, not just for drill. The soldiers had to use oil on them and any attempt to burn them clean with methylated spirits, as we had done at Sandhurst, would have ended in a court martial. I spent weeks on the rifle range, supervising the training of soldiers in marksmanship, though I was a very poor shot myself. I sat for hours in magazines and quartermaster stores, counting ammunition and entering rows of figures in ledgers, without knowing what I was doing, or why. I unlearned my Sandhurst drill and learned a new type, light-infantry drill, where all movements were executed with extreme speed and a minimum of orders. I attended courts martial 'under instruction'—the crimes were never very serious, but we scanned the *Manual of Military Law* and the *Rules of Evidence* as though a life depended on our diligence.

Yet Razmak was an unlovely place, and it was not really a pleasant life that we lived there. Its only value to me was that it introduced me to the Frontier, which, unless there was a major war, would be the core of my Indian Army career. Even so, I would probably have done better to spend my attachment with a battalion in Central India, or even in the dreamy damp of Madras, for at least I would have got to know something of India. The Frontier was a betwixt-and-between place, part India, part Central

Asia, just as I was a betwixt-and-between young man, serving with the British Army but intended for the Indian Army.

The Razmak barracks were low and made of stone and stood in straight lines inside a low stone wall three or four miles long that surrounded the whole fortress. At intervals of six or seven feet along the wall there were stones to give men head cover. Beyond the wall stood a row of electric lights on tall posts, and, just beyond the lights, three double aprons of barbed wire. Beyond the wire the tilted plateau sloped away to jagged mountains, and across the plateau tribesmen strode slowly with the full, free lilt of their kind, leading their camels behind them. We watched enviously from the safe imprisonment of the wall and the wire. In winter snow fell and in summer the sun burned the arid slopes. It was a good place for *cafard*, but no one committed suicide. However, a fine red setter belonging to a lance-corporal in my platoon got rabies. We shot the dog and the doctor gave the lance-corporal an anti-rabies injection. That was routine, but after a week the lance-corporal sickened, became paralysed, and, six months later, died.

Only in the mess was there any escape from the all-pervading sense of imprisonment. There Major Tom beamed kindly at us through his monocle, puzzled but patient in a world where all gentlemen were not sensitive enough to get their bootlaces at Peal's, where most officers of the 32nd no longer had at least a thousand pounds a year of private means—as things used to be when he took his platoon into the fires of Mons.

In the mess lived an echo from silver trumpets of the past. There impressions of light and tone were muted and wavering as in a cathedral under the sea. At dinner the Colours, cased and capped and crossed, stood like huge black rockets against the wall behind the president. On guest nights they were unfurled and lit the room with the embroidered battle honours of two hundred years. In their silken richness I saw all that glory, and all those muskets buried in the mud of forgotten fields, and all those men—my uncle's generation, Major Tom's young friends—who had died, broken, on barbed wire.

This regiment had a long association with India. As the 32nd Foot, it had held the residency at Lucknow through the famous siege of 1857, during the Mutiny. When the walls crumbled, the mess silver, crated, was used to plug the gaps. At dinner we now ate off some of that silver; the rest, the pieces that had been twisted by enemy fire, hung in glass cases on the wall. Among them was a soup tureen with a hole in it where a musket ball had entered—and dents where the ball had ricocheted round and round— and the leaden musket ball itself. A little farther along hung a long row of bronze medals, each with a short piece of dull crimson ribbon. These were the Victoria Crosses won by men of the 32nd at Lucknow. So, in the glow of the Lucknow silver and the self-effacing sheen of the Lucknow Crosses, we laughed and talked and quarrelled and felt ourselves lapped in the warm continuity of tradition—a tradition that reached years farther back than 1857. On parade every man of the regiment wore a single red feather in the front of his pith helmet. The light company of the other battalion of the regiment had taken part in a success-ful night attack on the Americans at Paoli on September 20th, 1777. The Americans vowed vengeance, and, in order that they should know who had done the deed, the light company stained red the white feathers they used to wear in their hats—and ever since then the Duke of Corn-wall's Light Infantry has worn a red feather or a red patch behind the cap badge.

I learned another lesson in that mess too. It was after a guest night in the summer, sitting outside with the adjutant, Richard Burbury, that I brought myself to complain about what I regarded as stupidity and unfairness in another officer. The adjutant was a fierce disciplinarian, but I liked and admired him. When I had finished speaking I thought for a moment that he was going to use his rank and position and blast me for daring to speak to him on such a subject. I curled up inside, ready to hate him and all of them. I was truly upset about what was happening, and I had asked him because I didn't know what to do. Also, it was not for myself that I had spoken but because I thought the officer was doing harm to the company and the regiment.

Burbury relaxed suddenly and ordered drinks. When the mess waiter had brought them, and we were again alone on the veranda, he said, 'Do you think you're being disloyal?'

I said, 'No.'

Burbury said, 'But you are.' He smiled at me, and I, in my turn, relaxed. I had wanted for a long time to be able to ask questions about loyalty, duty, and obedience, and have them answered by someone who would not snap my head off. Eagerly I explained my position.

Burbury said, 'Loyalty means backing up a man even when he's in the wrong. Even if he's stupid and inefficient. That's why it's so hard to be loyal. It's no boast to say you're loyal to Phil, is it?'

I had to agree. J. C. Phillippo, my company commander, was kind, efficient, generous, and understanding. I never heard of anyone of any rank who wasn't a better man for his association with Phil.

But I couldn't agree with Burbury's argument. I said, 'What about loyalty to the men, though?' I said that to be loyal to the man we were talking about meant being disloyal to the soldiers, for he was a bad officer.

Burbury said, 'That's the hardest of all. Look, suppose you have a corporal in your platoon. What would you think of a private who started to tell you that the corporal secretly did this and that, and had lied to you on such-and-such an occasion, and he, the private, could prove it, and so on?'

I said unhesitatingly that I wouldn't want to hear what the private said.

'Why?' Burbury added quickly.

'Because it's sneaking,' I said; then flushed, and quickly amended 'sneaking' to 'a dirty trick.' 'Sneak' was a schoolboy word, and I hadn't forgotten the incident of the cake. I added, 'I'd rather find out about the corporal myself.'

'Exactly,' Burbury said.

We stayed there drinking and chatting for some time longer, while I wrestled with my doubts. Loyalty was going to be a difficult subject. I agreed with what Burbury had said—indeed, he had hoist me with my own opinions—but I was left with an underlying unease. What if seniors were blind? There were some kinds of neglect and double-dealing that only the juniors, the toads under the harrow, could know about. How much did the man underneath have to put up with, on his own behalf and on behalf of those under him again, before his complaint changed from 'disloyalty' to 'public service'?

I saw no answer at that time. I am sure that if I had pressed the point Burbury would have told me what I found out for myself in due course: that a man must act by his lights and take the consequences, good or bad.

This talk with Burbury was a source of secret comfort to me a few nights later when my moment of tribulation fell upon me. A serious group of young inquisitors suddenly met me as I was going in to dinner and told me to join them in the ante-room after the meal. I asked Robin Hodson what it was all about. He said grimly, 'You'll find out soon enough.'

I looked at him in astonishment. Robin was my friend, and a most straightforward man. Yet I ought to have known, because it had all happened before. For the moment he hated me. I had done something terrible. I wished I knew what it was. . . . My code has never been quite the same as anyone else's. I ate my dinner in miserable anticipation and went to the ante-room.

All the subalterns of the regiment were there. They told me I had behaved badly at a cricket match in Tank, some hundred miles away, where a political agent and his wife lived. To be more precise, I had behaved badly at the P.A.'s bungalow after the match. I had made dubious jokes with, at, or to the P.A.'s wife. I had made too much noise. (They might have added that I hadn't bowled very well, either; that would have upset me much more. I was very proud of my fast bowling.) I pleaded guilty because, although I couldn't remember doing anything terrible, it was impossible to believe that all these people were off their heads. Then they talked back and forth for a time, decided not to proceed to the more awful disgrace of a subalterns' court martial, and dismissed me with a painful tongue-lashing. For a time I was humbled, even grateful to them for their forbearance. Later I wished that I had joined that select band—some good, some bad, none mediocre—who actually underwent subalterns' courts martial.

These affairs—subalterns' courts martial—were highly unofficial. They dealt with offences against the Code of Behaviour—a different code for each regiment—and their procedure was modelled on that of a real court martial. The charge described the offence, or, if there was no single offence, might be something like: 'In that he, being a four-letter man, failed to report himself as such.' Evidence was taken, sentence pronounced, and punishment administered. This ranged from tar-and-feathers to ostracism. The 'court' and all concerned were liable to a real court martial themselves if the victim complained, but I do not think anyone who complained would have enjoyed his subsequent life in the army—nor, probably, would he have been suited to that life. Many things are best borne in silence, and ability to do this is a real soldierly virtue.

Then one day it was all over and we were on our way to new lives. We four 'attached' officers shook hands all round and said good-bye to one another and to this step-mother regiment. We were half happy and half sad, with the tender, pleasant sadness of youth, which believes all things will come right in the end and all good friends meet again soon. Robin Hodson was going to the Guides Infantry, Bill Williams to the 14th Punjab Regiment, Chris Pulley to the 3rd Gurkhas. As for me, a groaning truck, loaded with leave men and kit, backfired and puttered steadily down the road to the plains, to India proper, and to the 2nd Battalion of the 4th Prince of Wales's Own Gurkha Rifles.

I knew where I was going, in both the metaphorical and the literal senses, for the 4th Gurkhas had not accepted me without sending for me and taking a look at me, as I explain later. Literally, I knew that where the blinding white road ended the narrow-gauge railway would begin. A little locomotive would chuff across the burning desert to the Indus at ten miles an hour. That train was called the Heatstroke Express, and it would rumble over the dark red girders of the Indus Bridge, and there on the other side would be the broad-gauge train. On, slowly north along the arid left bank of the Indus, in the Punjab now—two changes, two days, and I'd arrive at railhead. From there, another mountain road, another Indian bus. At last the red roofs of Bakloh, a little military colony crouched on a narrow, forested ridge in the foothills of the Himalaya. Bakloh was the home of my regiment, and my regiment was to be my home for as long as I, a young man, could foresee.

In the other sense I also knew where I was going, for decisions I had made at Sandhurst still stood. I was going to join the staff or the political service as soon as possible. I was ambitious, and I would head for the upper reaches, to join the men in the offices who told the men in the field what to do. But though the intention was clear enough the picture had become blurred during this, my first year of service. Visions of men kept edging in to distort it—men on the march, men drinking tea, men working under the sun, men smiling in the shade, men loading their rifles. And there were in my head unclear words and ideas, such as 'loyalty,' 'tradition,' and indeed 'the Colours,' which seemed to have no place in this prosperous future that I saw for myself. What would it be like without these things? Perhaps, somehow, it was possible to have both. There must be a way for a smart fellow like me. There must be.

Anyway, I didn't have to think about any of these matters just yet. I knew now that my Sandhurst dreams of getting on the staff within a year or so were sheer lunacy. I would have to do at least four years of regimental service, and more probably six. Well, there was nothing to do but make the best of it.

Meantime I had learned something of the pattern of this life that I seemed fated to follow. There would be more service on the Frontier, possibly among flying bullets. There would be more silver and mahogany, more tradition and comradeship. I could see myself in the new ante-room —in it *and* of it, this time—talking easily. I was one of that group of men in embroidered dark-green mess jackets, tight green trousers, and stiff white shirts, with rows of black cord looped across their chests and black-braided epaulettes heavy on their shoulders. With them I would share in cold-weather manœuvres, and as one of them I would see the dawn lend a short-lived beauty to the plain of battle or silver the water of the marsh where we waited for the wild duck to flight. With them I would stand parades and drills and audit boards, and share evenings of brandy and cigars and argument. (Ah, I'd never had a cigar. In the D.C.L.I. I hadn't dared, but in my own regiment I would!) They and I together would smell the sharp anxiety of a fighting night, more pointed than the waiting hedge of bayonets.

I did not think about the tides of tribulation that would certainly return upon me. Nothing told me which men would smile and which would sneer, or whose rusty hand would trail blood along the Frontier stones, or how a tiger's breath on my cheek would be both a danger and, from that moment, a part of my character—but so would each moment of duty or pleasure, each thought and action, each pang of wonder or disgust.

I realized suddenly that this was already and always true. The Royal Military College and the Duke of Cornwall's Light Infantry were behind me only in the physical sense that I had passed by them, as a train passes a wayside station. In the true sense of the spirit they were and are inside me, a part of me, and always will be.

CHAPTER TWO

THE journey from Razmak to Bakloh took two and a half days, and I looked out of the window, watched the unrolling fields, deserts, and salt hills, and thought. The future was a vaguely glowing ribbon ahead, and I could only wait for it too to unroll, like the fields. I thought of the past.

In Razmak I had been faced with a small practical segment of life in such detail that every wart and callus stood out, while my short Sandhurst training had shown a broader theoretical canvas, with no warts or calluses. The Razmak general asked me one day on the rifle range how I was getting on. I was not frightened of generals in anything like the degree I was frightened of full lieutenants. I had had very little to do with generals and, like most of my generation, believed they were so old as to be practically dead on their feet and so stupid they were lucky not to be in mental hospitals. I therefore answered easily that it was very difficult, and that Sandhurst did not seem of much direct practical use to a second lieutenant, though it had fitted me perfectly for some more senior rank—such as, say, major-general. He snapped, 'Oh, you think so, do you?' and walked away. The men on the firing point snickered, but I was not trying to be funny.

I went to Sandhurst early in 1933, being then a few months past my eighteenth birthday. After we had taken my bags out of the car my father shook me by the hand and said, 'Well, good luck, Jackie.' We did not embrace, because we never do, and anyway a sergeant with a red sash was talking to a group of young men beside us, and we would have been observed.

I said, 'Good-bye, Daddy.'

He got into the battered Rover and drove away, a small figure hunched over the steering wheel. He had a long drive back to Dorsetshire ahead of him, and the light of the February afternoon was already fading. I was rather glad he had gone, because he was wearing an overcoat that an elderly woman friend of ours had had made for herself many years before out of an ex-carriage rug, and had later given to him. The new pearl-grey homburg on his head did not make him look any less like a mysteriously sunburned refugee from Central Europe. 'Refugee' was a term of scorn in those days, when Hitler was a joke, and Central Europe wasn't so highly thought of either.

My suitcases and trunks lay at the foot of the wide steps. The sergeant said, 'What's your name, sir?'

I said, 'Masters, sir.'

He said, 'Don't call me "sir," sir. Call me "staff," sir.' He glanced at a paper in his hand and called over his shoulder, 'Bert, here's one of yours—Mr Masters.' A man in shirtsleeves came out, and the sergeant told me he would be my room servant, to be shared with two or three other cadets on the same floor.

Bert King, late of the Rifle Brigade, led me up the steps and into the low grey pile before me—the Royal Military College, Sandhurst. From that moment, for nearly a year and a half, I was Gentleman Cadet John Masters, of No. 5 Company of the R.M.C., as I soon learned to call it.

I was six feet tall—or five feet eleven and three-quarters, depending on how recently my hair had been cut—and I weighed one hundred and fifty-two pounds. I shaved every day, though I might have got away with shaving every other day. I had been a school prefect and head of my dormitory at Wellington, my public school. I was a fairly fast-running wing three-quarter back at Rugby football and a very fast but wildly erratic bowler at cricket. I ran quarter- and half-miles on the track, always finishing behind several others who could run faster farther than I could. I could not ride a horse. My sole athletic trophy was—and is—a silver cup the size of an egg cup, awarded to me for winning the hundred-yard dash. This particular race had been limited to men under eleven years of age, and was a handicap event.

On the other hand I had passed fifth into the R.M.C. in a competitive examination with some hundreds of other applicants, and had therefore been awarded a prize cadetship. I was destined for Indian infantry. I use the word 'destined' with intent. I did not want to go to Indian infantry—I thought myself far too clever to waste my life in that backwater.

My mother's family name is Coulthard. Her people came from the North of England, where, I believe, the family had been long established. Most of them worked in or had been associated with the coal-pits. But my maternal grandparents died before I was born, and I had never known that life; nor, when I was growing up, did I ever think that a coal-miner's life was the life for me.

It was through my father that my seemingly inescapable destiny had caught up with me. There he was now, driving past the Lower Lake among the pines and rhododendrons, on his way back to the pig farm. He had crossed the sacred gravel of the Square and passed below the main entrance with its colossal pillars and its brass row of Waterloo cannon. Once he had been a cadet here, but now he was what I would become unless I was clever enough to outwit fate—a retired lieutenant-colonel of the Indian Army.

He had served his time with the old 16th Rajputs. His three brothers had been in the 34th Sikh Pioneers and the 104th and 119th Hyderabad Infantry, respectively. His father had been in the Indian Police. He had uncles in the

Opium Department, the Central India Horse, and the Bhopal Battalion—all, of course, in India. His grandfather had been headmaster of La Martinière School, Calcutta, and died as a professor at Kishnaghur College, also in Bengal. His great-grandfather had gone out to India in 1805, was appointed quartermaster of the 8th (King's Royal Irish) Light Dragoons in 1812, and died at Cawnpore in 1819. His great-uncle discovered the tea plant growing wild in Assam in about 1847. His——

But the list, including tangential relatives and connections by marriage, is far too long and complicated to be recounted here. The essential point is that the Masters family had served continuously in India, in many fields of endeavour, since 1805. In fact they had neither served nor worked anywhere else. I myself was born in Calcutta, my younger brother in Karachi. No one tried to force me to go to India when my turn came—but where else was there to go? What else was there to do?

I had decided at an early age to become an engine driver. But a few years later I was persuaded that drivers did not get paid enough, and were, besides, *ex officio* members of those 'lower classes' from which we had emerged, by great effort, only in the past hundred and fifty years.

Very well, then, I would become a lawyer—a barrister in a wig, of course. But that would take money, and we did not have money. My father had retired after only twenty-six years of service, not because he did not like the army but because the army did not like him and his open-air type of soldiering. He was not staff-trained, which meant that he did not belong to what was called the 'trade union,' for whose members all the higher ranks were reserved. He had had to commute half his small pension in order to give my brother and me the education essential to young gentlemen. We were broke.

I decided to become an officer of the Royal Navy—and found I was slightly colour blind. So I faced the prospect of an army career. But there was still a way to avoid India. I would go to Woolwich instead of Sandhurst. That road led to the artillery, the engineers, and the signals, and all these were of the British as opposed to the Indian Army. In one of these branches I might occasionally be forced to go to India, but only as a visitor, a kind of military tourist. In them I would not have to spend my whole working life in that godforsaken country.

But what was I thinking? Although it was just possible for a young man without private means to exist as a subaltern in some of the more undistinguished British regiments, it was not comfortable. The Indian Army got more pay, and living on one's pay was not only possible but feasible. And, as I have said, we were broke.

Resentfully, in the manner of one choosing hair shirts from the stock on display at his tailor's, I submitted. I would become an infantryman of the Indian Army. I faced the prospect, that first day at the R.M.C., with sulky annoyance but no anxiety. I had passed in fifth. I was brainy, and good enough at athletic sports not to be labelled a swot. After a year and a half there I would become an infantry officer. But I would not stay one for long. I would not be caught the way my father had been— broke, with nothing to show for his service but a few fading photographs of himself among brown-skinned and turbaned soldiers, or in the jungle with his dog, or in the mountains in the dawn, or by the banks of a great river, rod in hand. I would get on the staff and wear polished boots and tell the infantry what to do. Or I would serve a few years and then get out altogether—join the Political Department with its vastly greater pay, or transfer somehow to the Indian Civil Service, the white Brahmins of British India. Better still, I would wangle my way into the legal department and thence out into the great, free civilian world and be a barrister after all. Or I would become an interpreter and spend my days in Paris, Warsaw, Madrid. . . .

But in fact I was a boy of eighteen, entering the army at a period when, in the fruition of years, I would reach some maturity as an officer at a time when civilization would need me. I would lead men and hold much responsibility in the greatest war ever fought, perhaps the last war where we soldiers were to lead, or hold responsibility, or be needed by our civilian fellow countrymen.

The war was even then foreseen accurately by a few men, of whom several were in the army and some in the regiment I later joined. In preparing us for that bridal night of September 3rd, 1939, they had a hard task. It was the young men of my generation who passed the famous proposition at the Oxford Union, 'That this House will in no circumstances fight for King and Country.' None of us at the R.M.C. went that far—though the behaviour of some regulars in Hitler's War would have led one to think so—but that was the intellectual climate that had surrounded us at our schools and which we still encountered whenever we left the tightly closed circle of the professional army.

Above all, this is a story of change and, I believe, of growth. In 1933 I disliked or despised more things and people than I loved or admired. In 1939 it was the other way round. It is not for self-glorification, but to show the path of growth, that I recount my life and thoughts from the year 1933 to that day in 1939 when, on the threshold of war, I stood ready to take a leader's place in the greatest volunteer army the world has ever seen.

But in 1933 I was rather too pleased with myself as I followed Bert King along the passage. Flames and smoke were billowing out of a room beside us. Bert poked his head round the door and said wearily, 'Now, Mr Murray, I told you it wouldn't be necessary to set fire to the whole ruddy place to clean the oil out of that rifle.' He shut the door.

Two young men passed, wearing grey flannel trousers and the loudest, horsiest tweed coats I had ever imagined. One said to the other, 'Come down to the Jesus with me. I've got to buy a packet of cigarettes.'

The Jesus? What on earth could that be? At Wellington we would have been beaten for that blasphemy. And cigarettes! So we were allowed to smoke here! I was a man, and among men. . . .

They took us in hand gently enough. They led us to a store and gave us fatigue suits of dark-brown denim, which we were to wear until our uniforms were made and fitted by a military tailor in Camberley—for this was the Royal Military College, and clothes off the peg would be unthinkable. They gave us bicycles marked with three stripes on the crossbars, to denote Five company, and painted numbers on the back mudguard so that we could recognize our own steeds in the long racks. My number was 5/32.

They taught us to mount our bicycles in a soldierly manner—that is, by pretending the bicycles were horses and we a troop of cavalry. The sergeant shouted, 'Move to the right in column of half-sections. Half-sections, right!' and we straggled off in pairs. Then came the old cavalry threat, 'Prepare to mount,' and we hopped along on one leg, the other foot on a pedal, until at the final command, 'Mount!' we could swing into the saddle and wind sedately across the Square to our occasions.

'As on sentry, fourteen paces to the left and salute!' Crash, two, three, crash, two, three, crash. . . . There were noises off, on the Square, where the intermediates and seniors were at drill. We heard screams and yells and the thunder of boots.

We learned one another's names and faces and what schools we had come from. We found our way to the Fancy Goods Store—the F.G.S., or Jesus—to buy cigarettes and cups of tea and buns. We sat down to meals at long, polished tables, and used our new freedom to order bottles of Tollemache beer and glasses of port. The mess waiters, who were also the room servants, hovered over us, wearing mixed expressions of tolerant affection and cynical scorn. They were all ex-soldiers and most of them had seen twenty or thirty batches of us arrive, learn, conform, pass on.

At the halt, on the left, form close column of—platoons! The noises grew louder and came closer.

And there was a mysterious disturbance that very first Saturday night. I was awakened late by loud gurgling and gasping from the floor above me. I jumped up, put my head out of the window, and withdrew it quickly, only just in time. A senior in the room directly above mine was vomiting out of his window. I listened for a time, heard much blurred argument, and decided that a friend had come to help the senior. I got back into bed. The poor fellow must have eaten something that disagreed with him. I went to sleep.

We discovered that the R.M.C. contained four companies of cadets. They were numbered, of course, One, Three, Four, and Five. There were juniors just like us in the other companies, but we saw little of them. One and Three lived in the New Building, a vast red-brick pile half a mile away across the Square, and Four was at the far end of our own Old Building. We had a special reason for not seeing much of those hoi-polloi anyway, even if we had been given the time and the opportunity. In the recent past our rooms had belonged to a company that consisted only of young men destined for the cavalry. It is well known that the function of cavalry in battle is to add tone to what would otherwise be an unseemly brawl, and those young gentlemen of the past had left an aura of 'tone' about the place, of which we were the most recent inheritors. Alone among the companies the juniors of Five were permitted to have their room servants clean their leather. We were expected to be efficient and win competitions, especially at riding, but we were on no account to be seen *trying*. In the other companies men might shout, 'Come on, Four,' or 'Well played, Three,' as the case might be. In Five we confined ourselves to a weary drawl—'Lovely Five.' In other companies juniors had to wait at attention beside any door through which it looked as though a senior or intermediate might want to pass within the next few minutes; but not in Five, for ours was the communistic egalitarianism of the high aristocracy, to whom rank and seniority meant nothing.

'*Mr Lord Greenleaf, you look like a bloody monkey on a stick—*

SIR!' *Terrible oaths, vile abuse, always preceded by 'Mr' and ending in 'sir.' We looked at one another out of the corners of our eyes and trembled in our huge hobnailed boots.*

We learned the grades of the hierarchy. In the clouds lived a major-general, the Commandant, whom we seldom saw after the first Sunday, when he gave us a talk on sex. Some day we were going to hope to be worthy of the love of a good woman, he said; that thought should guide us while we were here at the R.M.C. (Yes, but how can you recognize a good woman when you don't know anything about bad women? There was a lot to find out.) There were two chief instructors, and a teaching staff divided among the Army Education Corps and officers of the line, all posted here for three- or four-year spells. And the Adjutant, with a capital A, who was a captain in the Coldstream Guards. And the drill staff.

'*Fall in, now, gentlemen. In single rank, tallest on the right, shortest on the left. Mr Masters, you're not as tall as Mr Cleghorn. Get down three places.' We were there, the gravel crunchy under our boots.*

The drill staff were noncommissioned officers of Guards and infantry of the line—usually three to a company. There was another staff to teach equitation, but we wouldn't meet them till later, thank heavens. There were the cadets: the seniors, some of whom were under-officers and sergeants; the intermediates, some of whom were corporals; and the juniors, plain G.C.s.

Bedlam burst open its gates.

I had been in the Officers' Training Corps at Wellington and had reached the rank of sergeant. Wellington was a military-minded school, and we had prided ourselves on our drill. But this that they were expecting us to do at the R.M.C. was quite different. The sergeant shouted the opening or introductory parts of each command in a loud but fairly clear voice; on the executive word his voice broke into a meaningless screech. At the screech we were supposed to react as though a bomb had gone off under us. *Crash*, we hauled the rifles up into our sides, simultaneously

41

bawling '*One!*' Then we shouted, '*Two, three,*' in cadence, but stood motionless. '*One!*' we smashed the rifles on to our left shoulders and smote their butts with the heels of our left hands. '*Two, three*'—motionless. '*One!*' The right hands cut away to the sides and the movement was completed. We were sweating like young bulls.

The drill step increased from 120 to 150, 160, 170 paces a minute—anything, just as fast as our legs would carry us. Faster. The sergeants twinkled along beside us like demented sheepdogs, their pace sticks twirling, their mouths baying and yapping an endless series of commands, threats, and objurgations. 'Rightturnleftturnaboutturnleftturnforgodssakegetamoveontheresquadaltleftturnaboutturnorderarmsslopearmsquickmarchhurryupforchrissakelef'righ'lef'-righ'lef'righ' . . .' The sweat streamed salt into my eyes and soaked through my flannel shirt into my new heavy serge tunic.

Between parades we had five or ten minutes to change clothes and be on parade again, always spotless, puttees tightly tied. We learned the techniques of frantic hurry. We learned to stand still. Every morning at dawn they held a shaving parade, ostensibly to see whether we were properly dressed and shaved but in reality to order us to have another haircut. I had my hair cut three times in one week.

The lordly Adjutant, beautiful beyond belief with his dark blue hat, red face, glassy boots, and golden spurs, strode slowly around among our scurrying squads, communing in silent scorn with some Coldstream deity who hovered a hundred feet up in the air in front of him. Before his feet steps became level ramps, doors opened, potholes were filled, walls vanished. He never tripped or stumbled and he never looked down, round, or about. Everyone else senior to us—that is, everyone—looked at us as if we were mutinous lice and on the occasion of the smallest misdemeanour would mutter, drawl, or shout, 'Take his name.' From somewhere behind us an answering voice would instantly bawl, 'Gottim, sir.' May be the sergeant hadn't got him, but he scribbled fiercely on a pad and usually found out in the end whose name he should have written down. For serious offences, such as having a button undone, the cry was, 'Puttim in the guardroom'—that is, under close arrest. Again the yell went up, 'Gottim, sir,' and the recreant was rushed off between a couple of sergeants, up the great steps into the guardroom, his feet hardly touching the ground, the sergeants bellowing in his ear as they ran, 'Lef'righ'lef'righ'lef'righ',' as though he were a mile away. On one golden morning a sergeant of the staff made a bad mistake, and the Adjutant had *him* put in the guardroom. It was bliss to watch from the corners of our eyes as the sergeant sprinted off between two sergeant-majors. No one ever put the Adjutant in the guardroom.

I learned that hyperbole was the normal coin of R.M.C. speech. Two grains of Sandhurst's ubiquitous sand under the leaf of the backsight of my rifle caused me to be charged with having 'a disgustingly filthy rifle' on parade. I used to think a dirty soldier was a fellow with a stubbly chin, dirty fingernails, a cigarette hanging from his lip, and a generally raffish air of uncleanliness. I learned that I was wrong; the phrase meant a junior with a bit of fluff on his otherwise impeccable tunic. The other fellow, the one I had envisaged, was not a soldier at all. He was a member of the Royal Air Force or the criminal classes—the two terms were all but synonymous.

The word 'idle' meant anything the staff considered unsoldierly. We *were* idle; we *had* idle haircuts, idle rifles, idle bicycles; we *did* idle salutes, idle jumps. It was an excellent word. When a sergeant put his face an inch from mine and screamed, 'Mr Masters, sir, *idle!*' he was saved the trouble of more exact definition and I was thrown into panicky speculation as to the nature of my sin.

For nine weeks the drill parades seemed to be continuous and endless. We must have eaten and slept, and I know we went occasionally to the classrooms and the gymnasium, but I can remember only the Square. In the beginning I got into a good deal of trouble because I could not bring

43

myself to believe that grown men really meant all this fuss about drill—drill, for heaven's sake, which was a joke in the most intelligent circles! I thought the staff's paralytic rages were put on; that they were really just lovable old curmudgeons, Hollywood style. I had only to give them a knowing wink to show them that they couldn't fool me, and all would be well—surely?

I didn't actually wink at a staff sergeant, luckily, but I did try a cordially boyish smile on one who was shouting at me from point-blank range. His face grew even redder than before, and he bellowed, 'It's no laughing matter, Mr Masters, sir.'

Indeed it wasn't. I suddenly realized that at this stage my hopes of promotion depended solely on this same drill and my skill at it. In no time my rifle rattled louder than anyone's because I had put more and heavier steel screws in the magazine; my back was more painfully arched than any back; my comrades merely crashed their boots on to the gravel and sent up sparks, but I tried to get through to Australia; when sloping arms, they bruised the heels of their left hands, but I damaged the rifle butt. I developed a constant headache from jarring my spine when performing the 'about turn'—indeed this headache was an occupational disease of juniors, but mine was worse than anyone's.

I cleaned my rifle with methylated spirits, wax, and Silvo, to the point where it shone like the morning; and I loosened the mechanism and fastenings until the slightest movement caused it to give out a loud clank and any attempt to fire it would have caused an explosion. I polished the blade of my bayonet with Silvo and a square of steel chain; I undid the little screws that held on the wooden handgrips and polished them. Bert King polished my boots and belt and chinstrap with burning heelball, but I cleaned the hobnails under my boots and used up a toothbrush every three weeks on my brass buttons. I bought a set of old buttons and a cap badge from a senior; these were probably ten years old, and the design no longer stood out above the smooth surface to catch shadow and old dried polish.

44

Gradually the desperate pace slackened. The staff, having reduced us in drill matters to cataleptic automata, started working up our self-confidence on that foundation. Their new attitude could never have been called cosy, but a mistake was recorded with a brusque word instead of a spine-curdling shriek, and several times I saw a sergeant smile. We smiled too—cautiously—and began to take a pride in what we had achieved. That achievement was near-perfect unison in drill—not much, perhaps, but something. Its value would depend on what followed.

At last we passed off the Square at an inspection held by officers from the depot of the Brigade of Guards at Caterham. As we were getting ready for parade we saw a group of them standing negligently in wait for us, gorgeous persons in dark blue frock coats aflutter with broad blue ribbons, and gold-brimmed hats, and swords in metal scabbards. We fell in for inspection. The irregular *clink-clank* of scabbard and spur came down the line towards me. I became aware of cold blue eyes and a ginger-soufflé moustache scanning my strained and sweating face. The vision passed on, and imperceptibly I relaxed. The voices of the staff arose in falsetto command. We marched and countermarched, scattering gravel far and wide with our ballet-style kick-turns. We went through our arms drill. The frock-coated inquisitors wrote on their boards. The staff sergeants, who would be held responsible for our performance, quivered with anxiety on the flanks.

Our little offerings of Silvo and burned heelball and sweat and presented arms were found acceptable. They passed us off the Square. The company commander gave me and several others a chevron, which was said to be a sure sign of greater glories to follow. I was Lance-Corporal Masters, J.

We settled into the normal pattern of the R.M.C. The number of drill parades decreased, though they were still many. Academic work increased, and we were permitted to join the rest of the company on Adjutant's parade every Saturday and Church Parade every Sunday. We were allowed late leave and took trips to Aldershot on our bicycles to go to the flicks. On Saturdays we went to London by bus and there savoured the delights of the wicked capital—or we savoured as much as a young man can with seven or eight shillings in his pocket. We had our already short hair cut again in Camberley because a pretty girl worked in the hairdresser's there. We sat about in one another's rooms discussing life, women, and the R.M.C.

Cliques formed, the most noticeable being the foxhunting set, who spent a lot of time tearing down the long corridors, blowing hunting horns. This clique wore riding clothes whenever possible. One of them used to don breeches and polo boots to ride his bicycle to the Camberley flicks. Another bloc announced itself to be against foxhunting, perhaps because its members could not afford the sport, or perhaps because they didn't like the music of the horns at midnight. There was ill feeling, and one crowd murmured, 'The unspeakable in pursuit of the uneatable,' and the other crowd sneered, 'Oiks!' But whether we were huntin' men or not we all acquired the right clothes. These were: grey flannel trousers, a doggy tweed coat with skirts to the knees and two slits at the back, a tweed gorblimey cap worn well forward on the head, the peak sewn down to the rim of the brim. In this garb we were recognizable a mile off as Gentlemen Cadets, and a good thing too. We never wore uniform off the grounds of the R.M.C.

We came from every level of British society. There had been a few sons of titled families at Wellington, but they were of the pattern of the school, which was largely filled with the sons of professional, and hence penniless, officers. At the R.M.C. there were scores of titles and heirs to titles. Some were of the old land, and some of the new breweries and soap factories. Their only common denominator was that few had any intention of permanently pursuing a military career. They were here on their way to spend a few years in the Guards or the cavalry, because it was traditional, or because it passed the time while they were waiting to inherit estates, or because it was their only hope of an introduction into decent society. One young lord was sent a bottle of brandy and half a dozen pints of champagne every week by the peer his father, and had, besides, an inordinate amount of pocket money. Another cadet, much higher in the peerage than the first, was as broke as—as a Masters.

To one and all the staff N.C.O.s addressed themselves the same way: 'Mr,' followed by the cadet's name or title, followed by 'sir.' In the days when King George V's third son was a G.C. he was not yet the Duke of Gloucester but plain Prince Henry. There was a story that an exasperated sergeant had bawled at him, 'Mr Prince 'Enry, if I was your father, I'd——' A pause while the sergeant realized he could hardly, speaking of his sovereign, finish with the traditional words, 'I'd shoot meself.' Instead he bawled, '*I'd habdicate—sir!*'

At the other end of the social scale there were some young men from the lower-middle and working classes. These had enlisted in the ranks, had there been selected as officer material, and had been sent to the R.M.C. as 'A' (for Army) Cadets. Of course they varied as much as the aristocrats, the brewers, or the bourgeoisie, but this was a considerable discovery to most of us, for we had never before been exposed to such people on equal terms.

The Master of Wellington, which was only a few miles away, had once caused a great uproar by referring to the R.M.C. as 'the little hell over the hill.' While not agreeing with him, I began to find out what he meant. The R.M.C. was undoubtedly brutal, and it was an 'A' Cadet who was the occasion of my introduction to this notorious fact.

This particular man, several years older than the rest of us, let it be known that he had played Rugby football for the army and was, besides, a heavyweight boxer of repute. But when they put his name down for trial games and matches the poor fellow always seemed to be ill. Finally the football crowd cornered him and dragged him on to the field. It immediately became apparent that he had seldom played rugger and was a coward into the bargain. He suffered considerably during the game, what with boots and elbows flying in his vicinity, but that was not enough. Not at the R.M.C. That evening I heard a lot of gasping and banging in the corridor and went out to find a gang of G.C.s breaking up the would-be hero's room and shaving off half his luxuriant moustache. I wish I could say that I dashed to his rescue with my fists doubled, but I can't, because I didn't. I thought he had deserved what he was getting, although I did not take part in the administration of punishment. I was not invited to, and I don't think I would have accepted if I had been. I knew what unpopularity was.

Yet perhaps the vigilantes were right after all. They were trying to show the liar that the code of one's circle, whatever it may be, can be transgressed only by men who are prepared to take the consequences. The victim didn't heed the lesson, which might have been cheaply learned at the cost of a few bruises and half a moustache. I saw his name in the *News of the World* some time later. He was getting seven years for bigamy.

On the other hand, it is possible that the vigilantes—and I, because I didn't go to his help—were responsible for his fate. Perhaps it was we who taught him to hate organized society. An earlier generation of cadets so maltreated one young gentleman that he gave up all idea of a military career. Instead he became a politician of the coloured-shirt variety. Who was responsible? The brutal cadets? The system, which can be blamed with so much facility because it doesn't answer back? Society in general? The cadet himself? I don't know. I wish I did, because in milder forms the problem touches everyone everywhere.

It touched me very directly. One evening late in my junior term I returned from a visit to find my room wrecked and my clothes thrown out of the window. I didn't mind putting things straight again as much as the knowledge that everyone knew why I was picking coats and shirts out of the mud and sweeping my floor clear of water and cigarette ash and torn paper. I found that a gang of fellow juniors had done the deed, but I never found out exactly why. Clearing up the mess, I gritted my teeth and decided that this was something I was going to have to put up with for the rest of my life and it was no use getting worked up about it. I had already survived a prep school and Wellington, and had therefore twice been through this business of learning to live with a different set of people. This was the third time, and it conformed to pattern.

I started each new experience in reasonable popularity, because I had average acceptability, and no desire to hurt anyone. Weeks or months later people evidently decided, as though at a secret signal, that they had made a mistake in giving me their friendship, because Masters was really not a nice chap at all. This in turn was succeeded by phase three, when the same people discovered that, like anyone else, I am good and bad, pleasant and unpleasant. The trouble in my case seemed to be that people first discovered all the good and then a little later, all the bad.

As I have said, I wonder whether these punishments did good or evil. The R.M.C. had no such doubts. There was a Law, in Kipling's sense, and it was to be obeyed. A G.C. found pilfering small things from another cadet's pocket was tarred and feathered, horsewhipped across four hundred yards of lawn, and thrown into the freezing lake. He left.

You will notice that the crimes punished were lying to brother cadets, stealing from brother cadets, and, in my case (I think), seeking the limelight. The R.M.C.'s ideas of punishment may have been barbaric, but the cadets had an unerring sense of crime. No one cared how 'different' you chose to be in your way of living. You could write poems or paint, work hard or not at all, get drunk every night or stay sober—that was your business. Inside the limits set by the code—and they gave a reasonable man plenty of room—it was an amazingly free life.

But it was a violent life just the same. The ferocious set-tos I have described were not confined to occasions of punishment, nor to the actions of many against one. No notable inter-company fight took place during my time, but that was not due to any inherent gentleness on our part. It was because the stink from the last fight still hung in the air, and we knew that anyone who took part in another before the public had forgotten about the last would certainly get into serious trouble. In the previous affair a couple of hundred cadets had battled up and down the corridors that lay between two companies' quarters, for the space of an hour or so. Brass knuckle-dusters, loaded canes, chair-legs, and practically any other weapon that came to hand had been used; two cadets were injured for life, and thousands of pounds' worth of damage was done. News of this episode reached the newspapers, and people asked what the authorities were about to permit such hooliganism.

It was a good question. I do not think any good answer was given in public. The true answer, though satisfactory to realists, might not have been thought so by the parents of the injured cadets. That answer was: 'War is a dirty business, and we are training these young men for war; we are not running a kindergarten; we do not intend to snoop around seeing whether the cadets treat one another like Little Lord Fauntleroys; we have learned that a wild young man can learn wisdom as he grows older—if he survives—but a spiritless young man cannot learn the dash that wins battles. And, finally, we believe that a man's contemporaries are his fairest judges.'

In this manner life proceeded on the tenor of its way. No one but a G.C. of the 1920s and 1930s would have thought it 'even,' but we did. The two weary Camberley harlots made adequate livings from anxious libertines trying to find out about sex before their ignorance was discovered. Drunkenness was not common, but it was not rare either. I had long since discovered that the sick senior above me that first Saturday night had not been suffering from too many green apples. There were several well-known methods of persuading the sergeant of the guard that you were sober when you signed in. Sometimes friends stood close on either side and supported you; sometimes as you bent over to sign the book one friend talked to the sergeant while another, behind you, put his arm under yours and signed for you. The honour system as practised at West Point, for instance, was unknown, and we would have regarded it as the height of caddishness if we had heard of it, for, according to it, one cadet is expected to report the dishonourable actions of another. Our world was divided into two camps—us, and the enemy. Against the enemy no holds were barred. The code was something else again, and had nothing to do with written rules, regulations, and laws.

Cheating, which caused trouble for so many members of the West Point football squad a few years back, was recognized as a form of work and had its own customs. It was permissible, indeed almost laudable, to cheat if that was your only hope of passing out and getting your commission. What did book learning matter, anyway, to a subaltern of a fighting regiment? It was not permissible to cheat in the hope of improving an already secure position, and most especially not in order to get a reward. Winning any of the scholarships available meant a lot to me, but I never dreamed of cheating. On the other hand it was my duty, at an examination, to put my worked papers in such a position that a desperate neighbour could look at them if he needed to cheat to avoid dropping a term. Whether he did look or not was his business. And if he was stupid enough to get caught, that was his business, too. Damn it, a chap had to be good at something!

Some pranks that may be recorded as typical of the place and the time were: to tow the Waterloo cannons down to the London Road at midnight and leave them there, perhaps with candles balanced in chamberpots on their trails, perhaps without lights, as a lesson to civilians in obstacle-driving; to order expensive suits on credit at Bernard Weatherill's and then pawn them for a tenth of their price, in cash, at Ma Hart's, leaving your parents to foot the original bill; to loosen the brakes of your friend's bicycle, and the girth on your friend's horse; to play bicycle polo on the gravelled square, especially on machines with no brakes; on Sunday evenings, to collect stray bicycles which their owners had forgotten to chain into the racks, take them up to the company roof, and throw them down at passers-by; to line up in cars at Hyde Park Corner at 10 p.m. and race to Camberley down a busy main road—but this last not in my time. Too many civilians had been killed and otherwise had their lives dislocated, and there had been complaints to the War Office and letters to the newspapers, so the privilege of having cars was removed from us shortly before I went to the R.M.C.

All our jokes were not so bloodthirsty. One cadet had a date with a rich and highly titled lady at the Savoy, and, being broke, stole a road gang's steamroller and, in full evening dress, drove it to the Savoy. He was reported to have said that the ride up was great fun, and parking his steed in Savoy Court an absolute riot, but when he started back at 3 a.m. to return the steamroller to its place outside the R.M.C. gates the jest had somehow lost its savour.

Perhaps we were no worse than our contemporaries at Oxford or Cambridge. It gave me an odd feeling to recognize many of my R.M.C. acquaintances blended into the principal character of a picture called *The Rake's Progress* in England and *Notorious Gentleman* in America. That film was a masterpiece in the way it summarized the archetype of our between-wars generation. Of that type some had money and some none, but all were as wild as hawks. They seemed unable to find either happiness or release in peace-time, but came into their own and showed quite unsuspected qualities of generosity—most of them had courage anyway—when war concentrated their unstable energies in suitably destructive channels.

Yet I have probably given a false impression at that. When, in another volume, I come to write of my war I shall certainly describe with relish each bullet and shell and bomb that passed my way; but, although I was an infantry officer, I did not spend more than a few score hours actually

52

being shot at. So with the R.M.C. We were decent enough young men on the whole. At home we did not beat our mothers or kick our young sisters, and even at the R.M.C. our lives were, by and large, blameless. An old saying described the G.C. to perfection—he was almost an officer and not quite a gentleman.

However, as I have said, we did drink. Even if drinking is a greater sin than I think it is, it does seem to me reasonable that a man should be allowed his first drunk without too much fuss. We were inquisitive explorers of a new world, and sometimes our discoveries caused us as much discomfort as a bar of soap causes a puppy, but there was no call for master to beat us as well, and, on the whole, he didn't. I have not heard that a stricter system produces less alcoholism than do the free and easy methods of the R.M.C. I believe, in fact, that of all the drinkers I knew at the R.M.C. only one turned into an alcoholic.

A young Scot, who had better be nameless in case he is still alive, was the cause of my first experience in this field. The occasion was the June Ball of 1933. The Sandhurst June Ball was probably the most colourful function in pre-war England and was annually attended by about two thousand people. Five hundred of us cadets would be there in our dark blue 'patrol' uniforms. Some nine hundred women would come in evening dress—white, if they had any sense. Nearly all the rest of the guests would be officers of the fighting services. The servants converted the gymnasium into a ballroom and made it bright with hangings. The cadets and the women acted as a backdrop for the brilliance of nearly every mess kit of the British Empire—scarlet and gold, chocolate and French grey, royal blue and silver, dark green and light blue, white and crimson; kilts and trews, sporrans and aiguillettes and shoulder chains—and then the naval officers in their boat cloaks!

The sight of the officers gathering was intoxicating but awe-inspiring. How drab I would look, a twerp of a junior in dull dark blue with a minuscule red stripe down the sides of my trousers! Yet I saw the glory of what I would become. The most ornate mess kits were those of Indian Army regiments. (But I didn't care about regiments, did I? I only cared to get on in life.)

About an hour before I was due to join a party for the ball my Scots friend greeted me and asked whether I, like him, was going with strangers. I repeated that I was. Iain Murray, the same who had set his room on fire our first day, had been kind enough to take pity on my loneliness and invite me to join a party he was making up. As Iain is a relative of the Duke of Atholl it looked as though I was about to take an excursion into a walk of life where I did not know the ground rules. Then there were those overpowering mess kits to be exorcised. It is not in my character to be shy or afraid of such an adventure—just the opposite. I become keyed up and determined to shine. When the Scotsman produced a bottle of whisky from a parcel under his arm, and opined that we had better share it in order to get ourselves into the right mood, I agreed without hesitation.

I should have had enough sense to think over what I knew about the hardness of the Scotsman's head: that he smoked ten or twelve big black cigars a day, whereas one would have made me sick; that I had seen him drink forty-two single whiskies—about two bottles—in the course of a long afternoon and evening in London, and return to the R.M.C. hardly more than blurred in his speech—this at the age of eighteen. I should have refused, or at the least drunk with extreme caution. But we finished the bottle, with very little help from the water tap, before going down to meet our parties. I did not see the Scotsman again that night.

The wonder is that I saw anyone. The whisky was followed by champagne, and the champagne by beer, and I soon became intolerably garrulous, to the well-disguised alarm of Iain Murray's party. By midnight I was feeling very strange indeed, and at about that time went down to the men's room. I found it deserted except for a middle-aged major of Highlanders. He was holding up the front of his kilt with one hand and leaning his head against his other arm, which he had crooked against the wall. He turned to me while in this position and said portentously, 'Join a Highland regiment, me boy. The kilt is an unrivalled garment for fornication and diarrhœa.'

The remark acknowledged me as a member of his grown-up world, where people said these brave, true things, and I was much uplifted. I nodded cynically, carefully stubbed out my cigarette on the back of my hand, feeling no pain, and went back to the ballroom. There I heard from the Colour Guard, who were dressed in mid-eighteenth-century uniforms, that a well-known lady connected with the stage was raffling herself for charity at one pound a ticket. I didn't have a pound to spare, and on this occasion the tale may have been an echo from the past rather than actual truth. I was again much uplifted and felt that this raffling of the actress was undoubtedly the apex of military philosophy, very sophisticated indeed. Iain's party left—or left me, I don't recall which. Alone with my thoughts, I called for madder music, stronger wine, and began to drink life to the dregs. But first there was a lot more champagne, whisky, port, beer, brandy, and claret to be tossed back with the weary grace of your true connoisseur. It was a whole bottle of claret; I remember distinctly because I hated the stuff.

At 6 a.m. it struck. I went out of the ballroom to find the world as light as day. I decided that the floodlighting was beautiful, but I was wrong. It *was* day. I do not know how I got back to Five Company and bed. I do not remember throwing up, but I was lying there, fully dressed, unconscious and filthy, when the sergeant-major came to look for me. Because of my chevron, I was the orderly corporal that week, and it was my duty to march the sick to hospital. The sergeant-major awakened me and looked at me grimly. I threw up again. He said, 'The sick parade's waiting,' and went out.

I got up, washed, changed, went on parade, croaked the

55

appropriate orders, and tramped dizzily to hospital, vomiting twice more en route. I was far sicker than the youths with cut fingers and runny noses beside me, but there was no hospital ward for me. I came back, a dreadful green in colour, and dressed for the ten-o'clock Adjutant's parade. The staff would not let me march on. They told me to go to bed. The wine of life heaved like sour porridge in my stomach, the dregs of life tasted cold and nauseatingly bitter. Until late Sunday night every glass of water I drank made my head swim.

On Monday the company commander, Major Val Wilson of the 60th Rifles, sent for me. He looked hard at me for a time without speaking. Then he said in a flat voice, 'I hear you had too much to drink on Friday night at the ball.'

I said, 'Yes, sir.'

After a while he smiled, his thin face lighting up with the warmth of it, or perhaps at some wry memory. He went on, 'Well, every man has to learn *once* what he can hold, and I hear you did not disgrace yourself in public. But now you know, so don't do it again.'

He didn't make any threats about what would happen if I did do it again. He didn't have to. I saluted and marched out into the sunshine. I have not been drunk to the point of unfitness for duty, military or civilian, more than twice since that day, and both those backslidings were on wildly celebratory wartime occasions.

In my last term I was made senior sergeant of the company. I had hoped to be an under-officer, but the company commander knew what he was about when he placed Darling, Nicholson, Whiteing, Chetwode, and Borrodaile above me. I consoled myself with the thought that few field-marshals had been under-officers.

I had settled into a niche at the R.M.C. and worked it into a comfortable place. I was wild, but not the wildest. I was doing well academically and might expect to do better. I played rugger and cricket but not well enough to represent the company, let alone the R.M.C. I ran a half-mile for Five in the intercompany relay race and held, as though it were a precious jewel, the deficit the previous runner handed over to me. I knew nearly everyone but had few close friends. I was not particularly popular and did not expect to be, though the earlier, more positive dislike of me had evaporated, partly because of the hours I spent tutoring cadets in subjects where they were weak and I was strong. My aim was still to collect all available scholarships, pass out top, and enter the army with an *élan* that would carry me straight over the drudgery of service with troops and out into the realms of light beyond.

The principal obstacles then visibly standing in the way of my attaining these ends were my awkwardness at physical training and my terror of horses. I am no good at standing on my head, or leaping over five gym-horses placed end to end, or swinging upside down from parallel bars, or fencing, or bayonet fighting. I have never had either the physical strength or the sheer physical courage, the dash, to do these things well. As to boxing, I was a mutineer.

Early in my junior term the senior in charge of boxing came to my room and asked me what I weighed. I told him. He told me to report to the gymnasium for practice bouts at such and such a time, and started to leave with a perfunctory smile.

I said, 'No, thank you.'

He came back, looked at me in astonishment, and said, 'But this is for the company.'

I said I knew that, but I couldn't box, I didn't want to box, and I would like to make my effort for the company in some other sphere. I might have added that I did not want to get hurt without good reason, but that would have been against the code.

The cadet told me brusquely to be at the gym at the time appointed. Though near tears, I persisted in my refusal. I knew what would be thought and said. The cadet snapped, 'So you think more of yourself than of the company?' I didn't answer. What was the use? He stormed out.

I did not box until my senior term, when some of the company's champions needed sparring partners. I volunteered to get into the ring with them. It was an eerie but enjoyable experience. I went in with Peter Nicholson, hit him several times with great skill, and danced away. Peter shook his head, came after me, and knocked me out with a right hook to the jaw. I felt no pain, recovered in a moment, and got back into the ring with Douglas Darling, the senior under-officer. I hit Douglas rapidly and often and danced away. Douglas shook his head, came after me, hit me twice very hard on the forehead, and knocked me out. I think it was the only time he'd ever seen anyone knocked out by a blow on the forehead, because when I came round, still feeling no pain, he was standing over me with a look of near-panic on his face and saying to the instructor, 'But it was a mis-hit, staff! I hit him on the forehead.'

I offered to get into the ring again, but they told me to go away. They saw now that the lessons they would learn from me would not be the right ones.

If physical training was hard for me, equitation was immeasurably worse. I have always been afraid of horses. Horses are too big, and their feet and teeth are too big too, and they have no sense and no discipline and very poor manners, what with biting each other and dropping dung in public, and worse that I could mention. And I could not cheat at equitation, which was unfair, considering the help in other subjects I had given to some of the expert horsemen. And finally, I was not allowed to intimidate the horses with the correctness of my dress—no polo boots, no long coats, just khaki and leggings.

The horses, relying on their proverbial sense, found me out in no time. I fell off with amazing regularity. When I was not falling off of my own accord my neighbour was putting his foot under mine in the stirrup and, by a cunning jerk, heaving me off. Twice this caused me to fall off while the horse was standing still, a feat that made the rough-rider-sergeant's eyes bulge out of his head. Five or six times during every hour we spent in that damned manège I was the butt of the oldest joke in the history of cavalry: as I picked myself up, dusted off the tanbark, and felt my aching bones, the sergeant would screech, ' 'Oo told you to dismount, Mr Masters, sir?'

At last I found a horse that had heard of mercy and co-operation. His name was Carriard and he was about twenty-one or twenty-two years of age. He seemed to like me, would jump without too much fuss, and did not tittup and fart and hop about while I was trying to mount or remount him. I had begun to get a little confidence, when one day we went to get our horses and—no Carriard. The stable sentry said someone else had taken him, but I didn't believe that. They had hidden him from me. They wanted to see me fall off a different horse. The one they gave me was an absolute bastard and positively refused to jump at all. I beat him and cursed him, and the roughrider beat him, but the result was always the same. He would gallop down the lane as far as the first hurdle, gather himself for the leap, and stop dead. It became painful, landing on that hurdle. At last the sergeant said wearily, 'Go and get anotherorse.'

I went to the stable and asked for another horse. 'One that will jump, please,' I begged.

I turned pale, though, when they led out a monstrous gelding with white on parts of him and the rest pale brown. Also, he had a hunting saddle instead of the general-service type I was used to. The stable sentry told me this was Limerick, a show jumper about five years old, the pride of the R.M.C. I climbed up hand over hand and returned in a high wind to the squad.

That was the first and last time I ever enjoyed riding. Limerick strode down the lane at a canter that made me feel I was sitting in an armchair. Near the end I looked down to see what had happened to all those jumps. A jump meant a check, a bunching of muscles and a bursting out of sweat, a convulsive bound high in the air—I knew that from long, hard experience. The hurdles were still there. We had been over all of them. Limerick had floated over them with so little disturbance in his stride that I had not noticed it.

They never let me get near Limerick again. Perhaps he complained when he got back. Perhaps they shot the stable sentry as a warning to the others to be more careful of their horseflesh in future. I saw that equitation was going to be— as Wellington put it in a description of Waterloo—'a damn close-run thing.' I might fail altogether, or I might scrape through with the minimum possible marks.

For all this—education, equitation, fights, high life and all—our parents were paying large sums of money. Or some were. The fees for the complete eighteen-months course ranged down from £300 for a rich civilian to £45 for a poor officer or ex-officer. The prize cadetship I won on entry was worth £37 10s. 0d. It was not much, but because my father's finances were in a particularly rockbound state it was useful. About the time of my last term at Wellington he had decided we could no longer even eat unless he got a job, so he hired himself out as a labourer on a farm in Dorsetshire. The owner of the farm was a retired major, and thus one rank junior to his hired hand. The major gave Daddy charge of an isolated Nissen hut and thousands of pigs. We lived in the Nissen hut and Daddy stomped around the fields, calling the pigs with a weird cry, which he said was American hog calling. He also cut back the alders to improve the trout fishing and drew weekly a farm labourer's wage of thirty shillings. When the War Office sent him an inquisition on his finances, to assess what fee he should pay for my course at the R.M.C. he replied accurately that his occupation was 'Swineherd.' Since the information on the line above informed them that he was also 'Lieut.-Colonel John Masters, D.S.O., Indian Army, retired,' the War Office must have wondered what they were letting themselves in for. They found out a little later.

At the end of my intermediate term I won one of the £60 scholarships awarded from the funds of disbanded Irish regiments, at their request, to twelve 'worthy' cadets. This put the family £52 10s. 0d. ahead of the government, and I girded myself for the final assault, the objective being one of the five officer scholarships.

At this point disaster struck, with no more warning than in the case of the White Ship. With me too, youth was at the helm and pleasure at the prow and, over all, a complete confidence that life was good.

Once off the Square a cadet was allowed to go away for occasional week-ends, provided he produced a written letter of invitation from a proper person. Half these letters were, of course, written by the G.C.s to themselves. My old nanny's mother was the respectable widow of a country coal merchant, and had herself been nanny to a famous diplomat in India, Sir Francis Humphrys. She lived at Rose Cottage, in the Wiltshire hamlet of Bottlesford, and I had a standing invitation to go to this tiny place whenever I wanted to.

About half-way through my senior term I decided I would like to go to Bottlesford. Not having left enough time to get a letter from my hostess, I wrote one out myself and put it in with a formal application for week-end leave.

The leave was not granted. Instead I was ordered to appear in front of the company commander. I was marched in to the usual accompaniment of bellowed commands, salutes, and crashing boots. Major Val appeared to be in a bitter fury. He threw the letter over the table towards me and said very quietly, 'It has been suggested to me that this letter is not what it appears to be.'

I lowered my eyes cautiously, looked carefully at the paper, quickly at the major's blazing eyes, and replied with what man-to-man frankness I could muster, 'No, sir. I wrote it myself.'

Lightning crackled in the dusty room. Major Val leaned across the table and lashed me with icy words—lying, abuse of trust, forgery, letting down the staff, and many other things. Finally he ordered me remanded in open arrest, my case to be disposed of by the general in due course.

I crept out, handed my belt and sidearm to a sympathetic colour-sergeant, and went to my room. There I

61

tried to puzzle out why this thunderbolt had struck me. Everyone wrote these letters, and certainly every officer and N.C.O. knew that they were written. Could it be such a heinous crime just to be found out? (The answer, of course, was yes, but I didn't discover that truth till years later.)

I had, during the interview, quickly seen how the forgery had been detected. I had forgotten to fold the letter. That was a piece of inexcusable carelessness, but . . . One of the R.M.C.'s favourite jokes was about the staff sergeant who handed a letter back to the hurried applicant with the words, 'I'd take it away and let the ink dry first, sir, if I were you.'

Slowly I dug to the bottom of the affair where, curiously, light dawned on me. My hostess had the same surname as one of the R.M.C. staff. Major Val presumably thought I was trying to make fun of this man, and that I had invented Bottlesford. I went back and explained all to him. Unfortunately he did not believe me, and telegrams began to fly.

The first went to the police in Bottlesford, and I could almost see the quotation marks round that name. The major expected a reply that 'Bottlesford' was not traceable. But he was beginning to eye me with a certain reluctant respect as a youth of more than ordinary nerve and ingenuity.

The village constable did not answer the telegram till late the next day. Then he replied briefly that my nanny's mother had lived at Rose Cottage, Bottlesford, for thirty-eight years, and that he knew me and my brother well. The lady herself, who also got a telegram, replied that of course Mr Jackie could spend any week-ends he liked with her, and what was all this nonsense about a written invitation? My father chimed in from the piggery with a menacing letter to the general to the effect that anyone who called his eldest son a liar might take his choice of swords or pistols at any convenient but early date.

By the time I was marched in front of the general, my spine more fiercely arched than ever before or since, the affair had been reduced to its true proportions. Major Val, the Adjutant, the regimental sergeant-major, and a few others were grouped rigidly round the big room, and outside the windows the sun shone cheerfully on the Sandhurst lakes I might never see again. The general accepted my explanation, though perhaps with secret doubts, but the charge of forgery remained. He pointed out, not unkindly, that I might start forging cheques next, and reduced me to the rank of plain Gentleman Cadet.

Try as I might, I could not feel like a major criminal. Then, to my amazement, I found myself a very popular fellow. A man who had been no friend of mine, in fact one of the gang who had broken up my room, tried to refuse to accept promotion in my place. The authorities, on the other hand, eyed me narrowly for the rest of the term and seemed to be wondering what further crimes I would commit.

The immediate result of this affair, I saw, would be a loss of company commander's marks. Our passing-out positions were decided on all the marks we had amassed throughout our time at the R.M.C., plus the large number awarded for the final examinations. Among the marks to be allotted were a few hundred from the company commander. These were usually apportioned so that underofficers got the most, then sergeants, and so on down to G.C.s. Now that I was a G.C. I would get fewer marks from the company commander, and I might expect to lose some more for the episode itself. But I could not afford to lose any marks. Competition was keen in the upper reaches where I stood, and among the top ten were such men as Douglas Darling, who could ride and box and was a senior under-officer, besides having a first-class brain.

I saw that I would have to work hard. I had never had to do this in my life before. Worse, I was earnestly in love with a girl who lived, by chance, near Bottlesford; she must not be neglected. I would have to work *very* hard.

I began, tentatively putting in an extra half-hour every day—and then an hour, and then two, and so on, like a

63

bather entering a pond on a winter afternoon. Now for the first time I consciously realized that a misfortune can be useful, for I learned that hard work is not really painful and can indeed be fun. My tutorial periods also bore fruit, because in my efforts to explain the open-market system of controlling credit, for instance, to cadets who didn't know or care a damn about it but only wanted to pass out, I myself got a firm grasp on the subject, and in such a way that I could explain myself clearly and simply. A cadet would rush into my room after Adjutant's parade on Saturday morning, all dressed up for London in a pinstripe suit, stiff white collar, bowler hat, and rolled umbrella, and say, 'Tell me about the rules of evidence, Jack. Hurry up, I've only got ten minutes.' Then he'd sit, chewing the end of the umbrella, glancing at his watch, and mumbling responses after me, until it was time for him to go.

The great examinations came. I finished most of the papers in half the time allotted, or less. Unwearyingly tactless, I did not stay to pretend that I had found them difficult, but gathered my papers and walked out alone past the stares of my fellows. I won the Norman Medal as the top cadet for the Indian Army, an engraved sword for first in Military History, and awards of money to buy books as first prizes in Economics and German and second prize in Military Law. I had already been first in Map Reading. The end result was that I passed out second, with the much needed officer scholarship. Douglas Darling was first, and it was no disgrace to be beaten by him.

With the prize money I bought the following books: *Selected Prejudices*, by H. L. Mencken; *Horse Nonsense*, by Sellars and Yeatman (the authors of *1066 and All That*); *Great Events in History*, edited by G. R. Stirling Taylor; *The Intelligent Man's Review of Europe Today*, by G. D. H. Cole and M. I. Cole; *What Everyone Wants to Know About Money*, planned and edited by G. D. H. Cole; and *Point Counter Point*, by Aldous Huxley.

I started to pack. Daddy had had an argument with his

employer, and the family seat was now a cottage in Uplyme, on the border between Dorset and Devon. In a day or two I would be going down there by train. Meantime the attitude of the staff suddenly changed towards me. As I went about my final occasions my superiors kept showering congratulations upon me. The general stopped his car, leaped out, and pressed me warmly by the hand. The Adjutant, proceeding in one of his mystical straight lines across the square, momentarily shifted his gaze down from the face of the deity and said, 'Good show, Masters.' Lesser officers wobbled off their bicycles to clap me on the back.

It may have been good-heartedness that caused this display of bonhomie towards me, or it may have been relief. After all, they had reached the end of term without having that dastardly forger Masters set fire to the R.M.C. (they may have heard that Lord Roberts suspected my father of doing this in 1901; Daddy says he didn't do it), or inspire a mutiny, or put a grenade under a staff-sergeant's bed. As for me I learned from the whole affair, including these unexpected curtain calls, and at a fortunately early age, that: (1) there is no justice in the world, and (2) if you want to achieve a halo, grow some hair on your heels first. I never heard that the general congratulated Tommy Pearson, Peter Nicholson, Mike Gardiner, or any of the rest of them for their three terms of loyal and responsible effort.

A taxi took me seven miles to Farnborough North station, where a few of the main-line trains stopped on their way to the west country. A famous debutante was on the platform, walking up and down alone, also waiting for a train. I had spoken to her at my second June Ball, but I didn't speak to her now. She was a startlingly beautiful girl and had caused a furore in society by wearing a subaltern's stars as earrings much as a Sioux might carry a scalp about with him. I thought: she won't remember me, and anyway she's going to stay in England, while in another couple of months I shall be on a trooper bound for India. The train came in,

65

headed by the usual King Arthur class 4-6-0, and I got in, leaving high society on the platform.

The R.M.C. lay behind, and I had taken another stride towards the fate—which has since, surely enough, overtaken me—of becoming a lieutenant-colonel, Indian Army, retired. A few days later I became entitled to wear an officer's tunic of fine barathea instead of cadet's horsehair, and a brass star shone on each shoulder. A week or so after that I acquired a parchment signed in person by His Majesty:

George the Fifth by the Grace of God of Great Britain, Ireland and the British Dominions beyond the Seas, King, Defender of the Faith, Emperor of India, etc.

To our Trusty and well beloved . . . JOHN MASTERS . . . Greeting!

We, reposing especial Trust and Confidence in your Loyalty, Courage, and Good Conduct, do by these Presents Constitute and Appoint you to be an Officer in our Land Forces from the thirtieth day of August, 1934. You are therefore carefully and diligently to discharge your Duty as such in the Rank of Second-Lieutenant or in such other Rank as We may from time to time hereafter be pleased to promote or appoint you to, of which a notification will be made in the London Gazette, or in such other manner as may from time to time be prescribed by Us in Council, and you are in such manner and on such occasions as may be prescribed by Us to exercise and well discipline in Arms both the inferior Officers and Men serving under you and use your best endeavours to keep them in good Order and Discipline. And We do hereby Command them to Obey you as their superior Officer, and you to observe and follow such Orders and Directions as from time to time you shall receive from Us, and any your superior Officer, according to the Rules and Discipline of War, in pursuance of the Trust hereby reposed in you.

Given at Our Court, at Saint James's, the twenty-first day of August 1934 in the twenty-fifth year of Our Reign.
George, R.I.

Trusty? Well beloved of His Majesty? Especial confidence in my Good Conduct? Whatever I had done at the R.M.C. did not seem to have merited these words. It was a sobering document, and those single stars, which are less than thistledown, settled heavily on my shoulders and for a moment weighed more than the responsibilities of empire on a field-marshal.

I sailed for India in the troopship *Nevasa*, and in October of 1934 arrived in Karachi. The Union Jack flew over the harbour-master's office and over the fort at Manora, where the mouths of big guns gaped wonderingly at the Indian Ocean. All my family's hundreds of man-years of work now focused on me and gave dazzling power to the light that shone on what I saw.

This was India. The colours were bare and brown and harsh. From the ship we could feel the unrelenting heat sizzling on the bright metal of the railroad tracks. Nothing was green or tidy. Horse-drawn carriages clattered up and down the dock between travelling cranes, camels, and a chuffing locomotive. Ah, I remembered those carriages of Karachi! In 1919, when I was four and was travelling in one of those with my mother, I had seen the wheel come off another just like the one we were in. The wheel went bowling down the street, the carriage tipped over on its side, throwing out its load of British soldiers. The horse kicked and struggled in the roadway, and I was very frightened.

We set off by train for our various destinations. We crossed the Sind Desert. The scenery here was—but no one could call this 'scenery.' This was hardly even country. Grey, gritty soil, scrub, stunted trees in glaring groves, the whole earth flat to the horizon. . . . All day we sat in the cane chairs or sprawled on the berths, drinking soda water by the gallon ('Never drink unboiled water in India, my boy'). There was a tin box in the bathroom, and we kept it

67

filled with ice. The bottles of soda lay in the ice, making hollows for themselves as the ice melted, and the labels peeled off to float on the surface.

The bottle-opener is on the jamb of the bathroom door. Each window has three sashes—one of glass to keep out the dust, one of wire mesh to keep out the insects, one of wooden slats to keep out the sun. You can use them in any permutation or combination. How did I know this?

The black smoke hung heavy over the plains. Night came, and towns now, and in the night high-pitched cries. The clacking wheels were silent. I opened the door and stood on the step in my pyjamas, peering up and down. Lights burned along the platform in the hot, dark night; thousands of people in white walked and ran and lay and squatted. Men naked except for loin-cloths carried goat-skins of water and jars of milk, and it was they who uttered the cries and the meaningless chants. People bought from them and gave them money. I wished I understood, but no one came to offer me hot milk or peanuts or Moham-medan water, so I went back to bed.

In the morning the train hurried among pale fields, and patches of dark green jungle stood in the fields like silent, fierce watch-dogs. Bullock carts dragged their dust with them along the roads. . . .

Another train, another night, and Robin, Bill, Chris, and I were a group travelling alone, all the rest of the *Nevasa*'s passengers having, group by group, gone their ways. At two o'clock in the morning the conductor-guard came to awaken us, but we were all awake and sitting ready on top of our bags and boxes. At Bareilly a short, dark young man with pale-blue eyes was waiting for us. He said, 'I'm John Strickland. I'm Indian Army too—going to the Fourth Gurkhas in a couple of days.'

I looked around for a taxi, but Strickland said, 'You've got a hope! We'll take two tongas.' He beckoned, and two carriages clattered up. Each had two wheels and was drawn by a single small and underfed horse. The driver crouched half-way along the shaft as I got in, but even so my weight almost lifted the animal off the ground. After a bumpy, breathless journey the tongas stopped. Strickland led us into a huge, dark house. He struck a match and lit a hurricane lantern set on a table. We were standing in a vast central hall, stone-tiled and bare of furniture except for four beds, four mosquito nets, and four small tables. Five or six doors led off this gloomy barrack, but they were all closed.

Strickland said, 'You sleep here. Take your pick.'

I must have looked dismayed in the thin yellow light. This was not a room but a prison. Strickland said, 'Only for a week. Then you're going to Razmak.' He grinned and added, 'Don't put your nose out of the mosquito net. A mosquito might bite it—or a rat. Good night.' He went out.

We undressed, hardly speaking to one another, and climbed into bed. The mosquito net shimmered eerily all round and above me, and as soon as the light was out the rats began to scurry back and forth across the high ceiling cloth. I did not get to sleep for a long time.

Bareilly . . . train to Mari Indus . . . Razmak . . . twelve months . . . and here I was in a train again, thinking of Sandhurst. But now outside the windows the fields of India stretched and wheeled away from the line. Out here there were no actresses, no debutantes, no Guardsmen, no protective Daddy, and remarkably few peers. A first-rate country for second-rate people, someone had said. The R.M.C.'s gravelled Square faded among the scrubby crops. I was about to join the service of India.

CHAPTER THREE

THE train rumbled on a remembered landmark, the iron
bridge over the Ravi canal near Pathankot, and I
started to collect my baggage. The last time I had travelled
this route I had been coming to face the terrifying ceremony of being vetted, or approved by ordeal.

When an officer was seconded to the staff or the Militia,
or retired altogether from the service, his departure created
a vacancy in his regiment. If the regiment had a good reputation swarms of new officers like myself clamoured to fill
these vacancies. The Gurkhas had long ago taken the fancy
of the British people and press. They and the Sikhs were
the only Indian troops the general public in Britain had
ever heard of, so Gurkha and Sikh regiments usually had
three or four applicants for every vacancy. The regiments
made their selections by the good but cruel method of 'vet-
ting.' They invited the candidates, in succession, to spend
ten days' leave with them as their guests. On arrival each

young man was placed in charge of the junior subaltern—lieutenants and second-lieutenants are subalterns—who took him to military, sporting, and social occasions. Efforts were made to get the candidate drunk, because in *vino* there is *veritas*, and always his behaviour was unobtrusively watched. When the regiment had seen all the applicants a mess meeting was held, and the colonel asked every officer to give his selections. As a rule the opinions of the subalterns, who might expect to live closest and longest with the new boy, carried the most weight. The colonel, who bore sole responsibility, made the final decision. Sometimes he vetoed a young man approved by the subalterns. More rarely he insisted on taking someone they did not like. In nearly every such case events proved him wrong.

The wings of my luck beat strongly over me when I was vetted in July of 1935. One of India's typically confused religious disputes had been going on for some months in Lahore, the capital of the Punjab. It centred in the destruction by Sikhs of a small Moslem place of worship called the Shadiganj Mosque, which lay in the grounds of a Sikh *gurdwara*, or temple. That July the argument came to the point of serious rioting between the two communities. In India the worst riots flare up early in the monsoon—that is, in July or August—because months of murderous heat have frayed everyone's temper, and because the monsoon itself brings conditions that make it not too uncomfortable to get into the streets and work off ill feeling. In fact, it is very nice to be out in the cool rain, throwing bricks.

The Shadiganj affair boiled over while I was being vetted in Bakloh, one hundred and forty miles away. The battalion was ordered to Lahore *ek dum*—or English 'at once.' I begged to be allowed to go along. The colonel agreed, and I did my best to make myself useful on the move down and for a day or two in Lahore while the battalion got into position, reconnoitred alarm stations, and dodged flying bottles.

I believe the 4th Gurkhas accepted me only because of this lucky chance, that the Shadiganj riots gave me an

71

opportunity to show some military ability and at the same time cut off the social functions to which I would otherwise have been subjected. A few more days in Bakloh and there would have been trouble. I loved parties, and I was wildly excited at the idea of joining this regiment. I was just getting teed up to shine with an erratic brilliance my years were incapable of controlling. The colonel's final word would have been 'No'—regretfully, perhaps, but definitely.

But the blessed cantankerousness of India's religions saved me, and the regiment accepted me, and so this train was taking me at a dignified pace to join James and John, Beetle, Midge and Moke, Bullet, the Boy, and the rest, as an officer of the 4th Prince of Wales's Own Gurkha Rifles.

The broad-gauge railway ends at Pathankot. In the outside world Pathankot is probably known only by those who remember Kipling's story, 'The Arrest of Lieutenant Golightly.' To us, who used it frequently, it was famous for its station restaurant, where a decrepit staff rigidly adhered at all seasons and through many years to the best Indian tradition of catering for travellers. The menu for lunch and dinner was always the same—chicken curry and caramel custard. The bottles of Pan Yan pickle, Worcestershire sauce, and Beck's beer in a glass-fronted cupboard at the end of the room always looked the same and stood in the same relation to one another on the shelves. The hand punkah was always in the same state of dusty disrepair, its rope frayed but never broken. The *khitmatgars* preserved with religious care the identical egg and grease stains on the fronts of their off-white clothes. This was only my third passage through the place, but I greeted the familiar dead flies and cobwebs with affection and was happily stuffed full of curry when I set off to find the bus that would take me, I hoped, to Bakloh.

Indian buses were all built on the same lines. On an American chassis—Ford, Chevrolet, G.M., Diamond T.— local carpenters mounted an ill-fitting wooden body, painted the whole in garish colours, and added representations of a few temples, cows, and tigers. On the road the

72

vehicle rattled, squeaked, groaned, and swayed. The cautious traveller never put his finger or his person close to two separate parts because when the bus started they would become moving parts and would pinch him. Beside the driver there was one first-class seat, thinly padded. Behind this was a row of second-class seats, consisting of a padded bench with an upright wooden back, and five inches of knee room. Next there were two or three rows of plain wooden benches (the third class) with three inches of knee room each and no backs. Behind again was an open space for baggage and merchandise. Here, on cords of wood, sacks of rice, and cans of kerosene perched the driver's mate, known as the cleaner. On the roof were slats to hold more baggage.

I found my bus in its stable, its tyres looking wan. About thirty minutes after the advertised time of departure the Sikh driver appeared and started up the engine. Impatient now, I jumped into the first-class seat—and we were away.

We travelled fifty yards to the bus office and stopped. There seemed to be a hundred people and a thousand cubic feet of baggage to be loaded. After twenty or thirty minutes all was on board, the driver jumped in—and we were away.

We travelled fifty yards and stopped. We filled up with petrol. Many of the passengers, who had been hanging on by their nails or bulging through the windows, got out and relieved themselves in the dust. The second-class passengers began to look car-sick. The driver jumped in—and we were away.

We travelled fifty yards, back to the bus office, and stopped. The driver disappeared inside to check his invoices and bills of lading. Our tickets were inspected and three stowaways thrown off. After twenty minutes the driver jumped in—and we were away.

There were only two more stops before we finally did leave the town, one to pick up a goat and another hundred cubic feet of merchandise (charcoal in sacks), and one at the octroi post. In all my time in India I never saw a bus driver or anyone else actually pay any octroi, but there was an

73

octroi post on the outskirts of almost every town, and buses always stopped there. This time the resident tax collector, who was sitting inside with his feet on the table in the pompous trance of oriental officialdom, came out and went through a slow-motion routine of inspecting us, our baggage, and the merchandise. Then he waved a finger—and we were away.

We were away through the unspeakable squalor of the outskirts of Pathankot and then on the wide road between the mango trees. The world was green, and little convoys of overloaded donkeys and gaily shawled women walked along the grass verge under the trees. We honked at tongas—built to take three passengers but habitually loaded with eight people and a huge bale of hay—and made them swerve out of the middle of the road. The bus had an electric horn, but it was disconnected to save the battery and to enable the driver to show his virtuosity on the winding mountain road, where one hand perpetually honked at the rubber bulb of the old-fashioned horn and the other changed gear—'Look, no hands!' To the left as the road swung, the forested hills climbed up and away, rolling higher and higher till they disappeared into the hazy surge of the Himalaya. Once a gap in the trees, the line of the road, and the drift of cloud all worked together to unveil an austere, blue-white wall of ice a hundred miles away in the main chain of the greatest mountain mass on earth. A little later we rushed heedlessly under a cliff of conglomerate and the sign guarding it: DRIVE CAREFULLY, LOOKING UPWARDS.

After three hours of terrifying effort, after the radiator had boiled twice and twice been slaked with cold water, after everyone in the back of the bus had been sick many times, we stopped on the edge of a precipice and I got out. This was Tuni Hatti, and I had arrived. There was said to be a truck coming down the three miles from Bakloh to the road junction here. It would (perhaps) arrive in an hour, or (perhaps) two.

'Salaam, sahib,' said the driver. The bus roared away

down a curving slope, the engine switched off, out of gear, the top load swaying, the paper-thin tyres sliding on the loose surface.

I left my bags and boxes beside the road and started walking up the hill. It was hot in the afternoon sun, but trees covered the hillside and a footpath wound up through them to Bakloh. I knew the path, for I had hurried down it in July with clattering Gurkhas all round me, on the first stage of the road to the Shadiganj riots.

A thousand feet above the metal road and five hundred feet below the ridge crest I came to the 2nd Battalion's football ground. They had hewn it out of the hill, for there is no level place in Bakloh, and its sides were steeply built up from the valley. Below it, on the left, I saw a rifle range, and on the grassy knoll above the butts, a clump of trees. They were a rare kind of date palm and looked out of place among the pines. An exactly similar clump of the same rare date trees crowned the end of the next spur, three miles up towards Dalhousie. Thick forest covered the next lower spur towards the plains, but on the end of that too, among the trees, was another clump of palms. I sat down to draw breath, and to look at the palms. I felt the grip of the same awed fascination that had overtaken me when I first heard the legend about them.

The local hillmen said that these palms marked the line of Alexander the Great's outposts. The clumps were descended from the dates Alexander's soldiers had brought from the banks of the Tigris. Certainly the trees rose in the places any officer would have chosen for an outpost line, and history confirms that this was indeed the farthest limit of Alexander's penetration to the east. I thought: perhaps a young Macedonian officer climbed this path to inspect his posts. They were strangers here too, and the clangor of their shields on the rock echoed over twenty-two hundred years into my ears.

I went on and came to the little 2nd Battalion bazaar. The shopkeepers on their porches stood up to greet the new officer as he passed, but I could not say anything more

75

than 'Salaam' in return, for I did not know them. I reached the crest, which was occupied by the parade ground—another major feat of landscape engineering. Then came barracks, more pines, and the road wound down among the gardens of the officers' bungalows, past the tiny church and the German trophy guns from Flanders, and on to the mess lawn, into the mess itself.

The officers were at tea. They had been at tea when I came up to be vetted. 'Midge' looked up, said, 'Hello, Masters,' and went on with his cake, but in a friendly manner. He would have stopped eating cake had it been necessary to assure me of my welcome, or had I been a guest.

Another man, small, tough, young, with bright-blue eyes, tightly curled fair hair, and a furrowed brow, leaped to his feet and cried, 'Good God, how did you get here? Where are your things? You're early.' He looked at his watch with an unbelieving frown, shook it, placed it to his ear, and began to mutter under his breath, 'Christ—damn watch. Have some tea.'

James Sinclair Henry Fairweather, the next subaltern above me, was off again. He had been deputed to meet me and had forgotten, or had forgotten the time. He frequently did. Everyone else laughed, and after a moment James looked up with a beautiful shy smile and said, 'Oh, well, you're here, anyway.'

I wasn't going to make the mistake about the cake again, and firmly helped myself to a large slice. James bustled off to make sure the local bus picked up my kit from the road junction at Tuni Hatti where I had left it, and I looked around me.

The Victorian founders of our regiment had built the mess low, of stone, and set it on the edge of the ridge, its front turned to the Himalaya. The Edwardians had glassed in the back veranda, which faced south over the edge of the ridge, towards India. And so, near the end of the century-long dream we Georgians took our ease there, as on the promenade deck of a moored airship. Beyond the glass, forests and terraced fields dropped steeply away for two thousand five hundred feet, then climbed with the same precipitousness to a ridge two miles distant and only a few hundred feet lower than ours; and so on, and down and on in dwindling rise and fall to the flat lands of the Punjab. Beyond the last low smoky ridge the khaki plains reached round and on until, in the farthest light, only the visible curve of the earth's surface served to separate them from the sky. To the right the Ravi River burst through a cleft in the foothills and wound out across the earth in a spreading flood. The low sun sent us intermittent golden flashes from unseen water. To the left the Beas River curled out of Kulu, the Valley of the Gods, and moved off to the horizon. Far, far to the left again were haze and a loom of mountains. The light hung opalescent over all—not sharp, but warm and blue-green, washed by recent rain and split by the broad shafts of the sun. The undersides of the cumulo-nimbus cloud masses showed thick and solid and dark blue to the earth, but their anvil heads towered thirty thousand feet above the plains, and shimmered with a frozen gold in the upper light, and moved steadily on towards us.

I had come to my home.

CHAPTER FOUR

O F the officers at tea, only 'Midge' was in uniform,
though they had all been working and most of them
had more to do yet. In the 4th Gurkhas, as in most regiments, an officer changed into plain clothes after lunch
unless he had an outdoor parade with troops. Midge had
come in from machine-gun drill and wore our ordinary
working uniform. His nailed ankle-boots were of black
leather. His short grey-green puttees were wound in three
exactly superimposed folds over the join of boot and hose-
top, and each puttee was held in place by three exactly
superimposed folds of broad white tape. His pale grey
woollen hosetops were turned over for four inches just
below the knee, and held up invisibly under the turnover
by elastic garters. To the garters were sewn oblongs of

coloured felt so that a square inch showed on the outside of each leg. The colour denoted the company to which a man belonged—in Midge's case, red for D (Machine-gun) Company. His wide shorts were of heavily starched khaki drill. (The traditional way to put on these shorts was to stand them on the floor and step in.) The shorts had a deep waistband with three loops to hold the Sam Browne belt, and were tailored so that the point of the crease in front was level with the upper tip of the kneecap. His shirt was of a material called 'greyback,' a pearly blue-grey woollen flannel worn by the Indian Army, with plain black buttons and plain shoulderstraps of the same material, on which were sewn black cloth silhouettes of the rank badges—for Major Madge, a crown.

Around his sunburned face was the unmistakable brand of our calling, the clear white impression of his chinstrap. His hat was probably hanging on one of the pegs on the veranda, with his Sam Browne. The Sam Browne was not brown, but black. The hat consisted of two broadbrimmed felt campaign hats, sewn together to give better protection from the sun, and dimpled fore-and-aft down the middle of the crown. Several folds of very thin khaki cotton cloth were wound in a band round the outer hat and topped with a single black fold. The number of khaki folds varied with status—nine for a King's Commissioned Officer, seven for a Viceroy's Commissioned Officer, five for an other rank. Finally, on the left, pinned through all the folds of cloth, was the regimental badge—a great Roman IV in black metal.

I had come home. I sat back in the wicker chair with a sigh. James returned, and the duty bearer brought another pot of tea, a paunchy white pot with the regimental crest on it. I poured out tea into a cup and poured in milk from a crested silver jug. Glancing at it, I saw from the engraving that it had been presented to 'the Officers' by someone, a long time ago, 'on the occasion of his promotion.' I took a lump of sugar from a crested silver bowl—presented by someone else 'on appointment.' Soon my name would be on one of these little bowls or jugs or ashtrays. I felt good and comfortable. The sun shone level through the glass, the talk hummed lazily, china clinked; the 4th Gurkhas' private landscape lay like a dream before me.

Midge got up. 'We machine-gunners have some work to do, even if no one else has.'

James muttered something inaudible under his breath. Midge glanced sharply at him and walked out with quick, bird-like steps. Everyone drifted off. The sun went down.

James took me to a bungalow just above the mess. Half the bachelors lived there; it was called the Rabbit Warren. It had no electric light, so James lent me a small oil lamp. He went away, and I took a look at my room. I seemed to own—or be renting—a narrow bed, a chest of drawers, a wardrobe, two hard chairs, one easy-chair, a table, and a bookshelf. Attached to the room was my private *ghuslkhana* with its appropriate fittings, also rented.

A *ghuslkhana* corresponds in function to a bathroom, but it is a profound misconception to think of white porcelain, taps, or water sanitation. The *ghuslkhana* is small and square and has a hole in the outer wall to let out water and let in snakes. One corner, around that outlet, is fenced in by a low parapet the height of a single brick. In this enclosure sits an oval zinc tub. Outside the parapet is a slatted wooden board to stand on, and a wooden towel horse. Ranged along the inner wall are a deal table holding an enamel basin, a soap-dish, and a jug; a chamberpot; a packet of Bromo hanging from a nail; and a wooden thing on four legs whose proper name may possibly be 'toilet,' but which was never called anything but 'the thunderbox.' The thunderbox has a hole in the middle of the seat, and a hinged top. Under the hole, fitted into the structure, is a deep enamel pot called a top hat.

The *ghuslkhana* is the realm of the sweeper, whose Hindustani names are *mehtar*, *jemadar* (ironically; the word means 'officer'), and *bhangi*. He is the lowest of India's low, outcaste, untouchable, and hereditarily destined to deal with ordure. When a bath is ordered either he or the *bhisti* (which means 'man of paradise' or, in less flowery style, the water-carrier) heats the required amount of water in empty four-gallon Standard Oil kerosene tins over a wood fire in the compound, then pours it into the tub and dilutes it with cold water from the tap—if there is one. After the bath the bearer tips the soapy water through the hole in the wall. It flows slimily off down open drainage channels with the rain—if there is any.

When a sahib wishes to use the other conveniences of the *ghuslkhana* he shuts both doors and, when he has finished, opens the outer door, shouts, '*Mehtar!*' into the empty air, and forgets all about it. The sweeper, who spends his day dozing on his heels and smoking *bidis* within earshot of his life's work, comes, removes the top hat, cleans it out with a broom and by hand into a pit or a burning-oven, and returns it to its place. In prewar days his pay was sixteen rupees, or about twenty-three shillings, per month.

I did not fail to make a careful inspection of my *ghuslkhana*. I had read 'Rikki-tikki-tavi' many times, and through the years never forgot to search nervously for snakes coiled in the tub or—dreadful vision!—in the top hat. (I never found a snake, but was once bitten by a small scorpion that crept in and concealed itself in my towel.) I found that this was an ordinary *ghuslkhana* and, like all the others I ever saw, a fine miniature of the Indian scene—barren, ramshackle, by turns too hot or too cold, yet full of interesting corners, strange expectations, and a mixed smell of woodsmoke and human excrement.

A voice outside the front door said, 'Sahib!' I called, 'Come in,' and an old Gurkha entered with a note. The note read: 'This is your bearer, Biniram Thapa,' and was signed by James.

The Duke of Cornwall's Light Infantry had found me a bearer a year before, but he was so anxious to stay with the British Service that I fired him before leaving Razmak. In an Indian regiment his peculations would have been uncovered in no time, and both he and I knew it. Also, he was a sort of broken-down Pathan and I had been unnerved by a letter from Ashraf Ali, an old gentleman who had served my uncle and my father for thirty years. The last time Ashraf saw me I had been a boy of five, just about to leave India. This is the letter he sent me while I was in Razmak:

Ziarat,
Baluchistan.
dated 8th July

To:
Dear Master:—
    Sir. I was struck with wonder having come to know from Gordon Mem Sahib that you are appointed at N.W.F.P. i.e. Wazristen War. May God bless you.
    Please take every necessary step to take your care as it is very dangerous area.
    If you have to serve a Pathan bearer turn him out at once.
    Please write me once a weak. I know you are in a pitty condition as it is very hot there.
    Major Gordon, Gordon Mem Sahiba and Miss Sihibi are all getting on well and are residing in Ziarat now a days.
    Best compliments to all.
        Yours obediently
        Ashraf Ali bearer care
    Major Gordon No. 3 Rondavel Ziarat.

Now the new bearer, Biniram, was standing in the middle of my room, and we examined each other cautiously. He was old and grizzled and bent, and he had a dyspeptic eye. Within a couple of days the outlines of his personality were to become clear. He had no finesse and no professional charm. He knew little about being a bearer and he damn well wasn't going to learn any more, for he had gone to Flanders in 1914 as a rifleman with the 1st Battalion, and had taken the bayonet to the Prussian Guard, and stood patiently in the snow and sleet of the trenches under shell-fire. He had learned once over quickly how to make a bed and hang up clothes, but never how to hurry. I liked him and everything about him, above all for the greatest virtue any Indian servant can possess—he had no English. In fact, he had no Hindustani either, and only a mono-syllabic kind of Gurkhali.

Biniram unpacked my suitcase, threw my pyjamas on the bed, and stomped out. I set up the mosquito net and went to bed. It was a bare and untidy room, but the night was warm and still, and I was home. All in a moment the striving that others of my blood had put into this land had caught up with me. In England I had tried to ape the fashionable ignorance of India, but now already I found myself resenting England's total unawareness of this country which she owned and governed at so long a distance of distaste. I did not like hearing Indians spoken of as 'niggers,' 'wogs,' 'Hindoos,' or even 'black-bellied bastards' —the standard terms of the British soldier and often the British Service officer. To me already, from the evenings I had spent in the messes of Indian regiments in Razmak and on column, they were Dogras, Bengalis, Afridis, Konkani Mahrattas.

On the other hand I had never had the attitude of the average civilian tourist, so I did not think of India as quaint, picturesque, exploited, inscrutable, or other-worldly. I thought India was ugly, beautiful, smelly, pre-dictable, and as material as the West. It was inhabited not by yogis and saints, but by people—knaves, giants, dwarfs, and plain people—of various shades of brown.

Then there was Kipling, who was not a Eurasian, as has been suggested, but also was not by birth or circumstances one of India's self-appointed élite—the men on passage, the civilian and military tourists, from the Viceroy to Thomas Atkins. Why had Kipling gone out of his way to underline with sadistic approval attitudes of mind and habits of race-consciousness that must have caused pain to anyone who loved India? But his descriptions—the turn of a phrase that caught exactly some intonation I had just heard, some sight and smell of the Indian road I had just travelled, some breath from the mountains beyond my window—what of these? These proved that he did love India. No one could write like that except from love. . . .

I was sleepy. I would have to investigate Kipling later. What was all that recurring nonsense of his about 'Black Infantry'? Had he meant to speak of Gurkhas in that derogatory sense? If so, he was a colour-crazy ass. Perhaps he did not even know about the 2nd Battalion of the 4th Prince of Wales's Own Gurkha Rifles.

Come to think of it, neither did I. I knew nothing. I would have to learn, or I would never be a good officer. If I was a bad officer I would not be recommended for transfer to the Political Service when the time came. . . . The thought died away, stillborn. I was never going to apply for transfer from this regiment, unless they turned on me and hated me. So far there was no sign of that, but I'd only been here six hours.

I must wait, then, and be on my guard. Meanwhile, the road of learning stretched away from me into the unseen, uphill—'uphill all the way.'

CHAPTER FIVE

Second Battalion, 4th Prince of Wales's Own Gurkha Rifles.
It was a long title, though by no means the longest in the
King's armies. I wanted to find out what it meant. I knew
already what it connoted—nearly a thousand men, white
and brown, who wore the IV badge; hundreds of rifles, and
scores of machine-guns; an undying continuity of association in which, after I had passed by, my name and memory
would share a place, part of its immortality. But what did
it mean? How had it been built up?

'Gurkha' was the most important word. The Gurkhas
are the people of Nepal, an independent kingdom sandwiched between the north-eastern border of India and the
desolate mysteries of Tibet. Nepal is five hundred and fifty
miles long by one hundred miles wide, and lies stretched
along the Himalayan chain, north and north-west of
Calcutta. It is mountainous, wild, and almost completely
undeveloped. Few travellers have been permitted to enter
it and of those few only two or three had at that time been
allowed beyond the short, direct route between India and
the capital city, Katmandu.

The mongoloid Gurkhas conquered the original Newar
inhabitants in 1768. The immediately subsequent history
of Nepal is a tale of court intrigue, poisoning, murder, and
civil war that makes Renaissance Florence seem like a
kindergarten. Yet the Gurkhas also found time to fight the
Tibetans to the north, keep their independence against the

85

grasping, ubiquitous fingers of the Chinese Empire and, at last, spill out into India.

India was no longer a turmoil of warring princelings. The Honourable East India Company was on the march, and soon enough the two powers clashed. The Anglo-Nepalese War began in 1814. The British are a tradition-loving people, so at first the war went badly for them. The Gurkhas were the toughest enemy they had till then met in India, and they suffered several resounding disasters before muddling through to victory. But it had been a good, clean war and each side seemed to have enjoyed the other's company. They decided to make friends, and—an eerie thing in the annals of politics—they meant it, as subsequent history gave them ample opportunity to prove.

They signed a treaty of perpetual friendship and alliance. The British allowed Nepal its independence. Alone among the myriad principalities of the subcontinent, it owed no allegiance to the British and never became part of the strange growth later known to history as the Indian Empire. In return, the rulers of Nepal agreed to allow their Gurkha subjects to enlist as mercenary volunteers in three new regiments of the East India Company's service. These three Gurkha regiments formed the first strands of a rope that bound together the fortunes and affections of England and Nepal through the next one hundred and thirty years.

In its internal affairs Nepal at once reverted to a state of utter chaos until the year 1843. In that year a 'strong man,' Jung Bahadur Rana, came on the scene. Modern thought does not look kindly on strong men, but Nepal in the mid-nineteenth century needed one, and Jung Bahadur, not disdaining the use of petticoat influence and at least one full-blooded massacre, seized power. He appointed himself prime minister, maharajah, supreme commander-in-chief, and dictator of the country, and made all these posts hereditary in his family. He relegated the king to the position of a religious figurehead. In an unstable world this old-fashioned and undemocratic form of government gave stability to Nepal until the late 1940s.

The most important year in Anglo-Gurkha relations was 1857. In that year the flames of the Great Indian Mutiny engulfed the visible British power in India. All over the country Englishwomen fled with their babies from their burning bungalows, to be sheltered in the sugar cane by kindly Indians. Few Indian princes thought that the English could win India back again; but Jung Bahadur was one of those few, because he had recently made a trip to England and had seen with his own eyes that the power of that country did not rest only on the few thousand soldiers and the few score administrators actually present in India. Also, I like to think, he was a Gurkha and he had pledged his faith.

Jung Bahadur threw the whole power of Nepal into the British scales. Among other things, he permitted the East India Company to raise more Gurkha regiments. The first extra regiment so raised was called, with baffling consistency, the Extra Gurkha Regiment, and this was the regiment that later became the 4th Gurkhas.

In 1857, then, lit by the lurid glare of the Mutiny, there stepped on to the world stage these small men from a small kingdom, who were in the next hundred years to die on many fields, always with honour, in battle against the enemies of their friends. For the first time the world learned the Gurkha code: 'I will keep faith.'

There are many tribes and castes among the Gurkhas. Our regiment enlisted only from two of the biggest, the Magars and Gurungs, both from western Nepal. Each tribe is again subdivided into sub-tribes and families. A Gurkha calls himself by his given name, followed by the name of his tribe or sub-tribe. The most common of these latter are Rana, Thapa, and Pun (all Magars), and Gurung and Ghale (both Gurungs).

Most Gurkhas are Hindus of a sort, though their religion does not sit heavily on any except those of the higher castes, which the 4th did not enlist. In Flanders in 1914, when our 1st Battalion had had no food for a couple of days, food at last appeared in the trenches—several hundred cans of corned beef, each can clearly marked with the canning company's trade mark, a bull's head. No Hindu, however lax, can eat beef; but this time it was going to be beef or nothing. The colonel sent for the senior Gurkha officer and wordlessly pointed to the rations.

After a moment came the quiet reply, 'Sahib, we are here to fight the Germans. We cannot fight if we starve. It will be forgiven us. Remove the labels, and let it be corned mutton.'

Gurkhas vary in shade from pale wheat-gold to dull, dark brown. Their skulls are usually round—but, whatever the shape, always thick. I saw a Gurkha *havildar* (sergeant) bend down to tie his bootlace just behind a particularly fractious mule. The mule let drive, and both iron-shod hoofs smashed with murderous force into the *havildar's* temple. He complained of a headache all afternoon. The mule went dead lame.

Though there are, of course, exceptions, the distinguishing marks of the Gurkha are usually a Mongolian appearance, short stature, a merry disposition, and an indefinable quality that is hard to pin down with one word. Straightness, honesty, naturalness, loyalty, courage—all these are near it, but none is quite right, for the quality embraces all these. In a Gurkha regiment nothing was ever stolen, whether a pocket knife, a watch, or a thousand rupees. Desertions were unheard of, although once the men had gone on furlough to their homes in Nepal they were quite inaccessible to us. There were no intrigue, no apple-polishing, and no servility.

The perfect man—or, at the least, the perfect soldier? Not quite. The Gurkha was slow at book-learning, and he liked gambling, rum, and women; and, in his own home, he was apt to be unkempt.

But these large generalizations are vague and patronizing. It is impossible to give an idea of the Gurkha by such means, because each Gurkha is a separate man. I have talked of 'the Gurkhas' as doing this and 'the Gurkhas' as being that, whereas, like other people, the Gurkhas have the sameness and the uniqueness of a snowfield. We can say that the snow is wet or frozen or dry-powdered, but every snowflake is different from every other snowflake.

As the Gurkhas are an old-fashioned people, we can perhaps learn more about them by looking at a few old-fashioned magic-lantern slides than by trying to dissect the Gurkhas' characteristics.

A naik (corporal) was cutting scrub with his *kukri* in order to clear a field of fire for his machine-gun. His hand slipped, and the *kukri* all but severed his left thumb. He looked at the dangling thumb for a moment, then bit it off, put it in his pocket, bandaged the stump with a dirty handkerchief, and went on with his job. In the evening he went to the doctor, pulled the thumb from his pocket and said, only half joking, 'Can you put this back for me, sahib?'

One night on the North-West Frontier a sentry, after being relieved of his duty, left the little stone fort without telling anyone he was going, and wandered out to use the day bucket twenty yards off. A few moments later the new sentry saw his dark, armed figure loom out of the night. He took aim and challenged. The figure crouched quickly— wondering, perhaps, whom the sentry was challenging. The sentry shot him dead and was in due course promoted to lance-naik for his alertness. Next day the unfortunate careless soldier had to be burned with the usual Hindu rites. A senior N.C.O. collected a burning party with the necessary wood and oil and went off with the corpse on a mule cart. Later he described the ceremony. 'What a business! It rained the whole time, and the wood wouldn't catch properly. Old Dhanjit kept sitting up as the flames licked him, and raising his arms as if he were saying, "this is too damned hot." In the end we had to cut him up and burn him a piece at a time. You've never seen anything so funny!'

Those two slides have a rough light in them. But take the mind away from all that is past—the agony of mutilation, the years of comradeship with Dhanjit, the forgetful soldier—and see only the present actuality—a conjuring trick with a thumb, such as one does to amuse one's children; a dummy sitting up in a fire. Then there is a simple humour, something that any of us might laugh at.

Two more slides: A British battleship, lights out, abristle with fourteen-inch guns, moved slowly up the heavily defended Suez Canal early in 1915. The officer on watch heard a small voice shouting from the land. At length he understood the voice to be saying, 'Halt! Who-go-dah?'

The officer did not reply. The voice then said, 'Halt-or-I-fire!' The battleship switched on a searchlight, which illumined one Gurkha rifleman standing on the bank. His rifle was pointed at the side of the battleship. The battleship stopped; its captain sent an urgent message for help; and the strategic movements of the Royal Navy stood still while an officer of Gurkhas was found to tell the sentry that the battleship could pass. At last the Gurkha shouted, 'Pass-friend-all's-well,' and lowered his rifle. The battleship glided on, with a thousand British sailors cheering and laughing. . . .

Someone was shooting at us, on the Frontier again. The shots came from an enormous scrub-covered hillside. Five British officers searched with binoculars—one of them was an artillery brigadier who had a pair of Zeiss glasses of magnification x16. We saw nothing. Our colonel's Gurkha orderly—he had no binoculars—stepped up, pointed, and said, 'There he is, by that yellowish rock under the little cliff.' There he was indeed, one thousand one hundred yards away, motionless, and of the same colour as his background. The brigadier could just pick him out, with the huge binoculars held steady on a tripod, when the Gurkha had shown him where to look.

Now a round of legends, for legends have accumulated about the Gurkha until it sometimes seems he is almost invisible behind them.

Many people have told me that the Gurkhas throw their *kukris* at their enemies. Some insist that the *kukri* returns like a boomerang to the hand of the thrower. Neither of these statements is true. The *kukri* is an all-purpose cutting tool, equally useful in the jungle to cut wood and in the field to cut flesh, but it has no magic qualities, and it is never thrown.

I have several times been told the story of the Gurkha sentry at Peking, during the Boxer Rebellion, who was insulted by a Russian officer. The Russian apparently thought he was dealing with a muzhik and tried to force his way past the Gurkha; but there had been an order that no one should go that way without a permit, which the Russian did not have. The Gurkha stopped him. The Russian drew his pistol and threatened. The Gurkha drew his *kukri* and acted—a short swing from the waist, up and round. The Russian put his hand to his head and snarled, 'Drawing a weapon on an officer! You might have hit me!'

The rifleman replied grimly, 'Take your hand off your head.' The Russian did, and his head rolled in the dust.

I don't think this tale can be literally true. The only Gurkhas in China at that time were the 1st Battalion of the 4th Gurkhas. There is no trace in our regimental records of any rifleman having been able to speak Russian with the degree of fluency indicated by the story.

During World War II a Gurkha patrol went out in the vicinity of Cassino to locate German positions. After slipping by two enemy sentries in the dark of the night, they found the other four Germans of the post asleep in a row in a barn. They beheaded the two men on the inside, but left the two on the outside to sleep—to wake up, to try to rouse their comrades. . . . It was a brilliant improvisation, which went straight to the unlovely heart of psychological warfare.

And there is the tale of the unwilling volunteers. This is about a Gurkha regiment that called for a hundred men to volunteer to become parachutists in 1940, a year when parachuting was thought to be the coming thing by many keen soldiers. The British officers explained that the jumps were made at first from balloons, and later from nice comfortable aeroplanes at a safe height of a thousand feet or more. The officers were surprised and pained to find that only seventy men volunteered. They reiterated their arguments. The Gurkhas still looked glum—if anything, glummer, and one lance-naik was heard to mutter that in his opinion five hundred feet was quite high enough. The officers then called on the sacred honour of the regiment and vowed that parachutes never—well, hardly ever— failed to open, and explained the numerous devices that made parachuting so safe. The lance-naik's face cleared, and, speaking for all, he said, 'Oh, we jump with these parachutes, do we? That's *different.*'

Lastly, and to my mind most delightful and revealing of all, there is the case of the escaped prisoner-of-war. A Gurkha rifleman escaped from a Japanese prison in south Burma and walked six hundred miles alone through the jungles to freedom. The journey took him five months, but he never asked the way and he never lost the way. For one thing he could not speak Burmese and for another he regarded all Burmese as traitors. He used a map, and when he reached India he showed it to the Intelligence officers, who wanted to know all about his odyssey. Marked in pencil were all the turns he had taken, all the roads and trail forks he had passed, all the rivers he had crossed. It had served him well, that map. The Intelligence officers did not find it so useful. It was a street map of London.

So legend, slide, and fact combine with a little analysis to limn the tremendous quality of this man, the Gurkha peasant. I have said that the phrase 'I will keep faith' describes it. Yes, but on every level of human value. The Gurkha keeps faith not only with his fellow men but with great spiritual concepts, and, above all, with himself. He seems to be born with the ability to see the heart of a problem regardless of distracting circumstances, red herrings, or conflicting advice. He does not think, cogitate—he will tell you shyly that he is not clever enough for that—but he bends facts, arguments, and logic to fit what he somehow knows is right. The London street map is a perfect example on the material plane.

Here he is, facing us. Just over five feet high, he has a low forehead, slanting brown eyes with the Mongolian fold over the inner corner, thin eyebrows, and a face either hairless or lined by a straggling mandarin moustache. Sometimes he shaves the black hair all round his skull, but he always leaves a long tuft at the crown, by which he hopes his God will pull him up to heaven when he dies. In repose he is expressionless, but he frequently shows perfect white teeth in a smile or just a plain grin. When he speaks he hardly moves his lips or teeth. He gesticulates little, grunts rather than shouts, and points with his chin, not his hands. He looks you straight in the eye and is not very interested in you unless he knows you well. He is the world's best mimic and will use the gift whenever he feels like it—often to puncture the inflated egos of those who have the privilege of ordering him about. The muscles down his back, from neck to ankles, are tremendously developed; the thighs and calves are particularly strong and shapely. He runs awkwardly on the level, well uphill, and on a steep downhill no one on earth can touch him.

Perhaps he has been working for eight hours up to his waist in freezing water, helping to build a bridge. Now he has just gone to sleep in a blanket on the stones. Wake him, tell him there's an emergency, that we must dig a trench. He rolls out with a '*Jee-lo*,' takes pick or shovel, and starts to dig, joking with the men around him and with the officers. The task is finished in three hours, to the stupefaction of the experts, who said it would take six. We who know him are not surprised; we expected it. He rolls back into his blankets. Wake him again an hour later and tell him someone has blundered, that now we are to gird for the assault, and the enemy is numerous and well armed. He stands up, stretches, fixes his bayonet, smiles at us in wry comradeship, and moves forward. . . . 'At the last his unwavering lines disappear into the smoke and wrath of battle.'

CHAPTER SIX

GURKHAS enlisted between sixteen and nineteen years of age, and signed on for four years' service. At the end of four years a man could either 'cut his name'—that is, go —or sign for more service. His pay was sixteen rupees (about twenty-three shillings) a month. After fifteen years as a rifleman he had earned a retirement pension of five rupees a month, or about seven shillings. During his service he would receive promotion according to his ability —from rifleman (private) to lance-naik, naik (corporal), havildar (sergeant), havildar-major, and quartermaster havildar of various kinds and grades. Then came a much bigger step, promotion to commissioned rank.

Commissions in the old Indian Army were of two kinds, from the King or from the Viceroy. Officers holding them were known respectively as King's Commissioned Officers (K.C.O.s) and Viceroy's Commissioned Officers (V.C.O.s).

In a British or American battalion, all officers are second-lieutenants, lieutenants, captains, majors, and so on. In the Indian Army these ranks belonged only to King's Commissioned Officers, of whom there were about twelve in a battalion. The remaining nineteen officer jobs were carried out by Viceroy's Commissioned Officers. The V.C.O. started his military life as an enlisted man and, when promoted, was promoted in the same battalion. He was therefore always of the same caste and tribe as the rank and file. Thus the V.C.O.s in a Sikh Regiment were Sikhs, in a Gurkha Regiment, Gurkhas, in a Mahratta Regiment, Mahrattas, and so on.

There were three ranks of V.C.O.: jemadars, who wore one star, the same as second-lieutenants; subadars, who wore two stars, the same as lieutenants; and *the* subadar-major, who wore a crown, like a major. V.C.O.s were not warrant or non-commissioned officers, but officers in the full sense. They wore Sam Browne belts and swords, had powers of command and discipline over all Indian enlisted men, received salutes and were always addressed as 'sahib' —'Jemadar-sahib,' 'Subadar-Major-sahib,' and so forth. We never used the unwieldy designations of King's Commissioned Officer and Viceroy's Commissioned Officer except in official correspondence. We spoke of British officers and Gurkha officers.

The Gurkha officers were the backbone of the regiment and held much responsibility. Many lacked education, but that was what we were there for. Their job, beside the ordinary duties of command, was to act as a link between the Gurkha soldiers and the British officers. My Gurkha company was organized and armed in the same way as the British company of the Duke of Cornwall's Light Infantry that I had just left, but where the British company had had a major, a captain, two lieutenants, and two second-lieutenants, my Gurkha company had only me, a second-lieutenant. A subadar was my second-in-command, and subadars or jemadars commanded each of the four platoons. On any point of Gurkha custom, tradition, or religion it was these Gurkha officers' duty to give me the opinion and feeling of the enlisted men.

Commanding nothing, but omnipresent and almost omnipotent, was the subadar-major, the senior Gurkha officer. He and the colonel had probably grown up together for the past twenty-five or thirty years. When the subadar-major joined as a seventeen-year-old recruit, the colonel had been a nineteen-year-old youngster from Sandhurst. Now they knew each other, as soldiers, as men, as friends. The subadar-major kept the junior Gurkha officers in discipline and good feeling and daily reported to the colonel anything that might affect morale. He would say that Subadar X in D Company was getting mixed up with the wife of a 1st Battalion havildar and ought to be sent on a course, and that Jemadar Y was not fit for promotion to subadar because he had turned out to be a secret drinker.

Or the colonel might hear somewhere that Nepal was full of men of the tribe of Gharti who were anxious to join the army. He would ask the subadar-major whether we should make an effort to recruit them. The subadar-major would shake his head firmly. Why? Because when the Maharajah of Nepal freed all the casteless slaves of that country in 1925, the majority decided to call themselves Ghartis. If one of these *shivbhagti* Ghartis crept in as a genuine Gharti, which he could very easily do, the battalion would have to go through expensive and degrading purification ceremonies, and would be the laughing stock of all the other Gurkha regiments. Anyway, the subadar-major might add, a genuine Gharti is not all that good. The colonel would drop the idea.

So much for 'Gurkha' in our title. What about 'Rifles'? I found that this story had started in 1775—in New York! In that year a regiment was formed to beat the French and Indians at their own game, i.e. by making use of cover, woodcraft, and scouting. The regiment was called the Royal Americans, and the settlers who fought in it brought their short green jackets and long rifles with them, disdaining the scarlet coat and the official smooth-bore musket. So the corps of Rifle regiments was born. They wore darkgreen uniforms and black buttons, and boasted that they were always first into action and last out. They had to develop a special quick step of one hundred and forty paces a minute to enable them to get out ahead of the rest of the army in advance and catch up from rearguard positions in retreat.

Gradually the whole army discarded the musket and took to the rifle. Everyone learned to fight from cover, but the Rifle regiments alone kept the dark-green clothes, their black bone buttons, and their super-quick step. Their common badge, the stringed buglehorn of a forest hunter, was always found somewhere among their markings. Their private soldiers were never called privates but always 'riflemen.' They did not refer to 'bayonets' but to 'swords,' because at one time they alone carried the long sword bayonet, while the rest of the army had true toothpick bayonets. They still wore the full dress of hussar cavalry—busby, sabretache, crossbelt, frogged jacket, and the rest—for they had developed into the army's foot cavalry, though all the panoply of hussar colour was, with them, reduced to black or a very dark bottle-green, called riflegreen. They had no Colours, standards, or guidons, for they never formed a line. Instead they carried their battle honours on their drums and wore on all occasions an overweening pride. In a Rifle regiment the last insult was to refer to a happening, a custom, or a person as being thoroughly 'red.' This had nothing to do with the Politburo, but compared the bumbleheaded ineptness of the redcoat with the tensed alertness of the green-jacket.

At the capture of Delhi in 1857 British soldiers of the 60th Rifles fought in the same force as the 2nd Gurkhas. Shoulder to shoulder they stormed the great wall, and together battered in the Kashmir Gate with their rifle butts. In honour of this feat, and to commemorate the outstanding work of the other Gurkha regiments during the

97

Mutiny, Queen Victoria is supposed to have declared that they were all to wear the uniform of Rifle regiments. It is certain that they all went into the dark green and wore it until full dress died out after the Kaiser's War. After that the green lived on only in our officers' mess kit and in the uniforms we bought with our own money for the pipers, the mess havildar, and a few others. Our regiment, the 4th, was handed over to India in 1947 and is now Indian in every respect—but it still has the black buttons embossed with a stringed buglehorn, a super-quick marching pace, and an overweening pride.

'Fourth'—an honourable number. I soon came to believe with a passion worthy of a religion that there was no regiment on earth like it. The 1st Gurkhas were earnest, the 2nd idle, the 3rd illiterate, the 5th narrow-minded, the 6th down-trodden, the 7th unshaven, the 8th exhibitionist, the 9th Brahminical (they enlisted high-caste Gurkhas), and the 10th alcoholic. As for the rest of the Indian Army—well, the Guides weren't bad, but even they were not what they used to be in the old days, when they had a Gurkha company. The British Army, lock, stock, and barrel, was useless. But we—we were wonderful! We were stiff with battle honours. We had fought from France to China. We were witty, happy, carefree, tough, efficient, wise . . .

It was no bad state of mind to be in, and not inaccurate. The 4th Gurkhas would not have been even good unless we had believed it to be the best.

It may now come as a surprise to learn that this regiment of which we thought so highly did not actually exist. In the King's (or Queen's) infantry a regiment is not an organization that can be numbered and put on parade. It is not a tangible thing at all, but an ethereal idea. It has a page or two in the Army List, a roll of battle honours, a prescribed uniform and facings, and a home station or depot. That is all. In my time several regiments of the Indian and British Armies were indeed nothing more than that. Their battalions had been disbanded for various reasons, usually economy, but the essentials of the spirit were kept on record and could at any time be clothed with flesh by raising new battalions.

The King's infantry was, in fact, organized into units called battalions, each a collection of about eight hundred men and thirty officers, with many weapons and much equipment. A battalion was commanded by a lieutenant-colonel, officially the commandant or the commanding officer, unofficially 'the colonel' or the C.O. Every battalion belonged to some regiment—otherwise how would it have known what uniform to wear, what customs to follow, where its home was? In 1935 the ten Gurkha regiments had two battalions each. These two battalions went about their military business quite independently of each other and were not linked by any system of command. They met only by chance, usually in their home station, where the state of the frontier and the vagaries of peacetime reliefs sometimes sent them both at the same time.

The military formation into which battalions were grouped, quite haphazardly, was the brigade. So if we went to Razmak we would join the Razmak Brigade for the duration of our time there, while our 1st Battalion, serving in, say, Peshawar, would be part of the Peshawar Brigade. The brigadiers who thus had the honour of our services from time to time were the military seniors of our C.O.s and could order us to do whatever they wished—but they could not interfere with our customs or traditions. The 4th Gurkhas might have had a custom of standing on their heads whenever the name of the Viceroy was mentioned, and a brigadier might not like it, but he could do nothing about it.

These matters were in the hands of the only visible link between different battalions of the same regiment, the Colonel of the Regiment. Historically, when a sovereign needed troops he gave some important personage a colonel's commission and told him to raise a regiment. The personage was then the colonel of that regiment. Since he was usually a member of the high aristocracy and often a

99

courtier close to the sovereign's person he seldom actually served in command of his regiment, but left that to some lieutenant of his—hence the lieutenant-colonel. When still more soldiers were required the colonel would split his regiment into two or more battalions, and then there would be a lieutenant-colonel in command of each.

It is a long time since a British sovereign has raised a regiment by private commission, but each regiment still has a colonel. Nowadays this is a senior officer, often retired, who did his early soldiering with a battalion of that regiment and was later appointed by the sovereign, in person, to be its colonel. There was, for example, a man called B. L. Montgomery who rose from second-lieutenant to lieutenant-colonel in the Royal Warwickshire Regiment. He went on to become a field marshal and Viscount Montgomery of Alamein, but I do not suppose any of his numerous honours mean as much to him as the fact that King George VI appointed him Colonel of the Royal Warwickshire Regiment.

The Colonel of the Regiment is the arbiter in quarrels between the battalions of his regiment, has a big say in the selection of officers, and is the last authority in all cases of dress, tradition, custom, modes, and manners. And, whoever he is, he has the right of direct access to the sovereign on matters affecting his regiment.

Then, we were the 'Prince of Wales's Own.' A regiment honours a man who has served it well by asking the sovereign to appoint him its colonel. The sovereign honours a regiment that has served him well by appointing himself or a member of his family to be its colonel-in-chief. Many regiments have had royal colonels-in-chief at one time or another, and their names have often been permanently incorporated into the title of the regiment, as in 'The Rifle Brigade (Prince Consort's Own)' or 'Queen Victoria's Own Corps of Guides.' After the Kaiser's War, King George V appointed the Prince of Wales to be our colonel-in-chief, and our title and crest were altered to include his.

From then on our crest became the Prince of Wales's feathers and scroll with the motto 'Ich Dien'; below that crossed *kukris*, both blades down, both handles to the right; in the lower fork of the *kukris* a Roman IV.

Studying the Army List, where my name now appeared in small print at the bottom of the list of officers, I saw another name, another title:

Honorary Colonel:
> Honorary Lieutenant-Colonel His Highness Projjwala Nepala Tara Ati Pravala Gorkha Dakshina Bahu Prithuladesha Sri Sri Sri Maharajah Sir Joodha Shumshere Jung Bahadur Rana, G.C.I.E., Prime Minister and Supreme Commander-in-Chief of Nepal.

I closed the book slowly. There are boundaries of knowledge beyond which it is indecent to travel.

CHAPTER SEVEN

A GUEST night was approaching, at which I would be ceremonially 'dined into' the regiment. Days ahead I started to worry over the details of my dress and appearance. Biniram was neither excited nor frightened, which makes his negligence the more inexcusable. On the night my shirt was stiff and white as it could be, my black bow tie beautifully tied, and my mess Wellingtons polished like mirrors. After walking into the anteroom, I checked at attention with the proper carefully rehearsed carelessness, and said, 'Good evening, sir,' to the senior officer present. Alas, I had two fly buttons undone.

Major and Brevet Lieut.-Colonel David Murray Murray-Lyon, D.S.O., M.C.—more usually known as M. L.—said, 'Good evening, Masters. Stars in the east, I see. Good lord, that doesn't matter. Do 'em up. Well, this is the last time you'll be a regimental guest until you get married, so make the best of it. What d'you want?'

'A gimlet, please, sir.'

'Orderly, *yota* gimlet, *yota* gin-mixie-vermouth-cherry. Jim, can the C.O. come in tonight?'

'No, sir, he's held up at Dalhousie. You're the senior dining member.'

The room was full of officers. Many voices arose.

'Orderly, *dwui siano* whisky-soda.' '*Mero lagi pani.*' '*Ek* gimlet.' '*Dwui* sherry.' '*Tin thulo* whisky-soda.'

The orderly listened and said amiably, '*Huzoor, sahib!*'

The voices continued. 'Heard the latest about Sheepers? He persuaded some girl that . . .'

'Take Austria, now. *They* don't care, they're *gemütlich*. German in a way, but sort of carefree . . .'

'It's all very well for you, but we machine-gunners have work to do while you're bumsucking round battalion office. 7157 ought to be promoted and then there's 7493 too, and as for 6701 . . .'

'. . . Christmas Week in Lahore. The Boy's bought a racehorse. He gave me a tip for . . .'

'. . . crossed the Baralacha just ahead of a blizzard and came down through Zingzingbar behind forty Tibetans from the Patseo sheep fair. Stank like badgers, but one of them was a wonderful old boy. Lectured me on . . .'

'6573? That's Sarbdhan, isn't it? The one who got hit in the bottom in 'thirty-one?'

'Yes, but it wasn't his fault, you ass.'

A small Gurkha wearing bottle-green full-dress uniform marched into the room, saluted, and said, '*Sahib, khana tay yar chha.*'

M. L. said, 'Are we all here? Oh, you again, James, late as usual.'

'Good evening, sir. My watch—damned clock.'

Out on the green lawn under the lights the band struck up 'The Roast Beef of Old England,' and we straggled into the dining-room. The officers who chose to sit at the head and foot of the table became the president and vice-president respectively, for that meal. No one else had any special place except that the senior dining member sat half-way down the table to the president's left, with the principal guest immediately on his right. On this night M. L., the second-in-command of the battalion, was the senior dining member, and I was the principal and only guest.

I accepted a glass of sherry and looked around, while

cautiously toying with the hors d'œuvres. Outside, now that we were all seated, the band started on selections from *The Mikado*. The Gurkha in full dress, the three black chevrons on his right sleeve hardly visible against the dark-green cloth, stood immobile behind the president's chair. He was Machhindra, the mess havildar. The candlelight gleamed warmly on his wrinkled bronze face and glinted in his eyes as he glanced around the table and at the bearers who were serving up the food.

Around me the conversation rippled in comfortable waves. People spoke to me sufficiently to keep me in the current, and M. L. saw to it that my glass was never empty. I, on the other hand, saw to it that the level of the champagne in the glass did not go down too fast, for the disastrous June Ball of 1933 was much in my mind. Before I realized that the meal had progressed so far, the bearers were clearing the table. The decanters of port, sherry, madeira, and whisky circulated clockwise from the president. The orderlies took our water glasses away. This has been done in most messes since the day of King George I. Secret sympathizers with the Stuart cause would drink to the health of 'the King,' but would pass their wine glasses over their water glasses as they spoke, thus changing the toast from Hanoverian George to Stuart James or Charles, who were in exile in France—'the king over the water.'

The president rang a tiny bell, a silver replica of the regimental war memorial. We fell silent. The president rose to his feet and said quietly, 'Mr Vice, the King Emperor.'

The vice-president rose, glass in hand, and said, 'Gentlemen, the King Emperor.'

We all stood up and drank the King Emperor's health.

The president sat down, turned to the mess havildar, and asked him to invite the bandmaster in for a drink. Little Mr Adams entered and agreed to have a glass of port with the president. This was an invariable custom, but he managed to look shyly gratified at the invitation. As there was no place on our Establishment for a bandmaster of any sort, let alone a British one, we paid his salary from the Band Fund, which was principally supported by subscriptions from the officers.

While Mr Adams was still sitting there the president caught M. L.'s eye. The president nodded at the mess havildar, and Machhindra went out of the room. By now cigars and cigarettes were alight all round the table, and the decanters had made a second circuit.

A high, droning roar arose in the garden outside, and I started in my seat with alarm. Then high whines superimposed themselves upon the roar. I would have said then, in 1935, that the noise sounded like a hurricane a-building, but now I would describe it as an approaching squadron of jets. The mingled noises grew louder. I paled and looked around the table, ready to dive under it if anyone else showed a sign of doing so. But the officers went on with their talk, albeit now they had to bellow at one another above the din.

Machhindra flung open the double doors behind the president. Hard on his heels the noise burst upon us and overwhelmed us, and with it, one behind another in single file, came the four bagpipers who were causing it. The leader swung his shoulders and began to march around the table; the others followed. All wore rifle-green full dress. Silk banners hung from two of the pipes, one green, one pale silver.

I did not think I liked bagpipes, and their noise was very loud indeed. I crouched lower in my chair, but not too noticeably, for it was already clear that M. L. was a Highland fanatic and an expert bagpiper. He looked up keenly now, listening sharply to every note from each pipe, a slight frown creasing his rugged face as blurred fingering or a false grace note displeased him. The smoke curled to the ceiling from the cigarette held up rather high between his strong fingers. He smoked only his own special oval cigarettes of peculiar pungency, made in Aden by a Greek merchant, stamped with our crest, and sent to him in boxes of five hundred. I looked at the pipe programme in its little silver stand in front of him, and saw that they were playing the quick march of the first set, 'The Green Hills of Tyrol.'

The steady unison broke. 'The Green Hills' is one of the few pipe tunes that has a 'second' part, and now our pipe-major dropped into it. Suddenly the haunting minor harmony infused the steady cadence with a sad magic. As suddenly the plane on which I was experiencing the events of the evening moved from the directly seen to the indirectly felt, from the outside to the inside, from the senses to the spirit.

They had taken me into this family, and I felt the comradeship of those who had come before me to this table and been received into this home. I saw their graves on the banks of the Euphrates, in the Afghan snows, under the poplars beside the *pavé* to Neuve Chapelle, on the Russian steppes, in the seas and the mountains and the hills—oh, the green hills, the green hills . . .

The candlelight shone on the centrepiece. There, set on an ebony stand formally carved to represent waves, a Chinese junk rode, nose down, over the smooth surface of the table. Its silver-woven sails bellied to the imagined wind, its masthead pennants streamed forward, its tiny cannon peered out among the silver cordage, its helmsman stood steady at the tiller above the high stern. In front of the president stood a silver statuette of a Gurkha—Naik Chandsing Thapa of ours. It was in 1905 that he was a naik, and in that same year (the second of my father's service in India, the last of my great-uncle's) the 1st Gurkhas had given us this statuette of him. An earthquake had destroyed their home station of Dharmsala, and a party of ours, Chandsing among them, went to the rescue. Dharmsala is thirty-five miles from Bakloh by precipitous mountain paths. Every man of our rescue party had been given a pick, shovel, or crowbar and told to find his own way to Dharmsala as fast as he could. They all arrived before nightfall that same evening.

Farther down the table a monstrosity of Victorian craftsmanship, only less ornately symbolic than the Albert

Memorial, sent its pillars and cupids writhing towards the ceiling. In its vast shadow rested a delicate vase presented to us by Lord Curzon, the Viceroy of that time, in 1900. More silver gleamed everywhere—cups, candelabra, ashtrays, beakers; and on the wall hung presentation shields of wood and silver, and between the shields were the heads, horns, tusks, and skulls of animals.

This was our family's home. Here were the beautiful things any family picks up over the years. Here were the horrors presented by Aunt Hattie and kept on display because Aunt Hattie is a nice old thing and no one wants to offend her. (Our Aunt Hattie was usually the Maharajah of Nepal.) Here were purely sentimental pieces, meaningless to anyone outside the family, military equivalents of locks of hair—medals, swords, and photographs; the unspeakable watercolour old Colonel Snodgrass did the night the mess tent burned down after the battle of Umbeyla. Or was it Ali Masjid?

The pipers finished the set—slow march, quick march, strathspey, and reel—and marched out. While we banged on the table in applause Machhindra placed the quaich in front of the president. This was a small, shallow silver bowl with stub handles. The president half filled it with neat Scotch whisky, and Machhindra took it to M. L. The pipe-major marched in, halted with a clash of boots beside M. L.'s chair, turned to face the table, and saluted. M. L. rose to his feet, handed him the quaich, and picked up his own glass. All the others remained seated but took their glasses in hand, and I followed suit. The pipe-major raised the quaich in front of his face with both hands, looked round at us over the brim, and shouted 'Taggra raho!' ('Good health!'). He poured the whisky down his throat in one easy motion till it was all gone, and went on turning over the quaich until he could kiss the bottom with a loud smack. Then he reversed it again, bowed his head, and handed it back to M. L. All the officers cried out, 'Taggra raho!' raised their glasses, and drank to the pipe-major.

The decanters circulated again. The solo piper marched

in and played a set. M. L. was in serious doubt whether he should be given a drink, as he had been careless with his grace notes. Finally he relented, and again we answered, '*Taggra raho*,' to the piper's salute. The band struck up on the lawn, now playing 'In a Monastery Garden.' (They could also play a brass-band arrangement of Beethoven's Fifth.)

M. L. said, 'Drink up, and we'll go into the anteroom.' No one could leave the table until I did, for I was a regimental guest. The president and vice-president could not leave until everyone else had.

In the anteroom we slowly gathered again. Two captains sprawled in chairs, their long legs up, arguing good-humouredly about music. M. L. pressed a glass of brandy and soda on me. Someone began to do tricks on the mantelpiece. The orderlies were giggling, and Moke had one of their caps on. M. L. was in good form, and it looked as though a real party was developing. I began to join in.

Then I collected my wits. I was a regimental guest. Therefore no one might leave the mess until I did. I thanked M. L. for the regiment's hospitality, stiffened to attention, and said, 'Good night, sir.'

I thought I saw a momentary gleam of approval in M. L.'s eye as he said, 'Good night, Masters.'

Perhaps I had learned something already—a little self-discipline. I went out, and alone, to bed. But it wasn't lonely in the deserted bungalow, though I could hear the party going on in the mess until three in the morning.

CHAPTER EIGHT

Not until the guest night did I feel that I had truly joined the regiment, although the adjutant had taken me formally before the commanding officer on the first day after my arrival. The colonel did not say much, as serious words are never spoken on these occasions—only that he was pleased I had come to the battalion and hoped I would like it and do well.

Then he told me I was to take over both A and B Companies for a week, since their commanders were going on a short course. After that I would command A Company only.

This instantaneous transition from the command of a British platoon, whose language, at least, I knew, and where there were a company commander and second-in-command to supervise me and other platoon commanders to give advice, to the sole charge of two whole Gurkha companies was almost more than I could stand. I rushed out, found James, and wailed that I was sunk, my career ruined before it had begun. I didn't know what to do.

James did not seem worried. He said, 'Leave it to the G.O.s and the clerks. Do whatever seems to need doing, and ask me for help if you have to.' Since there was nothing else I could do, that is what I did. It turned out to be not so bad as I had expected. There was, besides, a humorous overtone that made the week a happy memory. A and B

Companies were arguing about responsibility for a lost piece of equipment and I went from one office to the other signing acid letters to myself about it.

James also told me that I would avoid a lot of needless badgering if I always walked about at a pace slightly faster than normal, carrying a bunch of papers, and working my lips as though thinking aloud. It was good advice, and still is, and not only in the army.

The true reason for the easiness of the work was that we were at a slack period in the training cycle. Buddhists claim that humanity is bound on the wheel of existence. The peacetime professional soldier was certainly bound to a more dreadful engine, the training cycle. It turned relentlessly with the year, beginning each new revolution at the time immediately after the best campaigning season, which in India is the cold weather, from November to February. From individual training it worked its way up through section, platoon, company, and battalion training to the exalted levels of 'higher' training. Just how high this was depended on how much money the Government was willing to allot the army that year. Brigade training was nearly always achieved, but division, corps, or army manœuvres were much rarer, since they cost a lot in terms of petrol, special trains to bring troops together from their scattered stations, compensation for damage to land and crops, and wear and tear on military equipment.

So it was that in March each soldier started once more to learn his individual skills. The rifleman turned to his rifle, the light-automatic-gunner to his Vickers-Berthier, the machine-gunner to his Vickers, the signaller to his flags and helios and buzzers. Once again each soldier learned about gas and wiring, digging and drill. For the old soldiers, who had done it all five or eight or eighteen times before, this blast of stale knowledge was tempered by much book-learning. They spent many hours having their education painfully improved, or in undergoing courses to fit them for promotion. The newly joined recruits and the young soldiers had the minutiæ of our trade ground into them until with them, as with the old sweats, it became second nature to reload their rifles once they had fired three rounds; to check pouch clips, canteen cork, bayonet hasp, and rifle safety catch with one circular sweep of the hand at every halt on the march; to put their shorts, tidily folded, under their mattresses at night, so that their own weight would press the shorts while they slept. It was mainly N.C.O.s' work. We officers had little to do but prepare the programmes and supervise the N.C.O.s, and we were, besides, undergoing our own individual training. The seniors taught us map-reading, and the signal officer explained the new field codes, and the junior major recounted, on a blackboard, the inexplicable changes that had occurred in the organization of other arms since the same time last year. In this period we wrote essays on 'Preparations necessary before undertaking action in aid of the civil power,' were taught double-entry bookkeeping, lectured one another on 'The role of the machine-gun in the attack,' and drew coloured diagrams showing the stages undergone by a wounded man between the time he was hit in the front line and the time he reached a base hospital.

Above all, individual training was the time for TEWTs. A TEWT was a Tactical Exercise Without Troops. It could be held in the open, or on a sand or cloth model made up to represent a suitable piece of ground, or even on a map. A senior officer prepared the exercise and gave us all pieces of paper that told us what troops were supposed to be taking part on our side, what we were trying to do, what we knew about the enemy, what the situation was when the exercise began, and what person we were supposed to be representing. Then at the appointed time we gathered at a viewpoint or round the sand model, and the director gave out Narrative 1. In Narrative 1 our make-believe commander usually appeared and barked out a series of orders. Problem 1 followed immediately: 'What is your plan to carry out these orders? Tell me here in thirty minutes.'

We looked at the ground, and at our notebooks, and back again, and straggled off in small syndicates to work out a feasible solution.

Time was up. We gathered again. The director said, 'Masters, let's have your syndicate's plan.'

'Well, sir, we don't know much about the enemy here, and—er——'

'Yes, yes, I don't want the whole appreciation—just your plan.'

'Well, sir, the guns are out of range and will have to be moved . . .' I ploughed miserably on. No comment was made when I finished.

'Murray, yours.'

'My intention is to capture Black Ridge—there—in sufficient time to enable consolidation to be completed before last light. Consolidation will take two hours. Last light is at 1827 hours, so I must capture Black Ridge by 1627 hours. Support—84 Field Battery from positions behind Tuni Hatti 1765. Battery to be in position by 1500 hours for ranging. Start line-copse 194032—track to 193030—house 193026. Zero hour 1530 hours . . .'

I hung my head in shame. Here was the only sensible plan, coming out in short, decisive phrases, with no ums and ers, carrying conviction, simple to understand. Our syndicate had had the same plan, but no one listening to me would have thought I believed in it myself, so they certainly would not have. I noted down on the tablets of my memory: make up your mind, know what you are going to say, say it briefly, then stop.

At the end of each TEWT the colonel summed up and pointed out our faults—tactical, technical, and psychological. We went back to parade ground, rifle range, or office, and turned again to the individual training of our men and the administration of our commands.

Towards the end of the rainy season in August the soldiers, now full to the gills with individual training, began to start section training. The emphasis changed from the efficiency of the individual as a soldier to the efficiency of the section as a team of seven or eight soldiers. The section leaders, the naiks and lance-naiks, now found officers breathing down their necks and pointing out the folly of moving their men across *that* ridge when *that* hollow would have been better. The soldiery did what they were told and relaxed. They knew the heat was moving up. Whatever they did, correction would not fall directly on them, for praise and blame alike always went to the top.

I was hurt at first when the adjutant took me a pace aside and told me venomously that 7550 Rifleman Deobahadur Gurung had no water-bottle in his equipment. Was that the way I looked after my company? He glared at me as though he had caught me mixing strychnine into their rice ration.

What did I know of 7550 Rifleman Deobahadur Gurung? I'd never heard of him, and as for his water-bottle—why, it was ridiculous! I soon learned that the whole lot of them, one hundred and thirty-two Gurkha officers and men, were my business—sleeping, waking, sober, drunk, on duty and off duty. I had to know them all, down to the third genera-tion, and their temperaments and capabilities, their homes, wives, fathers, children, cousins, next of kin, and inheritors. The way to deal with a case such as this of the water-bottle was to find in my list that Deobahadur was in No. 2 Platoon, walk up to the platoon commander, and say coldly—with-out, of course, giving an inkling of how I knew—'Jemadar-sahib, Deobahadur has no water-bottle. Is this the way you look after your platoon?'

Jemadar Sukdeo, with a quick glance full of dire meaning at his platoon havildar, pounced on Deobahadur's section commander, Naik Amarsing Gurung, and repeated the malediction as from himself. Finally Deobahadur ap-peared before me and received seven days' confinement to the lines for being improperly dressed on parade. But in the process we all had a lesson in responsibility, and we all knew that there was a weak link in A Company, and that it must be strengthened. I also learned that adjutants have eyes in the back of their heads, but I had known that already.

The quickening exercises began. The old hands reminded us that battle is full of the unexpected, and if soldiers are going to survive and win they must react quickly to the unusual without stopping to think. I learned to clap my hands loudly together and at once bring the right hand on into my chest. The resultant *crack-thump*, I was assured, made a noise just like a bullet. The *crack* was the bullet smacking through the air overhead—or, more accurately, the air filling up the vacuum caused by its passing. The *thump* was the noise of the actual explosion of the cartridge in the distant enemy's rifle, which followed at about 1,100 feet per second behind the bullet's 2,200 feet per second. The interval between the two sounds thus showed the distance of the firer.

We made these *crack-thumps* suddenly and without warning anywhere—on the march, during drill parades, in school. Every soldier within earshot learned to react on the instant—that is, dive for cover, and, if armed, prepare to return the fire and manœuvre to kill the enemy.

We gave absurd commands like 'On the backs—down!' in the middle of a drill parade, or 'Touch the ceiling— jump!' while the men were bent over schoolbooks, or, at any time, 'Everyone catch Banbahadur!' It was a lesson in comparative psychology just to watch the varying speeds at which the minds worked. There was a sort of chain reaction as each man jerked free from some other thought, fastened on to the idea of Banbahadur, then of catching Banbahadur, then of remembering where he stood, and at last began to move. Banbahadur, by the same process, at last reached the thought: Banbahadur? Good God, that's me; what am I doing here?—and broke off for his life with the quicker-witted of his pursuers hard on his heels.

Platoon training began. Sections coagulated into platoons, and we took our companies off, organized mock battles between the platoons, and afterwards attempted to sum up the lessons learned and apportion the day's crop of praise and blame. The seniors went round with copies of our training programmes in their hands, trying to find out what we were doing so that they could keep us on the right lines. We, in turn, tried to avoid them without actually cheating—that is, by leaving the area in which we had announced we could be found. I did not try to hide from M. L. because he never carped. He came, sat on a rock, smoked his vile Aden cigarettes, and at the end talked quietly about how one jemadar had used his intelligence and another had not, about why certain things made sense in battle and others did not. He never stayed long, yet saw all there was to see, put me right without showing me up as an ass in front of my company, and strode off with tremendous strides to find James or John or Moke.

Every Saturday, whatever the current phase of the training cycle, the whole battalion came together to do either a route march or a simple battle manœuvre. The route marches were done because it has been conclusively proved that there is no way of training soldiers for marching under load except by making them march under load. The manœuvres kept the mechanism of field command from rusting. Without them it would not have functioned when required for the big exercises of higher training, or for an unexpected war.

There is no apparent reason why route marches should not be very boring, since the essence of them is to march along a hard road at an even pace for a long time, with no excitements to help pass the time and no cross-country work to alter the scenery and ease the strain on the feet. Yet they never bored me. The men sang, the bugles blew *ta-ra, ta-raah* in the middle of the battalion, and I could look at the passing flowers and trees and animals, or could slide into a reverie and march along with my thoughts in England or China, the past or the future. I learned to bring my mind back every five minutes and sweep the company's faces for signs of fatigue or illness, to recognize the proper pace by instinct, so that I did not have to look at my watch to know we were passing each furlong post one hundred and twenty seconds after we had passed the last. I learned to feel the rhythm of the step so that a drag in it would drag at my brain and bring me back to correct it. This rhythm was important, and to keep it intact we marched straight through any streams or puddles that lay in the path. Wet boots and feet soon dried out, but a broken rhythm did not allow a man to relax while moving.

The route marches lengthened. Our early jaunts of eight or nine miles increased to marches of twelve, fifteen, twenty miles. At the end we always marched past the C.O. at a Rifle regiment's one hundred and forty paces to the minute. Then we really had to step out and march as though fresh from barracks for an Imperial Proclamation. Tired, hungry, sweaty, we willed ourselves to snap by with heads up, shoulders back; rifles sliding steadily along at the trail, exactly parallel to the ground, six inches between butt plate and nosecap, steel bootheels biting the road in the urgent step. Sometimes we used another Rifle prerogative and went past at the double, still trying to breathe easily and look as though we would be happy to do another twenty miles.

At the very last we did not even dismiss after reaching the parade ground, but performed half an hour's drill, and that too had to be perfect.

We were ready to take the road to the plains for battalion training and brigade manœuvres. I was looking forward to it all. I liked manœuvres. They were interesting, exciting, and comical, and were usually highlighted by a few impossibly ingenious tangles. The day always came when soldiers who should have been miles apart lay eye to eye in mortal combat, and soldiers who should have been breathing stern defiance at an onrushing enemy were found playing cards in a ditch while the onrushing enemy rushed on— in the opposite direction.

So, on a dry, cold November morning I buckled on my

equipment and hurried up to the parade ground, and there were the camels that would carry our baggage to the plains. There were scores of them, bubbling wetly as they dropped the insides of their throats out of their mouths, blew through them, and schlooped them in again. The reek of ammonia seeped into barrack rooms and offices, for there is no smell so sharp and pervasive as camels' stale. The ground was littered with tents, bags, boxes, and bales, and the Gurkha officers were in full swing. Subadar-Major Narbir rolled slowly about with his pigeon-toed gait, looking at people. He always wore crêpe-soled boots in defiance of army regulations and, although a man of even temper and few words, somehow projected his personality into every nook and cranny of the battalion.

Now as Narbir looked at them the soldiers froze like pillars of salt or flung themselves more desperately at their work, according to whether that wordless, expressionless glare had meant 'stop' or 'go.' From the hill above the scene looked like an ant-heap. I had no idea what was happening, or how order was to be achieved, until suddenly all the camels stood up, miraculously loaded, and swayed off down the road.

We fell in by companies. The pipe band struck up; the shouted orders drifted down to me on the light breeze; the boots started to tramp on the hard road. We snaked past the squash courts, the church, and the mess, past the corner of the 1st Battalion's lines, back round two hairpin bends, and down the side of the Bakloh ridge. All the women were out, waving alongside the road, babies in their arms and children at their sides.

The men shouted jokes up and down the column. Rifleman Dalbahadur ran past me till he was way out by himself, behind the colonel on his horse, and stomped along for five minutes in exact imitation of the colonel *and* his horse, as they curvetted sideways and tittuped forward in front of us all.

My company, in the lead, started to sing one of the Gurkha's favourite, endlessly repeated little ditties, a pleasant tune. The front half of the company began, then the back:

> *Raja-lai baipunki ghora,*
> *Sipahi-lai dwui kutta motor-ra.*

The rajah has a two-winged horse,
The soldier has a two-foot-power motor car.

The colonel turned in the saddle and shook his fist at Dalbahadur. The singing grew louder.

CHAPTER NINE

THE wild geese from Tibet were flying south with us.
At night in my tent in the mango grove I heard the
ya-honk of the skeins as the enormous squadrons arrowed
south over the five rivers. From down here, close to the
cold earth, I could see only the stars through the boughs
and the night haze over the wide-spreading crops, but in
my imagination, as I lay awake, I flew with the wild geese
and heard the thunder of wings as the following squadrons
echoed down the passes in the rampart of the Himalaya,
and beyond again I saw them circling into formation over
the salt lakes in the austere plains.

The ducks were on the wing too, and evening and morning we hunted their advanced guards, already settled for
the winter on the scattered water of the Punjab. Day by
day we marched south and east on a country road in a
timeless land. The road ran broad and unsurfaced and
straight as a spear, and huge trees marched with us on
either side and spread their branches over us to cool the
gorgeous sun.

All India must have been like this in the old days, green
and brown and quiet, for the noises of water wheels and
barking dogs were swallowed by the acres of crops and
jungle patches. My great-uncle had travelled this road in
1873. He was a young man riding a young horse in the
world's morning, a shot gun across his saddle and a little
Indian boy running at his stirrup with a bag of cartridges.
A pensioned rissaldar of cavalry might have come stiffly

to him over the fields, hurrying from a neat house at the corner of the sugar cane, buttoning his faded tunic as he stumbled along, his sabre rattling in his bony hand. Near the road he would slow to the dignity of his rank and age and give a greeting—'Salaam, sahib!' 'Salaam, Rissaldar-sahib!' The touching of a sword, words together in the sun-bright dust, and the little boy shifting impatiently from one leg to the other. He wants to get on to the birds. Farewells and parting. The old rissaldar has seen, perhaps for the last time, the regiment he served for forty years, embodied in a boy he never knew. The young cornet rides on into the morning, humming.

It was not difficult to see all this, for a pensioned rissaldar of the Hariana Lancers hurried to us across these same fields and stood very straight to talk to our colonel. Perhaps he had been the little Indian boy who had carried my great-uncle's cartridges, but he was not impatient now.

The dust lay inches deep in the road and rose in a cloud under the trees and would not blow away. We started marching at seven or eight in the morning, with handker-chiefs tied across our noses and mouths. After a few minutes, glancing back, I looked down a green-arched tunnel of hazy gold. The barred shadows struck down through it and settled in sharp relief on the moving frieze of Gurkhas' faces. Our boots made no sound in the dust and, muffled up, we could not sing. We marched in the removed trance of the professional infantryman, our minds miles away from this business of moving, but linked to one another by unseen cords, the rhythm of the step, the sound of the bugles.

Three or four times a day we passed the long string of camels. They moved at two and a half miles an hour and never stopped. We covered three miles and one furlong every fifty minutes, and then halted for ten minutes' rest. As soon as we swung clear of the swaying, padding monsters it would be time to halt, and they would lurch past us again, the dust thicker than ever, so that we never seemed to be free of them. They got on everyone's nerves.

Lance-Naik Dhansing of the buglers, a man very close to the animal in the directness of his feelings, did what the whole battalion would have loved to do, and showed in the doing a very true Gurkha humour. Sent with a message from the very back to the very front of the column, he swung out and began to hurry along beside the camels. As he went he leaped up and tweaked each male animal's testicles. The loads on our backs became as nothing from that moment, and as for me, apart from the satisfaction of second-hand catharsis, I shall never forget the sudden alteration of expression on each camel's face as Dhansing reached its hind end. Camels wear a conceited and abominably supercilious look, because it was into a camel's ear alone that Mohammed whispered the hundredth name of God. The memory of these ungainly beasts starting forward, the expression on their faces changing from pompous omniscience to alarmed outrage, has often made me wish to introduce Dhansing among a roomful of literary critics. I am sure he would see the resemblance.

The day's march usually finished between one and three in the afternoon. The camels arrived and dispersed to their places. There was a flurry of unloading, a pause, a minute's hammering, and the tents rose like ranked mushrooms. The Gurkha officers' mess baggage usually arrived before ours, and then the subadar-major invited us over to wash the dust down our throats with sweet milky tea laced with pepper and spice. An hour's rest, a late lunch, an hour's work inspecting arms and feet and giving out the next day's orders, and we were free.

I did not own a shotgun, but someone always lent me one, and we piled into tongas or went on foot to the best water in the neighbourhood. It might be three or ten miles away —it didn't matter. Crowds of Gurkhas clamoured to come with us and formed beating lines for snipe, or sat cheerfully up to their waists in water, waiting with us for the evening flight. Others took antiquated shotguns and went off to stalk the doves and green pigeons as they crooned unwary on the branches of the trees. For miles around each camp the air quaked to explosions and the Gurkhas' excited cries.

We would get back about midnight, rise again before dawn to take the morning flight, hurry back, swallow some breakfast, while the loading fatigue stood ready beside us, and get on parade.

This was my first hunting experience, and I put up a performance that still stands as a regimental record. During seven days' shooting I fired ninety-nine cartridges for a score of two snipe. The two kills were registered with the last three cartridges.

After the first couple of days my inaccuracy began to worry me. Sometimes an Indian bystander would say with grave politeness, and no twinkle apparent in his eye, that I was shooting very well, but God was kind to the birds. This did not seem logical nor could I really believe, though I tried, that all the guns lent me had curved barrels. Besides, it stung my pride when men to right and left of me leaned over with insolent disregard of my existence and blew the little birds out of my eyebrows. After God had been kind to ninety-six birds I saw a snipe stalking absent-mindedly towards me through low reed grass. The bird walked on, its head bent gloomily down. It had a preoccupied air, as though it were wondering whether its wife was faithful or whether it believed in Swaraj for snipe. One thing was clear: it had no more intention of flying than I had of allowing it to. Since everyone had told me that it was unsporting to shoot a bird on the ground, I looked cautiously around before dropping to a lying position. No one was watching. The bird raised its head and peered myopically down the left barrel, and I fired.

Not five minutes later a covey of the little devils, aroused from sleep by the beaters and in a bad temper, came zig-zagging towards the line of guns, going like the wind. A fusillade broke out. To left and right snipe crumpled and nose-dived *smack* into the reeds. In front of me their ranks remained unbroken, though I pulled hard at the trigger.

My safety-catch was on. I slipped it forward, again

swung expertly into the aim, chose a stupid-looking bird in the rear rank, and pulled the trigger.

I missed. The covey rocketed on over my head. I swung round after it, keeping my balance with easy grace. Immediately behind me my orderly, Jitbahadur, threw himself to the ground with a cry. I pulled the trigger again and again and again. By chance, it was the same trigger on each occasion—the one belonging to the barrel I had just fired. By the time I had examined the gun and found out what was wrong the irregular line of snipe was fifty or sixty yards away, going faster than ever, and jinking about in the eye of the setting sun.

Everyone else stopped firing and watched me. As the gun butt hit my shoulder I pulled the right trigger. Tiny in the farthest distance, a snipe crumpled and nose-dived into the reeds—*smack!*

A palpable silence spread from the reedbeds and covered the marshy fields. John and Moke and Bruce and James converged on me and took my (their) gun away. They unbuckled my (their) cartridge belt and gave both gun and cartridges to Jitbahadur as a reward, they said, for gallantry under fire. They said, 'Jack, three cartridges—two snipe. It's time for you to rest on your laurels.'

A Russell's viper slithered in the stubble behind James's feet, and further conversation was, thank heaven, forgotten until we had caught and killed it.

We crossed the wide Beas River in flat-bottomed ferry-boats poled by hand, and here M. L., who got a lot of shrapnel in his head in the First World War, lost his temper with a major. John Strickland and I, mustering three years' service between us, were witnesses of this scene between two men whose service totalled forty-two years. Embarrassed, I hurried off in one direction, and John in the other. As I went I saw the victim, shaken but undaunted, standing manfully silent against the blast, while fierce dispraise burst like gunfire over the dunes, and the mess staff had buried their heads in the sand and were praying to their various gods for deliverance.

Standing in the bow of the ferry-boat while the Gurkhas sang and the sun shone on the water, I thought about that incident. I was angry with them. Why did they have to shock me when I thought the world and them so wonderful? Then I considered a little deeper and realized that, though M. L. was in the right, the major had at least had a defence, if not an excuse, for what he had done. But he had said nothing. I jumped on to the sand of the eastern bank, feeling much better. I knew I had seen, for the second time, a soldier put into practice the motto of the professional fighting man—'Never explain, never complain.' What guided the major and Sergeant Broadhurst might as well guide me.

We left the river behind us and marched on, south by east across the fertile land. Impressions here were received not in a continuous chain, each linked to the last and to the next by a continuity of time, but in separate cameos that blend now under the recalled light of the Indian sun into one memory—*marching to the plains*. . . .

The sweet smell of death clung to the dust by a turn of the road. A dead donkey lay in a field beyond the low cactus hedge. Forty vultures crowded the boughs of a straggly tree, their naked necks red in the morning, their bodies grey and clammy cold. One of them lurched to the ground, ungainly and heavy, and plunged its head and beak into the donkey's anus and tore out the entrails in raw red strips.

In the night bullock-carts creaked and squeaked down the road past our camps, their loads of straw and grain piled as high as the arching boughs overhead. The drivers slept; the carts had no lights. Two cavalry officers had recently been killed running into one, not far away. We turned the patient bullocks so that the carter awoke in the morning back where he had started.

A *dak* bungalow, the traveller's rest-house of India, stood in a little garden outside a mud village. The fittings in its *ghuslkhana* had been built by a local craftsman who had heard, in the evenings round the wood fires, weird tales of

Europeans but had never actually seen one. We stood in silent awe in the little room, cramped against the door, so full was it with a colossal zinc tub, a chamberpot the size of a baby's bath, and a thunderbox towering grimly in the corner with legs like billiard tables', the seat three feet off the floor.

Each day Bruce Douglas went ahead to reconnoitre the next day's camp-site. Each day he rode away from us on a country-bred pony that had only one gait, a trot with its forelegs and a canter with its hindlegs. Lance-Naik Dhansing of the buglers capered in the dust, imitating the pony. We laughed, and the Gurkhas laughed, and every day Bruce turned in the saddle to laugh and wave at us all.

At evening, in my tent, I studied Gurkhali with the jemadar head clerk. We read together in the lamplight from a book of Gurkhali fairy tales. The stories carried me away from there, and from the earthy soldiers singing lazily in their tents outside, to the misty peaks and the fantasies of Sanskrit fable, where there lived gods and fairies, tortoises and eagles and wicked princes. Then the bugle called 'Lights Out,' and I was back in the army—but the Indian Army, the 4th Gurkhas, where these gods and legends were as real as the unshaven topknot on the bugler's head.

It was a golden season, and nearing its end, not only for that year but for ever. This was the last time and the first time that I went marching to the plains in the first snap of the cold weather. We knew we would be going to the Frontier for a year or two, but after that we thought that the familiar pattern would again shape our lives—Bakloh, marching to the plains, manœuvres, marching to the hills, Bahloh. But the year was 1935, the season Christmas, and Hitler did not hear our confident bugles.

CHAPTER TEN

IF war had broken out early the next year those cold-weather manœuvres of 1935–36 might have been of direct military value to me. As it was they formed only one link in the chain of experience that led me on to 1939. They were important, though, not because I was taking my first steps in the art of war but because I had begun to struggle with the nature of man—the Gurkha. I found that here, as elsewhere, knowledge does not come in a smoothly deepening stream but in unpredictable jerks and snatches. Experience, too, obeys the quantum theory. For weeks I seemed to stagnate in half-light; then suddenly some juxtaposition of events would cause a signal to flash out at me, illuminating the present and the past, and in turn becoming the half-light of the future. Three incidents in particular had this character.

Early in the manœuvres my A Company was scattered over a scrub-covered plain, digging defensive positions. I was talking to the subadar, whom I shall call Dallu, under a tree, when a confused commotion broke out from the direction of No. 2 Platoon, which was invisible in the scrub.

A moment later a man broke cover and ran towards us, bounding and whooping and waving a pick over his head. Our conversation stopped. Remembering stories of Orientals running amok I seized and loaded a rifle and held it ready to do my duty. Now my whole company burst from the bushes, all waving their hats, all shouting and brandishing *kukris* and digging tools.

A new Indian Mutiny! In the 4th Gurkhas! I glanced at Dallu to make sure he was not in the conspiracy and about to shoot me in the back; but he too was staring tensely at the extraordinary scene.

A hare broke cover near us. Dallu, an excitable man but a subadar none the less, leaped into the air and dashed, shouting, to head it off. My company, led by its second-in-command, disappeared in a cloud of dust over the near foothills, going strongly left-handed. Only the disconsolate sentries stood to their posts, and I could see that they too were jumping up to peer over the scrub and catch what they could of the progress of the hunt. If I had wanted the Gurkhas to love me I would have dashed off with them—they got their hare—but I was too surprised to do anything.

I had seen the only thing that can break the Gurkhas' discipline—game. Nothing else, not even a determined and ferocious enemy in the full swing of attack, has any hope of commanding a Gurkha's full attention when game is astir.

A week or so later, after a mock battle, I made my first attempt to explain directly to the company, instead of through the Gurkha officers, what I thought they had done well or ill. When we reached camp I gathered them round me in a half-circle and delivered my lecture. I narrowly watched them as I spoke, and, sure enough, they nodded in the right places and grunted appropriately, and no trace of a smile creased any of those Mongolian faces. I dismissed them, well satisfied, and we scattered to our various tents. Stopping to light a cigarette, I glanced round and was surprised to see the men flitting back through the trees to the open space. They had a furtive air about them, as if congregating for a black mass.

When all were gathered I stepped closer and heard Dallu say, 'What the sahib meant was *this*.' Then he gave a more succinct version of my talk. This was touching, but wounding too. How would I ever know if I had made contact?

The problem answered itself in the next few months. I found that joining a Gurkha battalion was like going to school again. None of the men, not even the recruits, accepted a British officer until he had been there several months and they had had time to adjust themselves to his presence. However well he spoke—and I soon spoke very fair Gurkhali, for I have a receptive and imitative ear—they would not understand him until they had decided to accept him. Acceptance did not depend on personal quality or military virtue. The men might thoroughly dislike an officer, and he might speak unintelligible Gurkhali, but suddenly he would be accepted. From that moment he became a member of the family, an obnoxious one, perhaps, but of the blood.

The date of one's acceptance was mysteriously chosen and impossible to predict. When mine came I had been making Gurkhali jokes for nearly two years, and no one had smiled. If I spoke to a man he would look woodenly to the nearest Gurkha officer for a translation. As I edged closer to the men—for it was chilly out there—they edged farther away. Then one day on a route march, still trying valiantly, I made a very stupid joke about someone's large feet. My company exploded in paroxysms of appreciative laughter, and word of what I had said was passed up and down the column. The next day I spoke to a rifleman on parade. The grapevine news about my acceptance had somehow not reached him, so in the customary fashion he looked blankly around for help. Everyone near him cursed him roundly, and the lance-naik gave him a sharp push and bawled, '*Jhanta!* Can't you understand plain Gurkhali?'

Jhanta means 'one pubic hair' and is a common term of mild abuse, but that was not what caused the expression of mingled bewilderment and anger to cross the rifleman's stolid face. What he was really saying to himself was, 'No one tells me anything.' I knew, because the same expression crossed my face, and for the same reason. I had been speaking exactly this 'plain Gurkhali' for months.

But during this cold weather, training in the plains, I was striving for acceptance rather than basking in full-fledged membership in the regiment. Again I felt stirrings of dislike in my friends. This time I was in a grown-up family and I knew that I would not be hailed before a subalterns' court martial or have my clothes thrown on the floor by secret visitors. All the same, I didn't know what was going wrong, so I summoned up my courage and asked Moke Murray whether he thought I was doing all right—and I meant socially, as a member of the family—and if not, what I could do about it.

Moke might have answered, 'No,' to the first and, 'Grow up,' to the second. Instead he said, 'Well, I shouldn't offer my opinions quite so often or so definitely, if I were you.'

I went away, shaking my head, but grateful. This made sense, and I knew that Moke was right. But it was a hard rule to obey at the age of twenty, when problems are so easy and clear-cut. Besides, I didn't so much want to hear my own voice or to pontificate as to be contradicted with the same positiveness so that there could be an argument, no holds barred.

I did not withdraw from the society of my brother officers, but I was a great deal more careful about speaking on any subject whatsoever. I found to my astonishment that it was as much fun to listen as to argue. Sitting in unusual silence in the mess, listening and ruminating, I realized that the regiment, without seeming to take any trouble over it, was beginning to train me on four parallel lines—one of the body, one of the brain, one of the character, and one of the spirit.

The first was easy enough. Every year we marched about one thousand five hundred miles under load and climbed perhaps eighty thousand feet up and down. We were always running and working and playing like young leopards and could not help being lean and hard.

At the same time the regiment imparted to me some of its many skills and my brain was acquiring army techniques that were, in essence, no different from typing or radio-telegraphy—indeed, each of these subjects formed the army skill of one kind of soldier. Simultaneously I saw that these skills are directed by the character, and without that have no purpose, being without guidance. The regiment did nothing overt to improve my character; it left that to me, giving me only good and bad examples and leaving me to draw my own conclusions. And I saw that ability was not really very important. It was for the conscientious, thoughtful, brave, and, above all, straightforward man that people gave their best.

The fourth and greatest gift was also left lying about on the ground—in the moonlight under the mangos, anywhere, on or off parade—for me to find and treasure if I had the capacity. This was the spirit of the regiment, and I think I found it.

Every army—every human organization of any kind—hopes to inculcate a spirit of some kind in its members. In an army the most usual rallying point is the flag—or the emperor, the national ideal. Call it by any name, it is still a form of wide patriotism. The British people do not take kindly to large abstract ideas, and many of them have always disapproved of and voted against the national policy. But in war it is necessary that all should pull together and fight with a will, whatever their opinions of the rights and wrongs of the case. So, in the King's armies, men were shielded from disturbing doubts by the interposition of a smaller cause, which no one could cavil at, between themselves and the great national cause. Their spirit was and is built on the regiment.

Whatever the country is doing, the regiment is clearly right in obeying the orders of lawful authority. This enables a man, by only a small exercise in schizophrenia, to be a disapproving citizen and an enthusiastic soldier at one and the same time. The regiment, besides, is a smaller thing than the nation. Every man in it can know every other man, and the idea of its unity is easier for the mind to grasp.

No man is an *Iland*, intire of it selfe; every man is a peece of the *Continent*, a part of the *maine*; if a *clod* bee washed away by the *Sea*, *Europe* is the lesse, as well as if a *Promontorie* were, as well as if a *Mannor* of thy *friends* were or of *thine* owne were; any mans *death* diminishes *me*, because I am involved in *Mankinde* . . .

Mankind has never been able to follow Donne and imagine itself as one whole, or there would be no armies. Yet none of us can stand alone against any real strain. At such a time we must know that we are a piece of a continent.

We British officers, being Christians, might have tried to find this continentality in Christ, as was done by many of the great Victorians, but that would have excluded the Gurkhas, who are not Christians. Besides, I think that most of us whose trade was war found it impossible, in this century, to be joined in Christ for the purpose of killing people. For myself, I believe that each fighting man can face Christ alone, if he believes in Him, and if he is able he can ask Christ's fellowship in war as in peace. I was not able. I felt none of that superhuman assurance that enabled the Victorians to ask, even to require, Christ's blessing in an enterprise of mass slaughter. Like most of us, I turned to the regiment and in it found the fellowship I needed.

The unspoken other half of Donne's parable—any man's *life* increases *me* because I am involved in *Mankinde*—went even closer to the centre of this spirit. In the regiment, if the bell rang out among us for one man's kindness, one man's courage, it rang for all of us. And if it tolled for selfishness, for death, for any meanness, I knew then— before Donne's blinding words ever reached me—that it tolled for me.

This was the regiment, a small ideal because humanity cannot encompass a larger one, and imperfect as its ends were imperfect. The spirit of the regiment took little heed of efficiency, discipline, or even loyalty. It had been built by generations of men, one after the other wearing the black IV in their hats, who all came to realize their continentality, one with the other, with those who had gone and those who had not yet come. It was for this spirit that we drilled together, got drunk together, hunted, danced, played, killed, and saved life together. It was from this spirit that no man was alone, neither on the field of battle, which is a lonely place, nor in the chasm of death, nor in the dark places of life.

And now again the bugles blew and the dust rose and we marched to Jullundur and pitched camp on the outskirts of the city. Every morning I bicycled to the rifle range to put the furlough men through their annual musketry course before they left for Nepal. At dawn the duty piper awoke me with the lilting quick-step 'Hey Johnny Cope,' and all the camp stirred as he walked among the tents. I got up and found the water frozen in the basin propped on three wooden legs outside my tent. Every day the sun burst over the horizon while the men were getting ready on the firing point, and the morning crackled with exhilaration, and the air bit diamond-sharp on the end of my nose as I huddled into my greatcoat and shouted 'First detail, ready!' Every Sunday our massed bugles sounded the 'Long Reveille' of the Chasseurs Alpins. The frosty silver waves of sound sprang clean and hard over the level plain, and some echoed back to me from the walled villages and the dark trees and the white temples, and some flowed on out over the thorn scrub to the faint horizon.

The furlough men left; higher training was over for the year; and the cold weather ended. Soon, even at nine in the morning, the low sun warmed my back, and by noon perspiration blackened the blue-grey wool of my shirt and soaked the leather lining of my hat. It was time to face the road again.

We started back for Bakloh, and one day we looked up and saw that ahead of us the Himalaya had silently risen out of the morning ground mist. The flat-country haze still covered all the forty miles to the nearest foothills of the Siwaliks, and all the gradually climbing, receding green hills that rolled back another forty miles. Above that, from horizon to horizon, the white towers and ridges of the Himalaya soared into the pale sky. Our companies began to sing, and we joined in with them: '*Kati ramro jhyal bhunyo bhane makura-le*,' again and again the same cheerful question—' "How many beautiful webs have I made?" said the spider.'

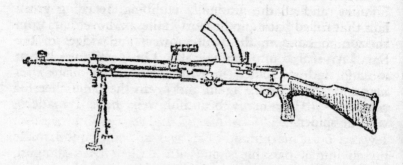

CHAPTER ELEVEN

No sooner had we returned to Bakloh than the colonel sent me to the Small Arms School at Pachmarhi, in the Central Provinces. This particular course was the first of a series that would punctuate my life from the time I left the R.M.C. until the time I retired. There were army schools for the study of gas, machine-guns, clerical duties, administration, gunnery, education, equitation, cookery (army cookery, that is), survey, animal management, physical training, hygiene, staff duties, imperial defence, and many others. The instructors at each school were fanatical devotees of their subject and tried to make each student who passed through their hands a missionary to spread the gospel. Susceptible young men would go back to their regiments in a frame of mind not unlike that of St Paul after his encounter on the road to Damascus. They would tell their colonels victory could be achieved only by men who could do six handsprings (Physical Training School); or that no one need worry about anything except gas—one whiff, and the war would be over (Gas School); or that the rest of the battalion existed merely as coolies and body-guards for the sacred, all-conquering machine-guns (Machine-Gun School); and so on. The colonels were not impressed; life in the battalions went on as usual in spite of the Word that had been brought to them.

The Small Arms School was the only one that every infantry officer had to attend, since it was an indisputable fact that rifles, pistols, light automatics, and grenades were the weapons on which we relied to kill the enemy. The Small Arms School, therefore, had more justification than most for its perfervid enthusiasm—in its case, for marksmanship. My ignoble talent for finding out what would please my masters came to the fore, and soon I was filled with unnatural zeal for musketry and set out to prove that I was a born marksman. This was not true, but I made myself into a passable shot (with a rifle, not a shotgun, remembering the snipe) and when the time came to fire our practices I got 109 out of a possible 120 and was first in the class.

But work was of secondary importance at this school. The students, twenty or thirty young officers from as many different battalions, were far from the overawing presence of their seniors, and the course lasted only six weeks. The atmosphere was joyous and irresponsible rather than studious and academic. Some of us worked hard, some demonstrated the insouciance we imagined proper to the particular cut of our tunic by not working at all. Some sowed wild oats and returned to bed at 5 a.m. every morning, to find others just getting up to practise rapid-fire drill on the veranda. Everyone wanted to emphasize the superiority of his regiment, so everyone refused to abate one jot of his regiment's peculiarities of dress, drill, or custom, and getting the group together on parade was in itself a circus. In mess a British Army officer sitting as president would obstinately instruct Mr Vice to offer the toast to 'The King.' If an Indian Army officer was Mr Vice he would, with equal obstinacy, pass on the toast as 'Gentlemen, the King-Emperor,' which showed a fine, pugnacious spirit but was bad etiquette, since the vice-president must offer the exact toast given to him by the president, whatever he thinks of it.

I was not present in this school on the night that a slightly fuddled vice-president made a far bigger gaffe. When the president rapped on the table and rose to say, 'Mr Vice, the King,' Mr Vice gave no answer. Twice the president repeated the instruction, while everyone waited in half-embarrassed amusement. Mr Vice suddenly emerged from his private fog and exclaimed, 'The King? The King? Show him in!'

Another cause of friction was the habit of some junior subalterns of saying, 'God bless him,' after they had drunk the loyal toast. In most regiments, including mine, this added phrase was, by tradition, allowed only to field officers. It was galling to hear another second-lieutenant, standing beside me, mutter the magic words as he lowered his glass; even more galling to tax him later with *lèse majesté* and be confounded by his explanation—that King William IV had once dined with his regiment and had, on that occasion, commanded all of them always to bless him when they drank his health.

Pachmarhi, besides containing the Small Arms School, was the summer capital of the Central Provinces. Since it stood only three thousand feet above sea level it was not a 'hill station' in the true sense, like the high Himalayan sanitaria—Gulmarg, Darjeeling, Simla, and the rest—but it was a pleasant little place. It was built on a plateau among ridges of jungle-covered trap rock, and its grass was green, its bungalows white, its flowers bright, and its roads gravelly red. All around the forests rolled away, scarred here and there with raw red precipices, split by deep gorges, and pierced by volcanic towers. Often ruined forts crowned these towers, which stabbed up five or six hundred feet out of the trees. The gorges were fifty or a hundred yards wide and several hundred feet deep, and down at the bottom there always flowed an ice-cold stream. There were hidden waterfalls and underground rivers everywhere, and places where the water ran between sheer sides and it was impossible to leave the gorge for a mile on end, and places where sunny banks dozed beside the water and steep paths led down to them from the plateau above.

The jungles were full of game—tiger, leopard, several

kinds of deer—and bees. The bees were the lords of the province. Not even snakes or man-eaters were so dangerous. Every year sudden disaster would fall on someone. A man would be out shooting, and the bullet or the echo of the shot would anger a colony of bees. Caught helpless in the open, the hunter would get a thousand stings into him and die before he could reach help. Or bathers resting on the bank would smoke cigarettes and fret the bees' delicate senses, and the murderous swarm would descend from their nests under the ledged overhang of the rocks, and sting and sting until the bathers jumped into the water and stayed under, half unconscious, and drowned. Or one of a picnic party moving down a narrow cliff path would put his hand on a concealed nest and be stung and shocked into losing his balance, and fall down the precipice.

Everything here was different from the north that I was beginning to know. Yet there was a familiar 'feel' to the forests of dwarf teak, and the dried teak leaves made a remembered crackling underfoot, and I had seen these white villages and these thin-legged peasants before. I could not understand until I looked at a map and saw, a little off to the east, the name 'Seeonee Hills.' This was the country of the *Jungle Books*. Kipling's genius for transmitting atmosphere had been here, and that was why I already half knew the place. Later, when I first went into the Himalaya, I was to recognize that I had travelled in them too, with Kim. It was in the pages of *Kim*, the best book that has ever been written on India, that I had felt the tang of the air and heard the silence, and seen 'the appalling sweep and dispersal of the cloud shadows after rain.'

The red blossoms of the flame-of-the-forest had fallen from the trees before I arrived in Pachmarhi, and I was sorry, because I had wanted to see them, but still I discovered something new and attractive there. The discovery came as a surprise, because to the desiccated veterans of the north this was the edge of the Sloth Belt. The Sloth Belt, they said, was all India south of a line drawn from Calcutta to Bombay. In it all Indians were black, timid, and uninteresting (*their* darlings were the pale, fierce Pathans and the unbending Sikhs). All the British were sunk in potbellied lethargy and conducted their business, if any, from their beds; the countryside was uniformly dull, wet, and sleepy. Recent history had indeed passed the province by, and it was buried in a peace that was only to be shattered six years later by the wartime discovery that soldiers destined to fight in jungles had better be trained in jungles. The province had many jungles. In 1942 divisions and brigades descended on it, and the average peasant saw more of the British and the bustle of government than he had seen since the Mutiny.

In 1936 it was peaceful, green, and lost. There was no large merchant community and little industry; trade and commerce flowed through the province along the railroad lines, but did not pause. Roads were bad or nonexistent, and all the great rivers were unbridged.

In our plentiful spare time a small band of us walked and swam miles in exploration of the gorges and jungles and isolated rock towers. We discovered, feeling that we were the very first ever to do so, ancient Hindu shrines, and overgrown paths that had once been trade routes, and ruined and deserted fortresses, and towns torns asunder by spreading tree roots. We also found a deserted *dak* bungalow, more desolate in its recent abandonment than any ancient ruin. It stood on top of a mountain in the jungle, and Jos Redman took a photograph of me standing outside it, laughing and waving my topi. I sent a copy of the photo to my mother, and she wrote back that it was interesting that I should go to Dhupgarh, because she had taken me there at the age of one and a half to recover from enteric while Daddy was a student at the Small Arms School.

Our fierce inter-regimental rivalries drove us to walk and climb a great deal faster than was comfortable in the heat of the day and I, as a Gurkha, simply had to arrive first at the top of every hill—and that without showing a trace of breathlessness. As we sweated along we asked one another at every rest whether we would honestly at that moment prefer a gallon of iced lager beer or an hour with a complacent Marlene Dietrich. It was not done to choose the lager. Then, when we reached the stream that was our destination, we lay on our backs beside the water and discussed a problem which tradition said was set to officers about to qualify from the riding school of the French Army at Saumur. I didn't believe the tradition at the time, but it is true; a couple of years ago I had the opportunity of confirming it from a French general and cabinet minister. When the French officer had passed all his tests in horsemanship and horsemastership, he had still another trial to undergo before he was passed as a true cavalryman, Frenchman, and heir of Murat. He was allotted three horses, three bottles of champagne, three whores, and a cross-country route of thirty miles. He had to cover the course in all particulars in three hours. The problem was, obviously, in what order should he tackle his fences? We reached no agreement on a single plan to solve the problem presented in this interesting TEWT, but we did a lot of laughing, and some wishing.

We were twenty-two or twenty-three on the average, and beginning to feel some of the peculiar pressure that our way of life exerted on us. Most of the earliest English to reach India, from the seventeenth century on, openly took Indian women as housekeeper-mistresses. In those times many of the women were ladies of breeding and accomplishment. Most old bungalows have *bibikhanas* (women's rooms) in the compound, and in Assam some tea planters still use them for the purpose for which they were built.

The practice was immoral but perhaps not inhuman. It took a man many months to reach India and, once there, he stayed for twenty years or more without a break, until he had made his fortune or earned his pension. The English were not yet conquerors in possession, but traders and soldiers manoeuvring about in a ramshackle and strife-torn subcontinent, so they were not concerned with putting up a godlike front. Few Englishwomen came out to India, because it was a hard and unhealthy life that faced them there. On the other hand, the men were always dreaming of their eventual return home and the suitable marriages they would be able to contract there with the money they had made in India, so they seldom married the Indian 'wives' of their youth.

There was also an increasingly strong colour bar, though I get the impression from reading old books and memoirs that the Englishman's initial aversion was from Indian customs and habits, especially those connected with Hinduism, and that he gradually transferred this feeling to the colour of the Indians' skin because, whereas the former could be explained, the latter could not, and was thus indefensible.

As the country began to develop and settle into peace increasing numbers of British soldiers were induced to stay on after their terms of service by offers of work on the railways. There were still few white women for them to marry, so they married or lived with Indians. These Indian women were seldom of good family or high caste, because the soldiers had no opportunity of meeting such women and because the women would have despised the soldiers if they had. These unions were the origin of the Eurasian or Anglo-Indian community which, until 1947, was still centred on the railways.

These affairs did not always come about in a deliberately cold-blooded way, and it gives a wrong sense of history to imagine a curt Englishman stepping off the ship, pointing sternly at a cowering Indian girl, and saying 'I'll have that one.' On our mess lawn in Bakloh is a low tree that could tell a warmer story. In some dim Edwardian frolic a Gurkha rifleman seduced and later married the young daughter of a Moslem barber. There was a great to-do. The rifleman lost his caste among the Gurkhas and was discharged from the battalion, while the Moslems read the girl in formal disgrace out of their religion and out of Bakloh's tiny Moslem community. But then the left hand of regimental charity tried to soften the stern punishment administered by the right hand of regimental discipline. The mess took on the discharged rifleman as a gardener. His family increased by three beautiful little girls, who were accepted by neither community and had no playmates.

On a quiet Sunday morning in the 1920s a subaltern of ours was sitting under the tree, drinking a flagon of cider and thinking far thoughts. The tree began to bombard him with twigs and leaves. He was used to the presence of the children, who were always gambolling about the mess—the only home they knew—and he looked up idly to see the eldest girl making faces at him and preparing to throw more twigs. Being a very young man, he joined in the game and scrambled up to spank her. In the course of the struggle among the bending boughs he made a discovery that the movies have always been extremely fond of portraying. As with those innumerable youths who have rolled in Hollywood's hay with freshly nubile childhood playmates, a look of wonder came into his eyes. The girl was not a child after all, but a woman, eager, young, and lovely—and the camera shifts meaningly to the ceiling of the barn.

For some years after this incident each of the little flock of girls slept happily and indiscriminately with any subaltern who asked her to. For a time the senior officers did not get to hear of it, though there were bitter controversies between the ribald and the righteous groups among the subalterns as to whether what was going on was or was not cricket. In the end, all was uncovered. One hot evening a major walked into someone's bedroom without knocking, and disturbed an operation only traditionally military. Then there were banishments and lashings of sensitivities with harsh words. In our time we used to look up at the tree and hope a golden dryad would throw leaves at us, but one never did.

Again, in the murky pre-1914 years, the regiment had an officer whose chief pride was his reputation as a lady's man. He never failed to attend the severe regimental ordeal known as the Tuesday Bunfight. Every Tuesday afternoon the ladies of the station, perhaps five or six in number, were invited to the mess for tea, cakes, and tennis. Every available officer had to be present to entertain them—all except one, a man who could hardly be induced to speak at all to any woman, and never spoke to one politely. This man had succeeded, through his known misogyny and addiction to work, in getting permanent permission to absent himself from the Tuesday Bunfights. What few people ever knew—and none at the time—was that every Tuesday, as soon as the ladykiller left for the Bunfight, the misogynist jumped on his bicycle, pedalled furiously down the steep road to the former's Indian mistress, and returned late at night with ardour quelled but misogyny unabated.

But long before these incidents took place the days of the recognized liaison with an Indian woman were past. In 1879 the opening of the Suez Canal markedly shortened communications with England, and English women began to come out in large numbers. The ladies exerted ladylike pressure, and the *bibikhanas* were turned into servants' quarters; the colour bar became a barrier.

And then, during the cold weather, from October to March, 'society' was organized much as it would have been in a small provincial town in England. Every year the onset of the hot weather changed all this with startling suddenness. The heat and the fear of cholera sent any European who could manage it to the hills, to stay there until September. The men could not leave their work in the plains for more than a few weeks, but the women and children could. So in April the hill stations began to take on their hot-weather aspect—a large number of women, mostly married, with nothing to do, and the usual flocks of servants to help them do it; a small resident male population, such as government officials in Simla or soldiers in Ranikhet; and a passing stream of male transients on leave, among whom would occasionally appear the ladies' husbands.

Perhaps it was the mountain air that caused so many of the women to cast away their inhibitions. Perhaps the friendly unfamiliar wood fires burning on the hearths warmed their blood and made them think with fervour of romps on tiger-skin divans. Perhaps it was moonlight and bulbuls—or perhaps it was human nature. But the explanation does not alter the fact, and the fact was that hill stations presented an unusual picture of a race that is supposed to be frigid.

The interested watcher—such as, say, Kipling or the present writer—saw strange things, no stranger than those that happen in New York or London, but unnerving because they were seen or known about in a way impossible in a great city. Captain A. comes up to join his wife in Mussoorie for his month's leave. The station forms a wordless conspiracy never to let him know of the existence of Mr B., a resident official who has, they all know, spent most of his days and nights with Mrs A. for some weeks past, and will resume this practice as soon as Captain A. has returned to Sweattypore. And around Mrs C. there are wonderfully public manœuvrings for position; she has really given up any pretence of being monogamous. Her husband eventually cites sixteen co-respondents in his divorce suit. Women who are thought to be, and in fact are, kind ladies and good mothers engage in pointed and bitter underground wars, where victory is not measured by beauty, clothes, wit, or intelligence, but by ability to annex the most desirable man and hold on to him in the face of all competition.

It is better to marry than to burn, said the Apostle. But army tradition said, 'Subalterns may not marry, captains may marry, majors should marry, colonels must marry.' Few junior officers could afford to marry anyway, and the army did not pay them marriage allowances till they were thirty, but the true power behind that tradition was that women and children were not part of the regimental *maine*. The men were part, one of another, but wives were not. They were part of a different, smaller, and rebellious *Iland*, the family. No regiment wished an officer to marry until he was firmly enough fixed into the *maine* to be able to support weeds and fungi without crumbling away. Until then the regiment demanded all. When a man was presumed to be indissolubly wedded to the regiment, the regiment permitted, even encouraged, him to commit bigamy by marrying a female animal of his own kind.

There were, in fact, few English girls for us to marry, though more than in the old days. Of those available, a fair proportion had ruined themselves in our lecherous but censorious eyes by their activities in the various hill stations. And finally, we could not marry if we loved our regiments, because if we did we would be invited to transfer to the Service or Ordnance Corps. In brief, it was a case of '*Enfin, il n'y a pas de canon.*' (A favourite 4th Gurkha joke was about a French mayor explaining to Napoleon why a salute of guns had not been fired when the emperor visited his city. The mayor said that the orders had not been received; there was no one who knew how to fire the cannon; the powder was wet; it was dangerous in this dry season; and, at the end, '*Enfin, majesté, il n'y a pas de canon*'—'Finally, your majesty, we have no cannon.')

The civilian reader might think that in these restricting circumstances the pastime of seeking women's company in dancing, wining, riding, tennis, picnics, and theatricals would not be frowned on; but he would be wrong. Such activities were called poodlefaking, and they were severely frowned on. When a subaltern applied for leave some colonels would ask him how he intended to spend it, and if it appeared that he was merely going to poodlefake they refused the leave. The young man must pursue animals, not girls.

Social life for the British in India was a goldfish bowl. The servants knew all about what was going on, and it was useless to attempt to conceal anything from them. Few people even tried, in spite of the danger of blackmail. Our riflemen, too, somehow always got to know, if not of an officer's specific doings, certainly of the nature of his inclinations. Some of the imitations they put on at the Dussehra carnivals were horrifyingly accurate caricatures of English tribal customs, as observed by them through ballroom windows and on mess verandas. Only once did I hear of the British turning the tables and successfully spying on a Gurkha. During a long spell of manœuvres a Gurkha rifleman crept out of his camp to a neighbouring village and succeeded by flourishing four annas—about fourpence —in persuading a girl there to accept his embraces. After searching about the fields for a time they finally found a suitably secluded spot and came to rest. Not very long after, but long enough to garner the whole cream of their embarrassment, seven searchlights leaped on the pair, and the night sky split with a single shout of applause from eight hundred British Tommies. The unfortunate couple had chosen the middle of a mock battlefield for their tête-à-tête, and a British battalion with artillery was there on the ridge, silent, watching the lovers' rites while waiting for the battle to begin.

But the Gurkha always displayed a sangfroid and politeness that we, with our Victorian traditions of prudery, were unable to match. During a minor war on the Frontier our colonel was in the tiny tent that housed the thunderbox when a gust of wind blew the tent away just as a platoon marched past on its way to the fight. No whit surprised by this sudden unveiling of his enthroned colonel, the havildar in charge gave him a perfect 'Eyes right!' The colonel, frozen by shame or laughter, did not return the salute.

Again, in one tiny cantonment town lived a Eurasian lady who claimed to be relict—her word—of a high post office official. She had an unmarried daughter she would very much have liked to marry off to an officer of the Gurkha regiment stationed there. At least, the officers thought that was her wish, for it was obvious that the girl had been told to offer the minimum of polite resistance to any advance. Well, one warm Wednesday in spring the mother gave a party at her house on the evening of a regimental guest night. One of the subalterns, full of sherry and passion, edged the daughter out of the house into the twilit evening. There didn't seem to be any privacy available. In despair, or perhaps reckoning that life is short and

soldiers don't care, he proceeded to the extreme of hetero-
sexual affection on the cement platform of a trophy gun
right beside the road. Round the corner swung the pipe
band on their way to play at the guest night. The pipe
major peered incredulously into the gloom and, having
satisfied himself that he really saw what he thought he saw,
gave the command 'Eyes right!' The rows of Gurkha faces
went by without the shadow or the suspicion of a smile or
a titter. Here and there one may have held a glint of
respect, but no more. The officer returned the salute, and
so in due course became a major-general.

It is useless to pretend that our life was a normal one.
Ours was a one-sexed society, with the women hanging on
to the edges. Married or unmarried, their status was really
that of camp followers. But it is normal for men to live in
the company of women, for if they do they do not become
rough or boorish and the sex instinct does not torment
them. In India there was always an unnatural tension, and
every man who pursued the physical aim of sexual relief
was in danger of developing a cynical hardness and a lack
of sympathy which he had no business to learn until many
more years had maltreated him. Of those who tried sub-
limation, some chased polo balls and some chased partridge,
some buried themselves in their work, and all became unmitigated nuisances through the narrowness of their conversation. And some took up the most unlikely hobbies,
and some went to diseased harlots—which didn't count as
poodlefaking—and some married in haste, only to worry
over who was now seducing their wives in the hill stations
where they had seduced so many other people's wives.
And a few homosexuals followed their secret star with
comparative comfort in that large and easy-going country,
where there are so many sins that there is no sin, except
inhospitality.

CHAPTER TWELVE

I T was against this background that the memsahib lived her life. Let us examine it for a moment.

In and about her bungalow she had a number of servants. First was the bearer, who probably had once been her husband's personal valet. He became a butler-valet when his master married, and probably much regretted the passing of the good old bachelor ways and days.

Then there was the *bhisti*, the water carrier, who carried water and was nearly always a likable man. Kipling did not make Gunga Din a *bhisti* without reason.

The *mehtar*, or sweeper, was the lord of the *ghuslkhana*.

The *khansamah* was the cook, a dirty and temperamental fellow who only gave his best in an emergency. Chinese cooks, who were supposed to be much more hygiene-conscious, were sometimes available. A lady who had a Chinese cook bet a lady who had an ordinary Indian *khansamah* that an unannounced inspection of the two kitchens would show how much superior the Chinese was. The Indian's kitchen was quite filthy, swathed in dirty dishcloths, and inches deep in dust and flies. The other was spotless in every particular; outside, the Chinese cook was washing his feet in the soup tureen.

Next came the *masalchi*, dishwasher and assistant cook.

Younger and dirtier than any of the others, he picked his nose while washing dishes, and spent his spare time gambling.

The *ayah*, children's nurse, always had an amazing collection of boy friends, and loved children with a warm, diffuse love, but cheerfully neglected them while going through the long routines of Oriental assignation.

The *syce* was the groom. Like other grooms, he smelled of horse dung.

Then there was the orderly, who was not a servant but a soldier. He came daily to the bungalow to clean the officer's equipment and arms, and could not be employed on any menial task. He was the only person allowed to touch an officer's sword.

Besides these there were *dhobis* (washermen) who washed and ironed the household laundry for about twenty-five shillings a month; *darzis* (tailors) who came and set up their machines on the veranda to make dresses and repair clothes, again very cheaply; *mochis* (leatherworkers); *nais* (barbers); and many others.

There was thus no reason why a woman should do a stroke of any kind of work. Nor was it easy to be house-proud or garden-proud when house and garden belonged to the servants. Domesticity was upset by a thousand factors. Everyone was camping out, ready to move on at the end of two or three years to some place a thousand miles away. Only a few household goods could be carried around, and most of the furniture was hired anew in each new place. The family was broken up for five months every year when the children and the wife went to the hills. Manœuvres took the men away every winter, and at any time a sudden Frontier campaign might call them away for six months, at a week's notice. Generally an infantry officer was stationed for perhaps only four years out of every seven in a place where women were permitted to follow him. Last and worst, when the children reached the age of five or six they went home to England, unless their parents wished them to grow up spoiled by too many servants. The wife could either accompany them—and for the next fifteen years see her husband only on his furlough every fourth year—or she could farm the children out on aunts, uncles, and grandmothers in England, while she herself stayed with her husband. Both situations were bad for all parties concerned, and the second has led to some of the most remarkable aunt-complexes known to literature, notably those of Kipling and Saki.

The details of material comfort varied from cities like Bombay, which had more amenities, to buried villages which had less; but in the 1930s the average woman existed without telephone, refrigerator, water sanitation, electricity, or gas. There were, of course, no symphony concerts, theatres, or dress salons. Drinking water had to be boiled, and fresh vegetables washed in a solution of potassium permanganate. British-type food was monotonous, tasteless, and not nourishing. Hens and their eggs were both minute. Bacon, butter, and often milk were obtainable only in cans. Mosquito nets hung round the beds most of the year; inoculations were frequent. The diseases always in the foreground were, in order of priority: dysentery, malaria, sores, and typhoid. In the middle distance stood typhus, rabies, and pneumonia, and in the background, bubonic plague, smallpox, and cholera.

The children had to be protected against the servants' affection, which would manifest itself in secret gifts of bazaar candies of sickly taste, poisonous hue, and unhygienic manufacture, from which the children were liable to catch many mortal diseases. Children could not be allowed to play anywhere without supervision because of snakes, scorpions, and sunstroke. Pet dogs were popular, but they would chase jackals at night, and many jackals have rabies. Anti-rabies injections for human beings are long-drawn-out and painful; the disease itself is 100 per cent fatal, and death comes in peculiarly horrible guise.

Forbidden by the custom of the community to keep herself busy as women in the rest of the world did, the memsahib would spend much of her time in feuds. Our Wilfred, our sardonic and brilliant Wilfred, made himself popular by announcing at a Bakloh cocktail party that all the wives of the officers of the 4th Gurkhas were either schoolmarms or barmaids. This was not true, but it had in it an element of oblique truth sufficient to make the remark sting like a viper's tooth. It had no bad effect, however, for it only unified the ladies in a temporary hostility to Wilfred, and unity was never likely to cause any trouble among ladies in India.

We were fortunate that the wives of Bakloh got on as well with one another as they did. The Senior-Lady complex, the bugbear of British India, hit us comparatively lightly, though I was once embarrassedly present when a woman burst out to another, 'I've been in the regiment ten years longer than you, and just because your husband is two years senior to mine you needn't think you can boss me about as if . . .' and so on.

The operative phrase in this outpouring is '*I've* been in the regiment.' She had not been in the regiment at all, really, as the 4th Gurkhas did not enlist women, but the phrase is indicative of the root of the trouble—enforced association with a husband's work and position.

Social life used to be governed by the Warrant of Precedence. A group of men sitting down together might not know or care whether a major with two years' seniority as such did or did not take precedence over an assistant director of public libraries with four years' seniority as such, but it was axiomatic that when there were ladies present some of them both knew and cared. Precedence had passed its prime when I went out in 1934, but it was not dead. It was always necessary to know who would be the Senior Lady at any given function, for she had important rights and duties. If there was no hostess the Senior Lady collected eyes when it was time to leave the gentlemen to their brandy and cigars. The Senior Lady must sit on the right of the host. The Senior Lady must have first go at the *ghuslkhana*. However, she surrendered all privileges to a Bride. A bride was a Bride for six months from the date and time of her marriage. Could a twice-married woman be a Bride? Well . . .

The remains of a sulphurous feud were hanging round Bakloh when I first arrived, and it had been fought out on this precise point. The actual questions were: (a) Should a divorcee, recently married to an officer of the regiment, be dined in as a Bride? and (b) if she were, should the colonel consent to having her sit on his right, as was her undoubted privilege? The colonel of that time finally ruled that the lady could be dined in, but regretted that he himself could not attend as he was ill. The officer and his wife very properly also fell sick, and a feud at once began between the backers of each side. Such a problem could then still exercise many sensible and really kind people who were in the main neither narrow-minded nor priggish. They held to a code that seemed to most of us younger people to be presumptuous. They tried to protect an absolute standard for the sake of the regiment. We thought that, without full knowledge, judgment should not be made, and no one ever has full knowledge.

This same conflict burst upon us again in 1936 when our colonel-in-chief wanted to marry a divorcee. Most of the juniors considered that it was no business of ours whom he married; most of the seniors thought it was. With us, as in England, the seniors carried more weight, and the colonel-in-chief abdicated.

In India the incidents that caused feuds were usually unimportant, and often forgotten as soon as the feud had begun. For example, there was the Battle of the Bedpan. In the dim past a lady had borrowed a bedpan from the tiny Bakloh hospital and used it while recovering from a minor illness. She was hardly well again when another lady fell sick. The second lady, knowing where a bedpan was to be found, borrowed it direct from the first lady. The second lady too recovered, put the pan away somewhere, and forgot she had ever had it. The first lady forgot that she had re-lent it without permission. Months later the doctor was faced with an inspection of his hospital stores and asked the first lady for the return of the bedpan. The first lady asked the second lady, who said she'd never had it and the whole thing was a wicked fabrication. The doctor expressed his annoyance at the first lady. The first lady passed this on to the second lady. That was the incident.

Then a subaltern went to tea with the first lady and was told her version of the story. Incautiously he said that it seemed to him that the second lady had been rather careless. His hostess wasted no time in telling two other ladies about the incident, and she also told them that young Tommy too thought the second lady's behaviour had been disgraceful; she added a curlicue to the effect that Tommy thought the second lady's husband really ought to speak severely to her. Without knowing it Tommy was now in the camp of the first lady. He received black glances and cold shoulders from the camp of the second lady, which had been growing in the same manner. The feud got hotter. Bachelors gathered at ten-minute halts on route marches and tried to find out what was going on. Husbands congregated in the mess and gloomily asked one another what the hell they were going to do about the bedpan. One suggested buying a new one and pretending they'd found the lost old one—but that would have been no use because the joy of the feud was that the fate of the bedpan had long since been overlaid with other things. Until another feud formed new factions there was likely to be no end to it. A feud could also be patched up in the face of calamity, as it was considered sporting at such a time to ask first for assistance from members of the opposing camp. No loss of face was involved in answering a call for help when an enemy baby was having dysentery.

These were the dangers and evils of a woman's life. The ordinary routine of living was not so lurid, nor so petty. The average memsahib did what she could to run a decent home and keep her sanity. She would make out the menus, keep the household accounts, do a little gardening (with the *mali* fussing around her like an old hen and insisting that the memsahib let him pull up those weeds), spend a reasonable time with the children, and carry out endless rounds of supervision to see that the servants were doing what they had been told to do.

In a sufficiently populous place she might spend a good deal of her time in mah-jongg, or bridge parties, which gathered in a different bungalow each day. When her husband came back from work he might join her at the club for a drink and a swim, or sit around and relax at home as any other tired man back from the office likes to do. Dinner parties were comparatively frequent and caused little bother. *Khansamahs* liked the chance to show off their skill, for in their way they were true artists and were seldom happy performing the same play night after night to the same miserable audience of two.

It was one of India's delights that a memsahib could come back to her bungalow at 7.30 p.m., tell the *khansamah* that there would be six guests for dinner at eight-thirty, and know that a five-course meal would be conjured up from somewhere. One clue to this mystery is the fact that guests would frequently recognize their own plates and glasses on their hostess's table, and would find themselves being served by their own bearers. No overt arrangement had been made to this effect, but as soon as the servants knew who the guests were to be they levied contributions from those households. The extra food for an unexpected mob often came from the same source, the guests' own larders, though there was not really much trouble, since chickens and eggs could be bought anywhere at any time and the *khansamah*'s specialties were 'boily-roast' chicken and soufflés. India's soufflés are the best I have ever tasted.

To sum up this brief review of the memsahibs' world, seldom in history have women been subjected at one and the same time to so many discomforts, so much monotony, and so many temptations. The proportion of women who became hard, idle, and selfish may have been higher than elsewhere, but I doubt it. These faults were just more obvious, as were our own, since privacy was, for the British in India, an unobtainable luxury.

CHAPTER THIRTEEN

I RETURNED from Pachmarhi to rejoin the battalion in Bakloh, and several of us took a week-end's leave to Dalhousie, fourteen miles up the hill, to go to a dance and see a picture.

The art of the cinema has given us all that power for which Burns wailed in vain—the power to see ourselves as others see us. It is true that the 'others' are limited to a few mysteriously anonymous people who singly have no existence, but collectively are Hollywood. It is also true that we have difficulty in recognizing ourselves or our surroundings in these films, but that is surely the whole value of an outside view.

The luxuriating tropicality we saw on the screen was strangely like, yet pleasantly unlike, this India in which we worked. It was as if one of the dimensions—the sixth or eleventh, perhaps—had slipped a little and we were experiencing a part of the continuum connected to our sort of reality only by this new dimension, which ran slantwise across all the humdrum known ones.

The features that made this India a pipe dream of bliss for us deserve a careful study, for they had been deposited, little cell by cell, from stranger thoughts and more fantastic reveries than Leonardo could ever have encompassed.

Yet behind it all was a wealth of detailed information subtly metamorphosed into near-fantasy by talent, industry, and flashes of pure genius.

It was not easy to find out how the initial research had been carried out, and there were in the regiment differing schools of opinion on the subject. Wilfred Oldham said that in 1921 a producer had actually come out to India, bought an exceptionally pithy topi, and been invited to spend a week-end with the Maharajah of Porbandar. John Strickland thought that the bulk of the information had been garnered from the unprintable and well-nigh unreadable diaries of an early movie magnate, Charles R. Snizzard, who emigrated to California in '92 or '93, having previously earned a transitory Indian fame as an importer of stuffed seagulls and wrought-iron pistol cosies. Others saw evidence that close studies had been made of the Bhagavad-Gita and the works of Maud Diver and Rudyard Kipling, and that the deductions and conclusions made from each study had then been interleaved, sentence by sentence, into one master volume labelled 'India,' which is kept in fireproof cellars at M-G-M and luckily contains no word of more than one syllable.

Whoever they were and however they did it, the men who created this wonderful India of the cinema, peopled it, and organized its history and economics have merited a better recompense than they have received. But there is notoriously no justice in the world and these heroes, who have deserved titles, jewels, slave girls, and *jagirs* of land—fairyland—have received only the spaniel-like devotion of the East.

Passing the cinema door—and that unseen barrier of dimension—we entered a new India, where motives were never complicated and the thermometer stood steady, rain or shine, at 114. It was a more convenient arrangement than the variations of heat and cold we had known such a short time before—the snow, the hard winter mornings, the dull grey glare of the hot weather. But now we were all either sweating heroes or sweating cads and, by God, how we sweated! Our sweat could be compared only with the Niagaras of rain that were Hollywood's monsoon—a capricious phenomenon that strikes, as the plot pleases, in January, April, or November. Here we all wore peculiar but attractive white topis of a mushroom-shaped pattern favoured seventy years ago by lady missionaries. We kept them on our heads till 2 a.m. to ward off the lascivious rays of the Indian moon, and seldom removed them except to greet the colonel's daughter, who wore jodhpurs, a similar topi, and a thin shirt, and carried a riding crop, but did not sweat, perspire, or even glow.

We met old friends. There was the Hindu Maharajah, his name redolent of all the religions in the universe—Sir Meer Chunder Oosmahn Gopalaswami Khan Singh, K.C., K.G., V.C., K.M.S.E. He was surrounded by a swarm of Mexican servants and eclectically garbed in an outcaste's turban, Sikh trousers, a Bond Street coat, and Mohammedan slippers. There was his Maharani, with a coolie woman's nose rings and bangles, Turkish trousers, Mohammedan yashmak, Hindu caste marks, and the healthy suntan and jutting breasts of a California co-ed.

There was an elephant, caparisoned for a fair in far Bengal and looking unhappy, as well he might. He was climbing unsteadily up a buttress of the Himalaya where no white man, and indeed no elephant, had ever trod. In his capacious howdah was a freight of sweating English privates on their way to a fancy-dress ball, and a knobbly-kneed Scots piper of the Gay Gordons (wearing a Campbell tartan). These fellows had succeeded, by God knows what feats of forgery and impersonation, in joining the Bengal Lancers, which did not, outside this obliquely tilted continuum, have any British personnel except officers. The elephant's mahout said he was a Sikh, but as he was very black, a foot or two under height, had no beard, smoked a hookah in blatant defiance of his religion, and appeared to have borrowed a turban from a Mahratta stable boy, we suspected him of being the hero in baffling disguise—perhaps George Raft himself.

A monotonous reedy whine filled every nook and cranny of the Maharajah's palace, the arid mountain pass beyond, and the dank green jungles on either hand. It oscillated in trembling rise and fall, but no one ever found where it came from. With it, now thundering menacingly near, now throbbing faint and far, was the sound of tom-toms. We saw a little group of men with burnt cork on their faces. They squatted under a tree by a temple wall and beat on tympani borrowed from the U.C.L.A. orchestra. Their faces were contorted with a dubious meaningfulness. Below the whining and the thudding there was another, lesser obbligato, a muted, continuous cannonade—the sahibs clapping their hands for chota pegs.

This dire diapason constituted the music of India. By a happy chance it is also the music of every other Hollywood country between Algiers and Shanghai. To this very wail and rattle Ah Sing Foo pops through concealed trapdoors, the Malayan bandit swings lightly from the hanging boughs of the rubber tree, the burnoosed sheikh canters on a white horse among the desert palaces of Akaba, the sepia torsos undulate through the Kasbah.

The Himalayan peaks that ringed the part of Madras where the action took place were each surmounted by an impassive cross-legged figure with a white beard, which blew quite freely in the fresh wind. He was a Yogi, balanced on the razor's edge between Nirvana and sheer lunacy. After a lifetime spent in examining his navel, he knew everything and spoke words of wisdom whose import could readily be ascertained with the help of a Hall of Mirrors.

It was time to return to the world, for the last inscrutable Oriental was rotating his eyeballs and honing a knife on his dastardly false beard. Everyone had had sixty-six chota pegs, and the colonel's face was turning purple. The colonel's daughter was about to impale her lover on the twin spears of her bosom, most inadequately guarded by the thin white shirt. The fool rushed on to his doom and expired among the lances. The Oriental was cornered; the

Maharajah's disguised mahout rotated *his* eyeballs and killed him with a single blow from a clubbed howitzer. And so, as the soft-voiced *khitmatgars* sang in the chutney bushes and the long lines of pink *chilamchis* wended their homeward flight across the golden path of the setting sun, we bade a tearful *koi hai!* to this colourful land of mystery, land of enchantment—and crossed the road, our minds lost in a shimmering wilderness, to have a drink at the club.

There was almost always a club, sometimes a dusty shack, sometimes a portentous mausoleum. However small, it contained a men's bar decorated with Spy's cartoons cut from London periodicals of thirty years before, and was occupied after working hours by a few cheerful young men drinking and a few not so cheerful middle-aged men soaking. In the larger clubs women congregated in the lounge, or snake-pit, surrounded by snakes in the grass, lounge lizards, or sofa cobras—i.e. poodlefakers. From 2 to 7 p.m. the card room was filled with women playing bridge and gossiping. At 7 p.m. the male bridge players arrived, and that took care of the card room till midnight or later. Outside in the cool of the evening men and women played tennis or squash racquets, swam in the club pool, or just sat around, smoked, and drank. On behalf of the community the club organized all these amusements and many others, for it fulfilled the functions which in a big city are shared between the hotels, the country clubs, the bridge clubs, and practically every other sort of human association. It usually had a billiard-room, a dining-room, a ballroom, and a library. The ballroom had potted plants and faded curtains and from Sunday to Friday wore a seedy air of forgotten splendour, but on the night of the weekly club dance it became a cheerful place and seemed smaller.

In Bakloh we had no club, for no one lived there but us, and we already had a home and a gathering place in the mess. Our mess had never been as gloomy a place as the messes of some other Gurkha regiments, sepulchral museums crouched among dank trees and flowing precipices, their insides musty with decayed Victorian pomps; yet in the rains Bakloh could look sufficiently forbidding to anyone who had no knowledge of the warm life beating within. In the twenties a young American girl visitor to Dalhousie, while being escorted on horseback round the rides of that pleasant little sanatorium, looked down and saw, through a break in the swirling clouds, our red roofs on Bakloh's gaunt ridge far below her. She asked her escort who lived there, and he told her—the 4th Gurkhas. She gasped and cried, 'For heaven's sake, what have *they* done?'

If she could have visited us then she would have thought we were rehearsing a play about the life of the Prince Consort. The colour themes of the mess were dark red and dark brown—leather chairs and sofas, long red curtains, mahogany tables, dull bronze ashtrays, and everywhere the skulls and bones of dead animals. Round the walls of the anteroom, which is the mess name for the combined living-and drawing-room, hung a grim legion of military faces. Here every officer who had commanded either battalion since the raising of the regiment stared masterfully at posterity, usually out of a beard.

In the card room an amorphously pink watercolour of a mountain scene, known as 'The Strawberry Ice,' struggled in vain to give an impression of size to the dark, cramped room. On the mantelpiece of the library, over a romping pair of bronze Italianate horses, hung an imaginative group-portrait of the principal commanders and staff officers who had accompanied Lord Roberts on his famous march from Kabul to Kandahar in the Second Afghan War of 1879. It was an amazingly posed collection of whiskers and attitudes. Even to look at them made me feel the iron clamp on the back of my neck. Inset below the men were their numbered and empty faces, with a key giving every man's name and rank. That picture we called 'The Dentists' Convention,' and there was something about the old-fashioned haughtiness of the expressions in it that made us want to shout, whenever we looked at it, the classic cry of the early sahibs, '*Boy!* Brandy *pawnee*—and wash the sweeper's daughter!'

The billiard-room was in a small separate building, reached by a covered passageway from the front veranda. The billiard table squatted in the middle, and leather-covered banks rose in two tiers around two walls. An enormous stuffed fish occupied most of another wall, and two or three long shelves were crammed with German *pickelhaubes*, Afghan knives, tribal shields, Burmese spears, and fable-encrusted swords. There was also a row of brilliant caricatures of officers, recently done by Bow-wow Borrowman, the artist colonel of the 1st Battalion—whose hand you see in this book, in the line drawings at the head of each chapter.

It was not a beautiful building, inside or out, but it was our home, and we loved it. All the same, those rhinoceroses and buffaloes, that carved Gothic splendour of fireplace, seemed right only under the candles in winter, when we tramped down from our bungalows and stamped the snow off our boots on the veranda, and even before we had got inside the anteroom raised our voices to shout, '*Eh choro!* Oh, my son, cherry brandy!' At breakfast the rhino would read the paper over my shoulder, and the buffaloes darkened the light with the menacing spread of their horns, and the ugly skulls of beautiful deer came between me and my porridge. I was glad when a mess meeting decided the place should be thoroughly redecorated; even more glad when the members of the committee co-opted Gwinyth d'Oyly Lowsley, the wife of a 1st Battalion major, to assist them in their work.

On being admitted into the anteroom with permission, for the first time in her life, to nose about and be critical, Gwinyth picked up three objects from the mantelpiece—two shallow bowls and a vase. Dull and dirty black in colour, they were said to be loot from the Summer Palace at Peking. They had been like that when we acquired them, and very poorly we thought the regiment had done in that uproarious bout of international burglary. Gwinyth took them home and carefully washed off the dirt. She brought back to the mess three delicate cloisonné pieces of robin's-egg blue and pale gold, the blue intertwined with golden dragons and formal Chinese patterns. Back on the mantel, they lit the room, and the committee decided to redecorate it, the most important room in the mess, round them. The room became a pastel masterpiece, with long velvet curtains of pale oyster, grey and blue Persian carpets, ashtrays and candlesticks of winking silver, stone-coloured covers on the furniture.

The committee could not do much about the dining-room, for it was over-heavy with traditions and gifts, but they transformed the library with pale-green curtains, light carpets, and bright copper ashtrays, into an attractive and airy room which admirably set off the books ranked to the high ceiling all round the walls. No one wanted to alter the long glassed-in back veranda, nor the front lawn with its trees and flowers, for in those two places flourished the special atmosphere, blended of wit, friendship, and unspoken discipline, that was the heart of the 4th Gurkhas.

One effect of the redecoration was to scare away our ghost. The mess used to be haunted—not seriously, but enough to discourage the orderlies from sleeping on the veranda at night. We could never find out much about the ghost, but the Gurkhas said it was a British officer who had committed suicide in the eighties. I don't think it was terrifying enough for that. From public report it seems rather to have been a diffident poltergeist who apologetically threw chairs about in the library and rattled things on the roof.

Personally I think the ghost was Tara, the mess bearer. He was a thin-legged Dogra and had been with us forty-five years when I joined. He knew no other home than this building, remembered no other people than the British officers of the 4th Gurkha Rifles who had passed through it, for five years or twenty-five years at a time, and said 'Salaam, Tara' to him as they passed. He did no work except carry round a duster, flick at the pictures and buffalo heads, and blow along the mantelpieces. He was bent and tortoise-slow, and often forgot whether it was in 1885 or 1935 that I had joined the regiment. Sometimes he called me by the name and rank of an officer who now lived only in Tara's brain. Or he hurried off, in the middle of a sentence, muttering that Grunt-sahib had ordered him to polish the dining-room table, and Grunt-sahib was a terrible taskmaster. But Arthur Grant had been nothing but a legend here since 1914.

We pensioned Tara off finally, after the Second World War. He was nearly blind and called pitifully on the dead past to prove that he could still work for the living present. I don't know whether we were right—we could afford to pay another man to do the work—but someone had found Tara in the mess, in the middle of the night, crooning an unearthly Dogra tune of his childhood as he pushed the furniture about, flicked aimlessly with his duster and acknowledged with sudden shouts of joy orders from the absent dead.

Our ghost, even if he was not Tara, was only a little one, and friendly, and not really to be counted among India's million haunts. The ghosts most terrible to British and Indian alike were the agonized spirits of English men or women or children murdered during the Mutiny of 1857. The Central Provinces, the Bombay and Madras Presidencies, and the United Provinces, were dotted with towns that had once held military cantonments. Even before the Mutiny the old strong-built bungalows must have looked lonely in their compounds, as if looking for lost children and buried sons, for nearby are the cemeteries of the British dead. They are large, out of all proportion to the size of the cantonments, and they are always full.

Here lies Ann Crawford who died of the cholera in
the 3rd year of her age, June the 4th, 1838.
Suffer little children.

Private John Hobbs, 39th Foot. Died of the cholera,
15th May 1827.

162

The headstones are difficult to read, but the story is the same—died of the cholera, died of the cholera, died of a fever, died in childbirth, died of the cholera, the cholera . . .

After the Mutiny the weight of the army swung north-west into the Punjab, to the new frontiers of British power. The old cantonments perished; creepers grew up inside the bungalows; the cemeteries lay silent in the hot, unbreathing embrace of death. If there were any ghosts in such places they were as lonely as the cobras and bats who were their only companions.

But some places, such as Meerut, Delhi, and Bareilly, were equally important before and after 1857. In them many of the pre-Mutiny bungalows were still inhabited and had their ghosts, and in the country around them each traveller's bungalow had its restless spirit of a woman murdered while flying from the scourge.

I had a friend, an officer of Indian cavalry, who had lived in one of these old bungalows. Something woke him one June night from a light sleep. It was very hot, and the room was airless and oppressive, but he could hear no sound. An irregular flickering light played on the wall above his bed, as though a big fire were burning on the lawn. He got up and looked, but there was no fire outside. For ten minutes more the reflected flames crawled on his wall, and then they died. The next night the firelight crawled again on his wall, and the next. The fourth night the flames were stronger, and as he could not sleep he went out on the veranda for a smoke. He thought he saw two strangely dressed figures moving across the parched grass of the lawn. He thought both figures were armed, but when he went down to look there was nothing.

The flames did not come again, but he did find out that his big garden had once contained another bungalow besides his own. On a June night in 1857 two troopers of the Bengal Native Cavalry regiment then occupying the lines had crept across the lawn and murdered their adjutant in bed there. It was the signal for the beginning of the Mutiny in that place, and an hour later the mutineers burned the bungalow to the ground as a funeral pyre for the bodies of the adjutant and his wife and two children.

There was a ghost in Lansdowne too. Lansdowne was a small cantonment town in the foothills of Garhwal and there, one night in 1937, the havildar commanding the quarterguard of a Frontier Force battalion noted in his log that his guard turned out at 2.20 a.m. to Grand Rounds. The field officer of the week had not made Grand Rounds that night. The havildar, on being questioned, explained that they had turned out to an officer with a pale face and heavy whiskers, wearing white mess dress uniform. He had ridden up in the darkness on a grey horse and had not said a word except to answer the sentry's challenge with the usual phrase, 'Grand Rounds.' The guard had turned out to the Lansdowne ghost, who appeared every ten years or so and was occasionally seen at a distance, riding slowly, head down in the moonlight, along a bridle path under overhanging trees. He was said to be a man who had lost his wife in the Mutiny, and, after a year's lonely brooding, shot himself in Lansdowne.

When an officer committed suicide in India some reason was usually found, but scores of British soldiers killed themselves without any cause ever becoming apparent. Many people read Kipling when they are young, for the zest and adventure of his tales, and to the child reader his stories of the *Soldiers Three* give an impression, carried on into maturity, that a private's life was a riot of jolly pranks and escapades. It is worth while rereading these stories as an adult, and noticing how much unhappiness lies beneath the surface. A private's life was no riot in Kipling's day, and it became even less so later. The young British regular usually did six years in India without a break, and during this time his government did nothing for him. For the officers there were clubs and messes and a few women; for the Indian sepoys, their own country and people and way of life. For the British private there were a flyblown bar and grill on the outskirts of the bazaar, where he was robbed of his scanty pay and given adulterated drink and skimped food; sand-harlots, riddled with every type of venereal disease; old-fashioned barracks, and the sour smell of sweaty socks and shirts; a cinema a mile away; and, close at hand, boredom, loneliness, and despair. And always, thank God, there was three o'clock of a burning afternoon, an empty barrack room, and a big toe on the trigger.

Every effort made to improve the soldiers' lot was made by regiments, not by the government. The regiments achieved a good deal, but the problem of providing female society baffled everyone. As always, in the absence of a normal amount of women's company, the men's thoughts rode on sex. Venereal disease went up to fantastic proportions from the negligible figure it was in England. Most British regiments once ran their own brothels quite publicly, and had the Indian girls who worked in them regularly inspected by the battalions' medical officers. Then, late in the nineteenth century, the wife of a commander-in-chief had that stopped, and boys went back to syphilis. Later a Member of Parliament suggested that soldiers returning from India should wear yellow armbands for a year, to show that they were probably disease-ridden and not fit for decent English girls to associate with. There was a counter-suggestion that Members of Parliament should send their daughters out to do a six-year spell in Multan and Ferozepore, at 125 degrees in the shade, on half a crown a day. It was thought they would probably need whole suits of yellow on their return.

Not infrequently men spent loving weeks and months preparing their own death in some complicated mechanical fashion. The occupation drove away the cafard by giving them something interesting to do and think about. One private soldier, who had a good rifle with him all the time, took twelve weeks to make a dummy machine-gun fireable. He added an unnecessarily devious contraption to enable him to fire it while sitting in front of the muzzle. He then sandbagged the walls of his little store—he was a storeman —so that he would not hurt anyone else, and, at last, shot himself in just the way he had intended.

This happened in Bareilly and was quickly followed by two more suicides. When, a little later, a series of unusual incidents troubled the cantonment there, some people thought the whole place should be burned down. John Strickland, who was mixed up in the affair, told me about it and whatever its cause it throws a useful light on what India does to people—or ghosts.

The quartermaster's daughter, aged twenty, ran into her father's room one night and said someone had bitten her lightly on the abdomen as she lay in bed. She had some nondescript toothmarks to show, and was very frightened. Her father got up and stumbled about the compound among the water channels and flowerbeds but found nobody.

A week later a sergeant's wife was bitten on the abdomen, not lightly, and thought she saw 'something' going out through the window. She went to the hospital next day with a nervous breakdown, and a reign of terror began in Bareilly. Wives snuggled nearer to husbands, and unmarried girls slept in their parents' bedrooms. The police came in, under a European inspector. He did not believe in ghosts and made searching inquiries about movements and examined everyone's teeth—the officers' too. John was one of many who had the right sort of teeth and no sound alibi.

After two hungry weeks the biter bit again. John shared a large bungalow with three other young men, all of whom happened to be away; the general's house was next door. The general had a grown-up daughter, and the whole family was sleeping out on the lawn in the hot weather. The general had gone away on tour, and that night John was awakened by terrified screams. He jumped up and burst through the low hedge on to the next lawn. The general's daughter, half collapsed through the torn mosquito net round her bed, was crying, 'He's bitten me,' and bleeding faintly through her nightdress. Her mother was there, quite as frightened as the girl. John's appearance was at first greeted with hysterical relief, but then the police came. They asked John a lot of questions and looked at his teeth like horse-copers. The general's wife and daughter said they did not need his help now and quickly went indoors with the police. For a month John went about his business in Bareilly almost alone. Everyone looked away when they saw him coming, and he gave up going to the club dances.

In the next dark of the moon a nurse was bitten, but John had an alibi; he was in a train coming back from Lahore with a very suspicious hockey team. His friends returned to him, the bitings stopped, and they never did burn down the cantonment—or find the biter.

CHAPTER FOURTEEN

A<small>N</small> Indian Army officer got two months' 'privilege leave' on full pay every year—three months if he was serving on the Frontier or in a non-family station. Every fourth year he also got six months' furlough on reduced pay, and in that fourth year he combined his privilege leave and his furlough and thus got eight months. This enabled him to go back to England and have a long rest in a better climate. My furlough was not due till 1938, but in 1936 I managed to get to England and back on my privilege leave.

It was a good leave. The weather was fine, the month was June, and I had already forgotten how green the grass was in England and how the sun could be a desired friend instead of a hostile companion. The people seemed smaller in stature than I remembered them, very pale, and all hunched and hurried in the morning when the dusty beams of sunlight streamed down through the grimed glass arch of Waterloo Station, and they looked to neither right nor left but scurried in their thousands down into the subway. For myself, I had a greater feeling of confidence than before. Whereas I used to seek everyone's approval and be downcast if it was not universally given, now I cared less than formerly what anyone thought about my clothes, manners, or way of living. There was a more fearsome censor inside me, made in India, and its force was stronger than any pressure to conform to established customs and ways of thought. I didn't have to live with anyone but myself—and my regiment.

After five weeks I returned the way I had come. Paris was the same as it always was for Indian Army subalterns returning from leave—a café on the sidewalk outside the Gare de Lyon, a sensuous ordering of food, the last of the saved money going down the gullet, uproarious recognition of old Bill of the Dogras (the sardonic waiters must have known half the Indian Army by sight after they had served in that street for a few years), a bottle of armagnac in the coat pocket, and on to the train, sitting packed in the second-class compartments, swaying and jolting down the P.L.M. to Marseilles. We made jokes about the ciné bleu in Marseilles (but no one visited it eastward-bound); and shouted at the porters in French, with Hindustani and Gurkhali words mixed in. The porters didn't find us as funny as we found ourselves, but they were going to stay here in this lovely steep city with the smell of fish along the Vieux Port, and we were going to sail on a P. & O. run like a warship, where the passengers would do as they were told and jump to it, and like it. They did, too. It is a pleasure to be on anything really well run.

I was glad to be back in Bakloh, and almost immediately went with John Strickland and Moke to pay a visit to the Gurkha officers' club. Narbir wasn't in that evening, and Parta Sing, the man who would shortly succeed him as subadar-major, was the senior G.O. present. Parta Sing did not enjoy the deep respect Narbir had earned, but things there were livelier than if the old man had been present, for Parta Sing was a character.

Seven or eight Gurkha officers were sitting outside the little building when we arrived, watching Subadar Dallu and Jemadar Sukdeo play tennis. It was almost dark, and anywhere else in Bakloh play would have been impossible, but the G.O.s' club and tennis court stood on a shelf cut out of the hill-side, facing west across the Ravi Valley. The last of the sun from behind the mountains of Jammu gave just enough light to play by.

When he saw us coming Parta Sing got up, saluted, and shouted to the orderlies to bring drinks. They hurried up, bearing tumblers containing five fingers of overproof rum, orange-scented in the way the Gurkhas liked it. It was sweet stuff and not immediately potent; its greatest effects were not felt till later, or after drinking water, and could be delayed overnight. Our attempts to have the rum diluted met with such expert obstructionism that they were quite pointless. After I had asked three times, Parta Sing himself passed a jug over my glass in a mystic wave that released perhaps 10 c.c. of water, and I gave up. We sat down to watch the end of the tennis.

Dallu was a steady player even without his skill at gamesmanship, and Sukdeo had rare flashes of erratic brilliance. We sat, drank, relaxed, and watched them bound about, feeling content and lazy. This place had an atmosphere of its own, half that of the disciplined Gurkha we knew, half that of the Gurkha as he would have been if left to his own improvident Mongolian devices. The orderlies were free and easy, happy and talkative, but none too clean. The G.O.s could not afford to dress them up in livery and probably did not want to. They themselves, except when coming direct from duty, always wore mufti. The clothes they chose were often startling. Middle-aged, iron-faced men, whom we knew well in khaki and grey, now lolled about in red and yellow shirts, purple suits, checked coats, and bilious heather-mixture plus-fours. All this was topped, even indoors, by an incongruous but comforting reminder of their trade, the plain round black pillbox hat.

Dallu won his match and came off the court, lecturing Sukdeo and pulling his long moustaches. Parta Sing suggested we all go inside. In a few minutes peace had fled, for he was in tearing spirits and soon the whole table rocked and the four oil lanterns shone redly on the ring of laughing Mongolian and Caucasian faces. In the dark corners behind, the orderlies came and went with rum for us and lemonade for Dallu, who never drank alcohol.

Parta Sing turned and shouted, '*Eh! anda le—oof, oof— brrrrk brwlck—cluck clk-clk-clk.*' He bent down to squat, still squawking, and felt about under his behind on the floor as if feeling under a hen. He brought up his hand, holding an imaginary egg, and shouted again, '*Oof! Oof! J'ai pas d'argent—mairçy, mairçy—bong jour, madame.*'

The orderly smiled in the way one smiles at a father's favourite joke heard for the twentieth time, and went to prepare the hard-boiled eggs. This was one of Parta Sing's favourite parlour tricks. Twenty-two years before, he had gone to France as a young lance-naik with the 1st Battalion, and there had learned a few murderous smatterings of French. He liked to air them and show again how, when all else failed, he used to make the French peasant women understand he wanted eggs by imitating a hen laying one.

The G.O.s started to teach me the songs the men sang on the line of march. Soon I had learned twenty or thirty sets of words, and my head was stuffed with muddled snatches of their tunes. The songs are called *jaunris*. Each has two lines and a catchy tune, but the rhythm is difficult until the ear becomes accustomed to it. The words vary from obscenity to nostalgia with every sort of weirdly pointless little fable in between. A few specimens, literally translated:

> One fish over the other in love,
> Then the bottom one laid eggs in the water.

> The train came, dear, going rumble-rumble
> At twelve o'clock on a June night.

> In '90 there was an earthquake
> And sure the Nepalis were frightened.

And, the best of them all in its phrasing and rhythm:

When you see mascara'd eyes winking
You know you're near Dehra Dun.

Eh jaun! jaun! pareli ankhen ma gazeli
Samajaunchhu Dehra Dun.

The orderlies brought in the appetizers, little saucers full of hard-boiled eggs, curried potatoes, curried goats' livers and kidneys, and tough pieces of fried and curried meat. We drank more rum and sang more *jaunris*. Parta Sing pushed back the table and dragged us out on the floor to teach us the simple dance that went with them, a crouching, rhythmic shuffle at full bend of knee, with sideways hops and shouts.

We were there till very late and came away in the moonlight. It was good to be back in Bakloh, with my regiment.

CHAPTER FIFTEEN

DUSSEHRA, most important Hindu festival of the year, was approaching. I had already seen something of the riotous indecencies of the Holi, when the Gurkhas threw coloured water on each other and capered at night on the parade ground with wooden phalli two feet long strapped to their loins. This was supposed to be not quite quite, and British officers took no part in it. But Dussehra we attended as guests of the Gurkhas. It is the festival that marks the opening of the Indian cold-weather season.

In most of the world armies used to go into winter quarters, hibernate, and begin their operations in the spring. In India armies have throughout history gone into summer quarters and estivated to avoid the glaring heat, the dust and disease of the hot weather. In June or July the hot weather is drowned in the monsoon rains and war then, from being unpleasant, becomes all but impossible because every track is a swamp and every stream a torrent. By September the rains have dried up, and the Indian kings could have been seen, in those departed centuries of their glory, drilling their armies, burnishing their armour, and caracoling out in silks and jewels for another season's aristocratic sport. In every country and every religion some great festival celebrates the turn of the year, the time when the blood again runs freely, and in Hindu India this festival is Dussehra.

One day early in October the Gurkhas began to arrange the arms of the battalion to form a hollow square on the parade ground. By dark the work was done, and the rifles stood in thick ranks, 'swords' fixed, their woodwork gleaming dully in the light of the bonfire burning beyond them. Jasmine flowers seemed to grow from every barrel; at the corners of the square garlands hung from the water-jackets of the machine-guns, and among the rifles there were posied automatics, wreathed swords, and flower-hung trophy cannons from forgotten wars. Sentries stood over the arms —shadowy figures who carried naked *kukris* cradled blades upwards in the crooks of their right arms and throughout the succeeding rites never ceased their silent patrolling, or took part in any of the celebrations, or even looked at the merrymaking so close to them.

As night fell the men worked hard, grunting and heaving and playing practical jokes on one another as they worked, to put up a line of tents around the parade ground. They pegged the backs of the tents down to the ground in the usual way but lifted up the fronts on poles and secured them well, so that the upper-crust spectators who were to sit there could see the show and yet be sheltered from the chills of our upland October night. In the centre of the parade ground, and right in front of the seats reserved for the colonel and the subadar-major they hammered deep into the earth a thick post that had a hole bored through it some eighteen inches above the ground.

Then riflemen came and put hand lanterns on every table in the row of tents. Others lit oil pressure-lamps and hung

174

them dizzily from basketball posts round the edges of the enclosure. The light came back sharp and clear from an eddying frieze of bodies, the Gurkhas. It shone on the starched white shorts and white shirts of their off-duty dress, and gleamed on their flashing teeth and high cheekbones. On their heads they wore either the flat round black cap, with our badge of the Prince of Wales's feathers in front, or a woollen scarf in bold black and red Fair Isle patterns, loosely tied after the fashion of an Indian turban.

The Gurkha officers began to arrive. Narbir looked at me, sitting there alone, with surprise and told me sternly that I would be hungry, having missed dinner in mess, and that it was not a good thing to drink rum on an empty stomach. I explained that I had wanted to see all the arrangements, and had invited myself to eat with my company at six o'clock and was now full of rice, curried goat, and vegetables. Narbir nodded approvingly. Parta Sing shouted '*Raksi le!*' and, like magic—the familiar, dangerous magic—a glass of rum appeared in my hand. Narbir sat down; the rest of the G.O.s went off to chivvy the riflemen or bustle round collecting together groups of singers.

A little after half-past nine my brothers, the other British officers, arrived. As they walked into the irregular circle of light they made a pleasant picture of bronzed faces, white shirt fronts, and scintillating medals. I felt temporarily isolated from them by having spent the evening eating, thinking, and laughing as a Gurkha, and now saw them— myself—anew. Let me describe Bill Mills. We all looked much the same, except that Bill was smarter than any of us because he was the newly appointed adjutant.

He had on black patent-leather Wellington boots, half-length with straight steel spurs three inches long fixed in small metal boxes let into the backs of the heels. Over the boots and under the instep were strapped very tight darkgreen trousers called mess overalls, with two-inch stripes of black mohair down the sides. Over his starched white shirt he wore a dark-green broadcloth waistcoat, embroidered with black silk, mohair, and velvet, and over that a short dark-green Eton jacket of the same broadcloth. The jacket had a stand-up collar and was loaded with five double rows of black looped cord across the front, designed to fasten over olivets. The ends of each set of cords were not in fact fastened but allowed to hang down the front of the jacket in careless profusion. On his shoulders were slabs of inter-woven black braided cord, six inches long by two inches across, and nearly half an inch thick, and perched on them were the rank badges of the King's land forces. Bill wore on each shoulder the two raised stars, in black metal, of a lieutenant. Each star bore, embossed, the badge and motto of the Order of the Bath.

I do not remember whether Bill had a medal or not but his predecessor, Jim Goldney, had one. The miniature of it hung among the cords on the left breast of his jacket, sus-pended from a green and black ribbon of watered silk, and on the ribbon was a tiny silver clasp engraved with the words 'N.W. Frontier 1930–31.' This was the India General Service Medal, always called the Frontier Medal, first issued in 1908 and awarded, with a different clasp, for every campaign that had taken place anywhere in the Indian Empire since then. A man who had joined the army in 1908 and had seen plenty of service would have had the ribbon stretched down to his waist to hold all the clasps. The 1908 Frontier Medal had just been made obsolete and had been replaced by the 1936 Frontier Medal, with a ribbon of a different colour, but none of us had won that yet.

When we were all settled down after the pushing back of chairs, the salutes and greetings, the circulation of rum and cigarettes, the dances began. It is more sensible to use the Indian word and say the *nautches* began, as 'dance' gives to Westerners little impression of these shuffled Oriental ballets, where dancers and assisting chorus act out in move and pause and countermove some long fairy tale of Hindu gods and devils. The Gurkhas' wives and families were there in the shadows on the other side of the parade ground but the *nautches* were done by the soldiers, some dressed as

176

men and some as women, for Gurkha women never dance in public except once a year at a special festival in their own hills. The 'men' wore loose white cotton skirts with many pleats, which hung nearly to the ground. On one ankle most of them had two chinking bangles. Above the skirts they wore black velvet waistcoats, white shirts and, on their heads, white turbans or the usual woollen scarves. The 'women' had been selected from among the young soldiers for their youth and good looks and made a surprisingly successful picture of laughing femininity, with full red and black skirts, embroidered bodices, and loose scarves of coloured chiffon draped over their heads.

The shuffling groups steadily looped and gyrated round the parade ground as they worked through the traditional dances to the music of massed singing and the beat of small drums called *madals*. The drums were carried by leaping and posturing soldiers, who used the heels of both hands to beat out an irregularly syncopated rhythm. The atmosphere was friendly and warm but far from concentrated. At times it seemed so diffuse as to be almost formless. Dancers drifted off to have tots of rum; the singing sometimes died out as the singers became bored or tired or went away to talk to their wives and friends; mongrel dogs wandered inquisitive and unmolested among the dancers; and all the spectators spent more time drinking and discussing their affairs than they did in watching the show.

Towards half-past ten the music faded, the dancers and drummers straggled off the parade ground, and a little procession came on from the left and behind us. Four soldiers led, dressed in white shorts and shirts and carrying rifles. Two more soldiers pulled and tugged at a short length of rope, and on the end of the rope was a big and angry billygoat. Behind the goat marched a Gurkha with bare legs and feet, white shorts and white vest, who swung in his hand a gigantic *kukri* all but thirty inches long, including the handle. In the rear of the procession waddled a portly Indian, who had a white caste mark daubed on his forehead. The Indian was our battalion Brahmin, whose functions were similar to those of a priest or padre in a Christian army.

The party wasted no time. They dragged the goat to the post in the centre of the parade ground. One herdsman pushed the rope round its neck through the hole and pulled it taut, jamming the goat's head up against the post. The other seized the goat's hind legs, jerked them back so that the animal was well stretched out, and held them firm. The Brahmin muttered in prayer and sprinkled the ground, the executioner, and the goat with holy Ganges water. The riflemen loaded their rifles with a little rattle of bolts that sounded very loud in the sudden stillness. The executioner stepped up to the goat, felt its neck with his left hand to find where the vertebræ lay, and shifted his feet till he stood well balanced with legs apart.

For a minute there was complete silence. Everyone waited. The executioner stood poised, looking down at his feet. The Brahmin muttered prayers and sprinkled ashes and water and made marks in the dust. A single shout rang down from the hill above us, where a rifleman stood on a high black rock among the pines, looking out to the east and waiting for the moon to rise behind the mountains. As the rim of the moon edged over the distant snow the rifleman called out in the silence.

The executioner slowly raised his *kukri* in both hands and slowly let it swing down again. He paused a moment, then with a sudden smooth effort of force whirled the broad blade up and down.

The goat's body sank sideways to the ground with heels jerking, and blood from the arteries of its neck spouted briefly over the dust. The choir burst into a Hindu hymn; the rifles banged away into the night sky; the herdsmen seized the carcass by the hind legs and ran with it, shrieking and shouting, round the arena; the Brahmin placed a live coal on the severed head; a whiff of singed hair blew down to us; everyone talked and laughed and hugged his neighbour.

The head had come off cleanly, in one blow. The

battalion would have good fortune in battle, and in all its activities, in the ensuing year. We were due for the Frontier the following March. No one was ashamed of the superstitious happiness we felt.

The rum flowed faster into my glass, and the dancers began a *Bagluni*, a dance worthy of the greatest stages of the world. Each of the twenty dancers carried in each hand a silver plate about a foot in diameter. They balanced the plates on their hands and swung them rhythmically round their bodies, up and down their sides, and over their heads, as they circled the ground with swooping steps. The lanterns caught the silver in rhythmic flashes, and the arena became alive with syncopated light and the changing pattern of the dancers' formal moves. When it was ended we sat silent, then roared our applause.

After midnight several of us younger British officers went into the arena and danced and sang with the rest. I was there, practising in public what Parta Sing had so recently taught me. We were not expert but we had learned enough not to be in the way, and our antics delighted the Gurkhas, who shouted encouragement and advice from the ropes and yelled applause when we tripped over our spurs or found that rum had disturbed our balance.

I woke next morning at 9.30 a.m. and drank a large glass of water. The rum reacted immediately, and my legs desynchronized. James came in, shrugged his shoulders, and said, 'We told you water was dangerous after rum. Come and have breakfast.'

Feeling slightly hilarious and very queer in the legs, I went down to breakfast in the mess. We sat down to the meal traditional after a night of celebration—very hot and peppery mulligatawny soup, with bowls of rice and fresh lemon, followed by devilled chicken and bacon-and-brain fritters. To drink there were the usual large pots of a warm grey gruel, made from sand and old bedsocks and humorously labelled coffee. This 'coffee,' made by *khansamahs*, was India's revenge, complete and unanswerable, for any or all British oppression in that country.

After breakfast we strengthened ourselves in another traditional way—brandy and ginger ale—for the grim but exciting rites to come. By eleven-thirty we were all once more seated in the row of tents, now wearing civilian clothes, as the day was a holiday. Three of the married officers' wives came up. The rest stayed at home, having been warned that they would not like the spectacle. The Gurkha officers and soldiers were dressed as before; few of them had been to bed. The sentries still patrolled the stand of arms, now bathed in hot sunlight. The glare from the parade ground made me wince, and I put on dark glasses. The colonel sat on the subadar-major's right, and on each side were ranged the five British officers who commanded companies. On the table in front of each member of this group—including me, in my capacity as commander of A Company—was a white cotton turban, neatly folded like a small towel. The whole battalion was there, laughing and joking and wearing flowers in their hats. At the end of the row of tents the pipe band stood about, smoking and chatting, their pipes and drums piled against the canvas.

Across from us were the Gurkhas' wives and families. The night before they had hardly been visible, and I had sensed them only occasionally from a high-pitched laugh or a few shouted words. Now in the daylight they were like an enormous flowerbed, gay with every conceivable colour.

The morning's programme began. One buffalo would be sacrificed on behalf of the whole battalion by an executioner selected by the subadar-major. Then one buffalo, three goats, six chickens, and six marrows would be sacrificed on behalf of each company, the buffaloes by executioners selected by the senior Gurkha officer in that company. Each buffalo-executioner, having carried out his task, would come up to the tables, and his commander would tie the white turban round his bare head in ceremonial endorsement.

The party of riflemen to fire salutes marched on, followed by a choir of thirty men led by one of the Brahmin's assistants. Then three herdsmen brought on the first buffalo. It was a big black beast with huge, curving horns, and it walked into the arena looking unhurried and unafraid. The herdsmen had no difficulty in securing it to the post. The battalion executioner, Havildar Khagu Pun from my company, appeared. Khagu was of medium height for a Gurkha and exceptionally powerfully built. He swung the big *kukri* in his hands, smiled to his friends, and danced about a little on his bare feet. He was very confident. The two-handed sacrificial *kukri* was always used at these executions unless some particularly strong and skilful man cared to take the gamble between undying fame and undying contempt by trying to execute the big buffalo with an ordinary service *kukri*, which is one-handed, half the size, and a quarter the weight. The feat had been done many years before by Subadar-Major Narbir, when he was a havildar, but today Khagu was taking no risks.

The ceremony followed the same lines as that of the night before, and the buffalo's head came off at the first stroke. The technique of these beheadings is not a matter of mere strength, as I discovered when I looked at photographs afterwards. At the moment when the head is severed, the executioner's hands, holding the *kukri*, are almost on the ground, while the blade has just passed through the neck and is about twelve inches off the ground. The blade has clearly been passed through the neck downward and towards the executioner, at an angle all the way, in a powerful slicing motion. A straight blow, however hard, would probably not go through.

While the colonel congratulated Khagu and tied on his white turban the battalion's untouchable sweepers dragged away the carcass, which they were permitted to eat; the Gurkhas were not. They left the head at one side, and the Brahmin placed a live coal on its forehead.

The herdsmen led on my company's buffalo, and I found that my hands were sweating. They had to do it right. We would be disgraced if anything went wrong. I shut my eyes, not because the blood sickened me, but because I could not bear to see failure—and I could do nothing to ensure success.

Shouts rang in my ears; Subadar Dallu was slapping me on the shoulder, and I opened my eyes. The buffalo lay dead, and the executioner was running towards me, his face split by a tremendous, proud smile. With shaking hands, and most inexpertly, I wound the white cloth round his head, and he ran back to the sidelines.

The third buffalo, B Company's, smelled blood as he walked on to the parade ground. He blew and snorted with terror, but the herdsmen dragged him remorselessly on. The executioner seemed to be infected by the buffalo's nervousness and kept spitting on his hands and shifting his feet as he waited at the post. The arena was now dotted with B Company's other sacrifices—three goats, each held firmly by two men; six chickens, held by the men who were going to execute them; six marrows, each supported on four short wooden legs, the subadar's eight-year-old son standing eagerly over them with his father's sword in his hands.

But no one looked at anything but the centrepiece, the straining buffalo and the anxious executioner. The man swung the blade up and down twice, then raised it higher and more slowly than I had seen the others do, and put every ounce of his strength into the downward blow.

The edge bit deep into the buffalo's neck but did not go through. The buffalo knelt down and died as the executioner hacked frantically at the remaining shreds of flesh and skin. The battalion gave a roar of disappointment. The executioner threw down the *kukri* and started to run, but he was not quick enough. One herdsman dipped his hands into the buffalo's reeking blood and rubbed them in the executioner's face and hair. The other picked up the severed head and hurled it at the executioner, hitting him in the chest and knocking him over. In the excitement, with the executioner running to hide his shame and everyone shouting, the efficient dispatch of the company's other offerings went almost unnoticed. They had all gone cleanly, and littered round the arena were heads, blood, bodies, split marrows, and headless, running chickens.

The morning wore steadily on and the smell of blood grew thicker in the dust and glare. One of the British wives turned green and went away, escorted by her husband, who was almost audibly saying, 'I told you so.' The row of heads, each crowned with a live coal, lengthened. The smell of burned hair grew stronger, and I was glad of those brandies. At last the sacrifices came to an end. We hardly had time for a cigarette before we were on our feet as the pipes began to wail and the drums to thud.

The first notes of the Regimental March froze the scene. Eight hundred men stood still, facing in toward the severed heads and dead bodies of the sacrifices. The band played the Regimental March at the Rifle quick-step, once up and once down the parade ground, while the colonel took off his hat in salute. Under the sun there was standing colour in the red of the blood and the red of flowers and the red of women's clothes; and there was white of drill and yellow dust of earth and brown sheen and steel light from the arms; and through everything and among it all flickered the khaki and silver and green-black of the band.

The bass drummer struck two double beats, a magician waved his wand, and there was life again. The pipes wailed more slowly to another tune and the Gurkhas broke ranks to follow the band, shouting and throwing flowers. The whole mob, like an ill-jointed and riotous snake, writhed round and round the square of arms. They dragged the wreaths and garlands off the barrels and threw them to and fro in a battle of flowers. Their dancing, stamping feet raised the dust so that in five minutes nothing was visible except a noise-filled haze from which caps and flowers suddenly bounded toward the sky and curved down again to be lost in the tumult.

CHAPTER SIXTEEN

Dussehra was for the Gurkhas and Christmas was for us, but on the Regimental Day we celebrated together the festival of the spirit that had brought us together and made us one with each other.

On March 11th, 1915, the 1st Battalion of the 4th Gurkhas went into the battle of Neuve Chapelle. On March 11th, 1917, the 2nd Battalion was among the first troops to enter conquered Baghdad. After the end of the First World War we celebrated the Regimental Day on March 11th each year. Its full title was Neuve Chapelle— Baghdad Day, though men of the 1st Battalion were likely to call it Neuve Chapelle Day, and we of the 2nd, Baghdad Day.

Several pensioned Gurkha officers always came back from Nepal for the day, though not many of lower rank could afford the time or the money, as it averaged a man twelve days' travel each way between his home and Bakloh and on the journey he had to use several railway lines, two or three buses and in Nepal, for days on end, his feet. The biggest attendance was from the men who had retired to settle round Bakloh. The Nepalese Government did not like us to encourage this settling, for it wanted the pensioners and their rupees back in Nepal; but there was no good way to prevent it, and in the seventy years we had been in Bakloh a big colony of pensioned men, their wives, children, and grandchildren had grown up round us.

Early in the morning of each March 11th pensioners began to arrive on the parade ground with their families, to be greeted according to their age and rank by our reception committees. The parade ground was ringed, as at Dussehra, with tents, awnings, chairs, benches, and enclosures for the women and children. Bent old men, grey-haired and wearing steel-rimmed spectacles, hobbled on with the aid of sticks, and the subadar-major respectfully saluted them and reintroduced them to the colonel. Young men who had only recently cut their names after the minimum of four years' service went straight to their old companies and mingled with them cheerfully, not yet knowing the compulsion that had made Narbir weep as his Gurkha officers gathered round to touch his feet and knees and wish him God's blessing in his retirement. The women squatted on their heels in little clusters, talking of birth and death. Hundreds of children ran about in the crowd, falling under everyone's feet and getting cuffs when they crossed their fathers' paths.

Then all the officers gathered to greet our two greatest old men. The first was a retired subadar-major, a very special one. Honorary Captain Rannu Thapa, Rai Bahadur, seventy years of age, had followed a grandfather, a father, and one brother into the regiment. One of his two sons, the subadar-major of the 1st Battalion, saluted him and led him to a chair. The ashes of his other son made fertile a piece of the soil of France, for that son had been killed in action at Givenchy in 1914. Eight grandsons, in our uniform, came to touch his knee. His great-grandfather had enlisted in the service of one of the Honourable East

India Company's Native regiments in 1790. This was 1936—146 years of service. He spoke English well and sat at the colonel's right hand, his thin face and faded eyes smiling, his veined hands one over the other on top of a stick between his knees. He looked like a wise and tired old mandarin.

On the colonel's left was someone far, far older. No one knew quite how old he was, but he had been a jemadar of Gurkha irregular cavalry in the Mutiny of eighty years before, and he was said to be 108. He walked with a stick, slowly but uprightly, and spoke no English but understood our Gurkhali perfectly if we bawled in his ear, for he was deaf. He thought the regiment was going to the dogs and whisky was not what it used to be in the days when he had chased the Nana Sahib across the United Provinces and seen Lieutenant Roberts of the Bengal Artillery. Weaker men who had not yet attained his freedom from the wheel of existence would say 'when' after four fingers of neat whisky had been poured into their glasses, but not this old hero. He looked speculatively but wordlessly at his tumbler until the colonel, some sixty years his junior, had filled it up to the brim with seven or eight fingers of the best Scotch—and then, without fuss, he drank it back and had another. He got tired quite early in the afternoon and walked off, slowly but uprightly still, acknowledging the salutes of us all as he passed, and carrying a load of years and whisky that would long since have put anyone else in the cemetery of a DT's hospital.

The main items of the day were the sports in the afternoon, the ceremonial beating of 'Retreat' in the evening, and dances and feasts during the night. The sports were of the gymkhana pattern—very serious competitions and relays between companies, less serious events between the various ranks, races for children, and handicap dashes for pensioners. The climax was a tug-of-war between the British and Gurkha officers.

The year before, the crowd, moved by a common impulse we later traced to some hints dropped among them by the subadar-major, had edged right forward round the tug-of-war contestants, and the British had soon found themselves being irresistibly drawn over the line in both the first two tugs, thus losing the competition. We learned that five extra Gurkha officers, concealed in the crush, had attached themselves to their end of the rope. We acknowledged that we had been defeated by superior cunning and organization, and remembered.

This year Wilfred Oldham announced that the tug-of-war ground must be prevented from getting churned up, and had it covered with straw. At night three of us secretly hammered a post deep into the ground under the straw. Next day the colonel tossed for ends with a double-headed coin, most of the straw was cleared away, and the tug-of-war began. The Gurkha officers did not show much originality and their team of eight rapidly increased to ten, to twelve, and at last to sixteen. Meanwhile Wilfred gave our end a couple of turns round the post. As each new opponent crept deceitfully into the battle one of us stretched, left the rope, and lit a cigarette. Finally only Wilfred was left as our anchor man, yawning and holding sixteen enemies with one hand.

A tremendous argument disrupted the Gurkha officers. Parta Sing rushed up, saw the post, and began to bawl at the crowd to pull it up. But the riflemen were on our side this year, so Parta Sing led a sally of Gurkha officers to attack Wilfred. The grinning riflemen tripped them up. We all dashed back to the rope, and in utter pandemonium easily pulled the white handkerchief over the line, for there was by then no one on the other end. The colonel said that as he had a stomach ache all further pulls would have to be cancelled, and we had therefore won by one pull to nil.

Round the sides a fairground was in full swing, all run by the regiment, with booths for innocent gambling. Aunt Sallys, coconut shies, miniature rifle ranges, fishing in buckets—all the fun of the fair. The N.C.O.s in charge barked and shrieked in the best tradition; the customers eddied about like shoals of mackerel; and the band played selections from *The Mikado*. All profits from the sideshows went into the Welfare Fund, and the surest money-spinner was a British officer taking the place of the regular Aunt Sally. The prospect of throwing things at us brought scores of men running and laughing.

Towards six o'clock the adjutant disappeared to inspect the band, pipes, drums, and bugles. This was their big show of the year, and they had to be good. They made a fine muster, for by ingenious wangling and improvisation we could turn out from both battalions together some forty bugles—of whom twenty-four were also drummers—forty pipes, and a fifty-piece brass band. Now they were all fallen in in solid ranks behind the bugle major. In a Rifle regiment the bugle major does not carry the heavy staff of a 'red' drum-major, but a light stick four feet long or less, usually of ebony with a silver top.

The bugle major snapped round to face the band and shouted 'Fanfare Number Three! Buglers—ready!' The silver bugles flashed up in two sharp movements. In the quarterguard the memorial bell struck the first double stroke of six, the mellow notes coming up out of the trees across the silent parade ground.

'Sound—up!' Forty bugles shrilled out the intricate harmonies of the long fanfare and snapped down again. Around the parade ground the men sat down or clustered along the ropes. Above us the women banked on the stone-stepped and terraced hill-side again formed their great border of colour. Below, in the sunlight, the band was a khaki hedge on the pale earth, black-topped, speckled with dark cords and black belts, and winking with silver. For half an hour the men marched up and down. The band and bugles played the contentious, rousing quick-step 'Marching Through Georgia.' The harsh bugles sang alone; then the pipes wailed and the drums crashed; and then all were again silent and still. Behind them the ridge crest dropped away sharply past the 1st Battalion's lines and then, miles across the hidden valley, rose to the snows. It was twilight but not dark.

The bugle major looked at his watch. This was for form's sake only, because when 'Retreat' is being beaten half-past six occurs when the bugles start the call, no matter what the clock says. Below in the trees the quarterguard sentry held the bell clapper, listening and waiting.

' "Retreat"! Buglers—ready! Sound—*up!*'

The buglers sounded the call, again in harmony; the quarterguard flag slowly dipped; the bell rang; the army's night began. The bugle major stepped quickly across to the colonel, his stick swinging jerkily in front of his body. He saluted and said in Gurkhali, 'Programme finished, sir!'

The colonel returned the salute, congratulated him, and ordered him to march off. The bass drummers beat faster as the pipers swung into the march-past; the side drums rattled and banged in the lifting, urgent Rifle step.

Formality and the obvious unity of discipline slipped away with the band. We, who had stood for a moment as a regimented body, broke up into laughing and talking groups. Before the thunder of the emblazoned drums had faded down the hill we were individuals, men and women, scattered over the level square of earth hewn down and built up on the spine of the Bakloh ridge, all eddying off to other open places in and among the barracks. The *madals* began to throb in the night, and the havildars passed round rum in huge jars.

I fell down a small precipice that night. I was following a drainage cut on the left side of an unfamiliar path in the 1st Battalion's lines, where I had been dancing *jaunris*. I kept the dim line of the drain carefully on my left, but it turned and crossed the path, and I kept it on my left and walked over the edge of the cliff. A pair of riflemen found me winded and half unconscious at the bottom a few minutes later. They carried me tenderly to my bungalow and told Biniram they thought I was drunk. But I wasn't, I was in physical pain, and very happy.

We were due for the Frontier the following year.

CHAPTER SEVENTEEN

ON November 25th, 1936, the Frontier, which had been simmering since the Mohmand Campaign of 1934–35, suddenly exploded. The first incident in what was to develop into the biggest campaign since 1919 took place at Biche Kaskai in Waziristan, where Waziri tribesmen ambushed the Bannu Brigade on a carefully laid, well-concealed, and boldly executed plan. The brigade suffered one hundred and thirty casualties and lost many arms and much ammunition. The tribesmen, elated by this early success, went on to higher things. The rallying point of tribal hostility was a man called the Faqir of Ipi, a man who still in 1955 occasionally hits the headlines, as he is currently the leader of the movement to form a separate Pathan country, to be called Pakhtunistan.

Waziristan contains two great and well-armed tribes, the Mahsuds in the south and the Wazirs in the north. The whole area, which is about the size of Wales, had been fairly quiet since the big campaigns of 1919–23, but many young men had grown up who had not fought in the old battles and were eager to take up their national pastime of war and emulate the feats of their elders.

At a time when several sections of the Wazirs were complaining of other grievances a Wazir abducted a young Hindu girl from Bannu, on the edge of tribal territory, and forcibly converted her to Islam. The political authorities had to exert all their power to get the girl back and return her to her parents. This recovery of the girl from the arms of Islam aroused the strongest feelings among the fanatically Moslem Wazirs, who began whispering, then shouting, the magic word *Jehad!* Affairs moved steadily towards an explosion though all those on the government side tried as hard as they could within the limits set by policy, justice, and the bands of history to avoid war. But war it had to be, war it was, and the guns—*ultima ratio regis*, a king's last argument—poured into Waziristan in increasing numbers.

The first arguments were the normal methods of diplomacy—persuasion, conferences, minor bribery, rewards, and threats. The civil government's second argument was the *khassadar* system. A *khassadar* was a local tribesman who wore an armband labelled 'K,' but was otherwise indistinguishable in his dirty grey or black cotton from any other tribesman. He received a small pay and sat on hill-tops near his village with the task of shooting at disaffected or excitable friends who tried to kill soldiers and rob convoys. The tribesmen were reluctant to shoot at *khassadars* for fear of becoming engaged in a blood feud. Unfortunately the *khassadars* were equally reluctant to fire on their naughty fellows for precisely the same reason. Furthermore, all *khassadars* seemed to be permanently in a temper about pay or promotion, and a high proportion of the stray shots fired at the army in Waziristan was fired by peevish *khassadars*. We thought they were an unmitigated nuisance, but they were probably a necessary step in the development of local responsibility for law and order, and we had to put up with them.

The third argument was the militia, or Scouts, or levies— they had many names. The whole length of tribal territory, from Gilgit in the north to Mekran in the south, was patrolled by the volunteers of these highly disciplined corps. They were armed, but their pay came from civil funds, not from the army budget, and they were under the control of the local political authorities, not of the military commander-in-chief. In ordinary times they could keep the peace because they were light-armed and fast and because they were themselves Pathans, usually from another part of the Frontier. Their officers were British officers of the Indian Army (or Indians holding King's Commissions) who were lent or seconded to them for three- or four-year tours of duty. The various corps had romantic titles, romantic crests, and romantic tasks: the Gilgit Scouts, with their ibex-horn badge and the duty of patrolling the Karakorams and the Pamirs on the verges of China and Russia; the Chitral Scouts, circling always within sight of Tirachmir's 25,230-foot cone on the edge of the Wakhan, the Afghan panhandle; the old Khyber Rifles; the Kurram Militia, safe in a nest of anxious Shia Moslems among hostile surrounding Sunni Moslems; in Waziristan, the two biggest and most warlike corps of all, the Tochi Scouts and the South Waziristan Scouts; farther south again, the Zhob Militia; and last, patrolling the deserts that run down to the Indian Ocean, the Mekran Levies.

North Waziristan, roughly the water-catchment area of the Tochi River, provided a clear-cut example of the system. The Political Agent, North Waziristan, had his headquarters near the middle of his area, at Miranshah, where there were a fort and an airfield. He lived inside the fort, where also were the headquarters of the Tochi Scouts. The Scouts also held a few small *Beau Geste* forts scattered around the country, each garrisoned by perhaps two hundred and fifty Pathan officers and scouts, and one British officer. The Scouts' only armament was rifles and a few immobile machine-guns for defence of the forts.

Once or twice a week each post commander would leave a part of his force inside the fort and take the rest out on patrol. If the patrol had no particular purpose it was called a *gasht*; but if it was specifically punitive in purpose—in which case the Political Agent would usually accompany it —it was called by the delightfully onomatopœic name of *barampta*. *Gasht* or *barampta*, the Scouts covered enormous distances at high speeds. Each man carried thirty or fifty rounds of ammunition, a water bottle, a bag of raisins, a few disks of unleavened bread, and a lump or two of coarse sugar. The whole party, numbering perhaps one hundred and eighty, shared the burden of the heavy baggage—four stretchers and a basket of carrier pigeons. The *gashts* swept along the ridges and past the loopholed towers, loping ceaselessly on at five miles an hour, and returned after a circuit of twenty-five or thirty-five miles to their fort. The *baramptas* pounced before dawn on some fortress village within fifteen miles of their post, arrested the startled headman, and whisked him lightfoot to headquarters, there to explain just what hand the young men of his village had taken in last week's mail robbery, and why he had not come on his own in answer to several polite summonses.

Scouts on the move were a magnificent sight. The British officers were indistinguishable from the men—all brown as berries, all wearing khaki turbans, grey shirts flapping loose outside khaki shorts, stockings, and nailed sandals. The Pathans—in uniform or out, fighting on one side or the other—are rangy, hawk-nosed, and seem to be made of whipcord and steel. British officers of Scouts had hard work at first to keep up, but in time they all developed astounding endurance and matched it with an equally astounding ability in drinking and revelling. Several famous mountaineers, including the great Peter Oliver of Everest, had served with Scouts at one time or another. The only people who could outmarch Scouts, and then only on roads, were Mountain Artillery moving with their guns and their huge Missouri mules. (On manœuvres in 1939 one mountain battery covered seventy-three miles in twenty-three hours at a steady pounding trot; the men hung on to the mule saddlery or to the stirrups of the few horses.)

When a situation passed beyond the power of the Scouts to control it the army emerged from its posts in tribal territory and lumbered into action under the direction of the Political Agents and their boss, the local Resident. Sometimes even this was not enough, and then the Resident whistled up still more soldiers from the nearby garrison towns in India proper—Peshawar, Rawalpindi, Kohat, and the rest—and a full-scale Frontier war was on.

In the last stage the Resident handed over his civil powers to the army commander. This amounted to martial law. All the politicals took one pace sideways and one pace backward and, instead of telling their military opposite numbers what to do, assumed a knowledgeable air and advised them of the probable political effects of the action they intended to take. But this happened only when violence was so widespread and so clearly out of hand that the problem was not to calm the tribes but to restore conditions in which the politicals could begin to think what was the best way of doing so.

An army exists to advance by force or the threat of force civil policies that cannot be advanced by civil methods. The Government of India's Frontier policy was always the same—the quickest possible re-establishment of tranquillity. The army's immediate task to achieve this invariable object depended on the circumstances of the particular trouble. It might be to break up the big armed bands, or *lashkars*, with which a tribe was defying the government. It might be to force the tribe to recall a *lashkar* of theirs that had gone over the border and was raising hell in Afghanistan. It might be to build a road, an airfield, or a new Scout fort in a hitherto inaccessible area, and so destroy the usefulness of that section as a refuge for outlaws and troublemakers. It might be to capture an important ringleader and arrest his personal followers—though the army was singularly unsuited to such a role.

In 1937 our tasks were to be all these, and a few more, and between 1936 and 1939 the theatre of operations was to spread over the whole of Waziristan, though keeping in the main to the north and centre of the area.

The core of our problem in the army was to force battle on an elusive and mobile enemy. The enemy, while he retained any common sense, tried to avoid battle and instead fight us with pinpricking hit-and-run tactics. We had light automatic guns, howitzers, armoured cars, tanks, and aircraft. The Pathan had none of these things, yet when he tried to even up the disparity, and cumbered himself with stolen automatics or home-made artillery, he suffered heavily, because they constituted impediments, things that were difficult to move but were worth defending. And when he stayed and defended something, whether a gun or a village, we trapped him and pulverized him. When he flitted and sniped, rushed and ran away, we felt as if we were using a crowbar to swat wasps.

Even so, the scales were not so heavily loaded as it appears, for we fought with one hand behind our backs. We were usually denied a soldier's greatest weapon— aggression, the first shot. Again the government remembered its object, the re-establishment of tranquillity, and reminded us that there would be no tranquillity among these proud and fierce people, however quickly we forced them into mere surrender, if we fought our campaign on unnecessarily ruthless lines. In 'normal' warfare armies bomb cities and destroy the enemy food supply without compunction, but we had to be careful not to harm women and children if we could help it, and we could not shoot on suspicion, only on certainty, and we could not damage fruit trees or destroy water channels.

In the warming-up days of a Frontier campaign the rules and regulations governing our actions were irksome in the extreme. The troubled area was delimited and called the 'proscribed area.' Outside the proscribed area we might not take any action at all until shot at. Inside it we might not fire at any band of less than ten men unless they were (a) armed and (b) off a path. These were dangerous conditions in a country where arms can be concealed close to flowing clothes, and where paths are tracks invisible from a hundred yards. One day in this war, after a minor shooting affray, my company caught a young Pathan wandering along a goat track that led away from the recent fight. He was admiring the scenery and looked very innocent, but he had a rifle tucked inside his robes. We inspected him closely and found four empty places in his otherwise full cartridge belt, and the chamber and barrel of his rifle were dirty. He had not had time to clean it. It was a moral and legal certainty that he had taken part in the fight and my subadar, a bloodthirsty little man named Naule, wanted to shoot him on the spot—or rather, after a small exercise in legalism. He urged me to let the young man go and, when he was a hundred yards off, fire a bullet past his ear. He would jump for cover off the goat track and would then be off a path, armed, and in a proscribed area—in brief, lawful game. I was sorry that I had to say no to this suggestion, and I still don't know why I did. I was here to kill Pathans and look after my company, and this would have been a step towards both aims. But I sent the prisoner back under guard to the adjutant at battalion head-quarters, who in turn would pass him on to the Political Agent for further questioning.

That evening I heard the sequel. The adjutant ordered the armourers to inspect his rifle again. Under pretence of examining it they took the weapon in a vice and secretly bent the barrel a fraction of an inch, not enough to notice but enough to cause an explosion and perhaps blow the young man's hand off next time he fired. They did this because they knew the young man would shortly be delivered to the politicals and, like all soldiers, they were not sure which side the politicals were on.

The Political Agents would have been useless if they had not identified themselves thoroughly with the tribesmen's thoughts and feelings, but we felt they often carried it too far. At the end of one day of fighting the Political Agent's young assistant came into our camp mess for a drink. M. L., in command, was in a good humour. After a confused beginning, the battalion had fought skilfully and well and several men were certain to win decorations.

The young political put down his glass. 'I thought our chaps fought very well today, sir,' he said.

M. L. beamed. 'So did I. Not at all bad.'

'And outnumbered about three to one, too, I should say.'

M. L. looked a little puzzled. 'Well, only in one or two places. On the whole I think the tribesmen were out-numbered.'

The political said, 'Oh, I'm sorry. It's the tribesmen I was talking about.'

Two of our men had been killed that day, and the Pathans had mutilated the corpse of one of them. My Signal Naik Karnabahadur had lost two fingers, and several more men had been wounded. Our mess that night was not the right place to say 'we' had done these things, though no one minded honest praise for 'them'—the enemy.

I said above that we were not to be ruthless. Ruthlessness, however, is relative, and the definition used on the Frontier was the Pathan definition. On the government side, armourers removed the propellant charges from cartridges, replaced the low-explosive cordite with a high explosive, and then dropped the doctored clips about. The tribesman, always short of ammunition, picked them up, with bad results for his hand or face when he fired his treasure trove. We took few prisoners at any time, and very few indeed if there was no Political Agent about. The government's rules for the conduct of the war mattered less to us than the lives and confidence of our men, and we interpreted them in that sense.

For their part the Pathans mined and booby-trapped the roads with dud shells and stolen grenades. They never took prisoners but mutilated and beheaded any wounded or dead who fell into their hands. They took advantage of the rules to disguise themselves as peaceful passers-by, or as women. They simulated death and pounced on anyone foolish enough to relax his guard.

I had heard many Frontier stories, of course. The most illuminating were about an officer of infantry, a man who had been a major in an earlier campaign. Whatever his over-all faults of character there is no doubt that he had a superb, almost supernatural tactical sense. Once he ran up and ordered a group of soldiers to open fire, without warning, on a funeral procession of Pathan men and women that was wending peacefully along the road a hundred yards from the battalion's camp. Doubtfully they fired. The sudden slaughter was seen by an appalled brigadier, who soon arrived to put everyone in sight under arrest. But the 'women' had other things besides rifles concealed under their *burqas*, and the coffin contained two alive and badly wanted outlaws, and also two thousand rounds of stolen ammunition. No one ever found out how the major knew these things. He just did, in the same way that, tactically, he could see through a hill and know what the other side was like.

Again, two unarmed men led a camel loaded with vegetables slowly past the camp along a track towards a low saddle, where the track disappeared over a ridge. The major was leaning on the wall, smoking; it was a hot, still afternoon. Suddenly he turned, ordered a somnolent pair of machine-gun sentries to aim their guns at the saddle and sit with their thumbs ready on the double buttons, with the safety bars up. The little procession disappeared over the ridge and the machine-gunners began to relax. A spatter of bullets smacked into the camp from the saddle, where two heads and two blazing rifles were just visible. Ten seconds and they would have gone, but the instant and accurate blast from the two guns killed them both.

These stratagems, wiles, and strange examples were not confined to the Pathan side. Indeed, there is little doubt that something of the harsh bitterness of the scenery entered into everyone who spent any time there. . . . It was during another campaign, at the end of a day of hill-side fighting on another part of the Frontier, that a British officer of Indian infantry was severely wounded. Twice his battalion tried to rescue him, but had to give up at last when they had lost more men than even the disgrace of leaving him out there was worth. Next day they found him. He had been castrated and flayed, probably while alive, and his skin lay pegged out on the rocks not far from camp. The senior officer present made every man of the battalion file past this Pathan practical joke and then told them that he did not want to see or hear of any prisoners. A few days later a jemadar arrived from the battalion's depot in the plains and, on his first night in one of the camp picquets, was severely attacked by a party of tribesmen. His picquet beat off the attack at some cost and in the morning found blood all round where the tribesmen had removed their dead; and also one wounded man, who had been overlooked. Both his thighs had been broken by grenade splinters. He was helpless and unarmed. The jemadar took him prisoner and sent him down on a stretcher to camp. The senior officer got into a cold fury, but there was a prisoner, whether he liked it or not. He had much the same idea of a good joke as the Pathans, so he ordered the prisoner to be pegged out, face up, in front of the quarter-guard. There was no shade and the sun temperature was probably about 130. The further order was that every man who passed should kick the prisoner in the testicles. When he died, towards evening, his body was carried out and left where the British officer's skin had been.

It is doubtful whether the Pathans who found the corpse gave the matter a second thought, for if they captured any soldiers other than Muslims, and especially if the soldiers were Sikhs or British, they would usually castrate and behead them. Both these operations were frequently done by the women. Sometimes they would torture prisoners with the death of a thousand cuts, pushing grass and thorns into each wound as it was made. Sometimes they would peg the prisoner out and with a stick force his jaws so wide open that he could not swallow, and then the women would urinate in his open mouth till he drowned. This kind of cruelty was not confined to war, but was as much a part of the Pathans' normal lives as were their sturdy independence, their physical hardihood, and their occasional flashes of quixotic generosity. If a man suspected his wife of the most minor infidelity he would cut her nose off. Murderous blood feuds were waged for generations against innocent children and tired old men. The Pathans punished an adulterer by forcing a thick and knobbly thorn twig down his penis. They rewarded infringements of lesser laws by tearing a man's tongue out by the roots.

This background to life lies near the surface anywhere in the Orient, and certainly in India. It is still customary among some tribes in Assam, one thousand six hundred miles east of the North-West Frontier, to punish an unfaithful woman by tying her to a post with her legs apart over a quick-growing kind of bamboo, and leaving her there until the bamboo grows up into her womb and stomach and she dies. Shortly after I returned from the Frontier war I saw some of the pamphlets put out by one of India's submerged terrorist societies. The coarsely printed sheets started with a lecherous description of the soft white thighs of white women, and followed with detailed instructions on how to use burning slivers of wood between them. The authors had a superstitious faith that the European's blue eyes gave him supernatural powers, and the reader then learned how to put these eyes out with a maximum of pain, how to perform drooling cruelties on English babies when the Day came.

The Day did come. The madmen did all these things, and worse, in the Calcutta bestiality of August 1946, and again when partition of India split the Punjab—but not to the British, to each other.

So these things were a part of the Frontier, like the heat and the holly oak and the winter sleet. The Pathans had fought like this against the Sikhs when they ruled, and against Alexander when he forced the passes of the Kabul River in 327 B.C.

All the same, it is wrong to think of the Frontier as an unrelieved study in barbarism. The tribesmen looked on war as an honourable, exciting, and manly exercise. When they had no quarrel with the British or the Afghans they arranged one among themselves. Many of them clearly thought the Government of India organized Frontier wars on the same basis. At least, there seems no other reasonable explanation of the fact that when a campaign was over scores of Pathans used to apply to the Political Agents for the Frontier Medal with the appropriate clasp. I think their request was reasonable. As they pointed out, they were British subjects and they had fought in the battles so thoughtfully organized by the King Emperor Across the Seas. Indeed, without their co-operation the war would have been a complete fiasco and no one would have got any medals.

Lawrence noted the tendency of the Arabs to homosexuality. It was the same among the Pathans. 'A woman for business, a boy for pleasure, a goat for choice' is an old Pathan proverb, and one of the most famous of Pathan songs, the '*Zakhmi Dil*' ('Wounded Heart') begins with the words, 'There's a boy across the river with a bottom like a peach, but, alas, I cannot swim.' I do not know why homosexuality should affect various peoples so differently, but there was something startlingly incongruous about the idea when associated with these fierce men, physically the hardest people on earth—they use sharp stones for toilet paper—and with the vast, grim jaggedness in which they live. A Pathan walks with the grace of a man-eating tiger, in long and unhurried strides, with a lift to them. He carries his head insolently up and his shoulders carelessly back, but without any stiffness as from drilling. Pathans often have pale-blue eyes, untamed and a little terrifying, and the young men's eyes are rimmed with kohl. Gritty dirt is ingrained in their skin, and the soles of their feet are like cracked leather. They often wear roses in their long hair, and I frequently wish I could see a Pathan entering a gay cocktail party given by Manhattan fairies.

Against this nomad and patriarchal civilization the use of air action presented certain problems. At first the Pathans thought aeroplanes were unsporting, and pilots had to be protected in a special way against the fearful savagery waiting for them on the ground if they were shot down or had to jump. So the Frontier invented the system, later much used in the Second World War, of giving air crews papers that offered a large reward to anyone who brought them to safety, and guaranteed safe conduct with no questions asked.

There was a lot of shouting at the League of Nations and in the world press about the iniquitous use of bombing planes on the Frontier. The criticisms were either disingenuous or caused by an amazing ignorance, and amounted to statements that the airmen rained bombs on defenceless women and children—their own enslaved but peaceable subjects, at that. The tribesmen were not peaceable citizens in quite the sense that the words convey in Oxford, Cleveland, or even Lahore. Nor were they unarmed, for reasons discussed in the first chapter of this book. By the 1930s they had become adept at shooting down aircraft and no longer thought the use of planes unfair. Sometimes they welcomed their arrival because there is a lot of loot in a crashed war-plane, and, by Pathan standards, the chance of getting it was well worth the price of a few bombs and machine-gun bullets. It is possible to argue that no government had any right to prevent the tribesmen from kidnapping Hindu girls or raiding into India and Afghanistan, or shooting up Scouts, Political Agents, and soldiers, since all this was to them life, liberty, etcetera. But, if it is granted that the tribesmen had to be held within certain bounds of behaviour, how to do it?

Someone had the idea of using aerial proscription—that is, instead of sending in troops to achieve whatever was the immediate object, the government used air forces alone. Aerial proscription was subject to many rules and much rigid form, and the case of the kidnapped Hindu girl will serve as a good example, though I am not sure that air power was actually used then.

Let us suppose that the Political Agent hears that the girl and her abductor are being sheltered by the Tori Khel section of the Wazirs. Conferences and threats produce no result. The Tori Khel headmen merely deny they have ever heard of the girl, and at length refuse to attend meetings. The Scouts try to investigate and get badly shot up by superior forces. The Political Agent, who has very accurate means of information, knows the girl is there, and suggests that aerial proscription be authorized against the Tori Khel, who live in an area roughly twenty-five miles long by fifteen miles wide.

The P.A. warns neighbouring tribes not to shelter out-laws or join in the fight. To add point to his warnings, Scouts *gasht* through these surrounding sections in in-creasing numbers and with increasing frequency. The request for aerial proscription works upward through the Resident in Waziristan to the Governor of the North-West Frontier Province, and perhaps to the Viceroy. If sanction is given, aircraft at once drop notices printed on white paper all over the Tori Khel's country, warning them that proscription will begin one week thence unless the girl and her kidnapper, and a fine of a hundred rifles, are produced before then. The notices also define a safe area, a small enclave big enough to hold all the people of the tribe with their flocks but not big enough to graze the flocks or to live in with comfort.

Twenty-four hours before proscription is due to begin, aircraft drop thousands more notices, these on red paper. They say that since the required action has not been taken proscription will begin as promised, failing a last-minute compliance. From H-hour aircraft continuously patrol the area and attack with machine-guns and twenty-pound bombs any man or animal seen outside the safe enclave. The airmen are not allowed to attack buildings unless they can clearly see that the buildings are being actively used, at that moment, for hostile purposes.

Ideally aerial proscription sent all the tribe into the safe enclave and forced its surrender, without bloodshed, by the complete disruption of its normal life. In practice the threat alone was often enough. If not, the tribal determination usually went still further. Aircraft attacked the sheep and goats surreptitiously sent out to graze, or fired on bands of people, sometimes containing women, as they scurried about in forbidden territory. The tribesmen tied out a few useless old women in the hope of collecting blood money for them, and sometimes the airmen could not see the ropes or the disguise of male clothing, and duly killed them. Build-ings were occasionally damaged by accident, though I suspect this was done by the tribesmen in the middle of the night with picks and crowbars since, from what I saw, the twenty-pound bombs could hardly knock the plaster off those strong towers.

Aerial proscription against a Western city would have been a terrible thing. Hospitals cannot be moved; the complex organization of life cannot be altered; and people would starve. Furniture cannot be moved, and children would die in the shelterless fields. The tribesmen had no hospitals, few schools, no power houses, and no furniture. They frequently slept in the open, and their wealth was in their flocks. Great discomfort there was; that was the idea. The tribesmen may even have been as uncomfortable as the Hindus they kidnapped, robbed, and forcibly circumcised. But there were not the calamitous hardships which the shouters, unaware of any pattern of life other than their own, seemed to be imagining. Aerial proscription was as sound, humane, and economical a weapon as any, granted a government's right to refuse to fight its strong-willed subjects on the level the latter choose—i.e. man to man.

The air forces also acted in direct support of the army under another and equally rigid set of rules. They could take offensive action only (a) in a proscribed area, and (b) against bodies of armed men, specifically pointed out to them by the soldiers on the ground as a legitimate target, or (c) against bodies of armed men indubitably hurrying to or away from a fight, whom the army could not see. Even with the speeds of the bumbling old Audaxes, Harts, and Wapitis this threw a considerable strain on the pilot, who flew miserably along at low level in fierce mountains, his thoughts muddied by a host of instruments, his responsibility to the soldiers, a lapful of instructions, and dire thoughts of castration.

For a year the regiment had been training for this particular game—'a Frontier show'—trying to weld the rules for successful warfare with the rules laid down by the government for Frontier campaigning. The two conflicted violently and we, girding for war, heard ourselves being advised by contrapuntal voices. The first voice, that of military experience in all the wars of recorded history, was hard, unequivocal, and merciless. The second voice, that of the civil government, was oleaginous, ambiguous—and merciless. The chant went like this, and I sang it gloomily to myself to a psalm tune:

Get there fustest with the mostest men.

Do not get there at all until we have referred the matter to the Governor-General-in-Council, which will take months.

Shoot first, shoot fastest, shoot last, and shoot to kill.

Do not shoot unless you have been shot at, and then try not to hurt anyone, there's a good chap!

Mystify, mislead, and surprise the enemy, then never leave him a moment to gather himself again, but fall on him like a thunderclap and pursue him to his utter destruction, regardless of fatigue, casualties, or cost.

Announce your intentions to the enemy, in order that he may have time to remove his women and children to a place of safety—and time to counter your plan. At all events, stop what you are doing as soon as he pretends to have had enough, so that he may gather again somewhere else.

Casualties, damages, losses, cost, are only some of the many factors to be considered when making a battle plan. If any factor is given undue weight, the plan is likely to fail.

Pardon us, but your plan does not interest us. We are happy to say that that is your business. However, casualties cause questions in the House, damage brings complaints in the Assembly, losses get into the newspapers, and cost we cannot stand, in view of the depleted state of the country's finances. Remember all that, and get the war over quickly. And if you should fail . . . Ah, but there—you won't fail, old chap, will you?

In the end a reasonable compromise was reached and the thing was done, in an attitude varying between the soldier's downright description of the Pathan as 'enemy,' and the political's opinion of him as a 'misguided fellow citizen.' It was seldom done as quickly or as thoroughly as the army would have liked, given the men, the money, and a free hand to make a job of it; nor as pleasantly and as cautiously as the politicals would have liked, given the time to alter circumstances. Sensible soldiers, in spite of furious grousing and bitter complaints—more bitter every time we saw our mutilated dead—realized well that we were not in fact fighting a true enemy. We accepted with good will most of the limitations placed on us, but always remembered our overriding duty to the men who trusted us.

This was the Frontier theatre: a tilted wilderness of rock and scrub; hard, barren, and jagged; split here and there by stony watercourses in which little water flowed; in summer, a blinding glare from the ochreous ridges; in winter, a cold breath shaking snow off the holly oak on the mountainsides; intense heat, intense cold, vivid storms, violent people—everything excessive.

Here were the actors: on one side the ponderous army, the handcuffed air force, the racing Scouts; on the other, anonymous thousands of tribesmen; in the middle, the Political Agent; on both sides, as the whim of the moment dictated, the *khassadars*.

After graduation from the Signal School, I joined the cast at Bannu on March 29th, 1937, and was given an obscure place near the middle of the fifth row of the soldiers' chorus —that is, as commander of the battalion's A Company, and also of its Signal Platoon. I did not have many lines to speak, and my view of the scene was often obstructed by the other actors, but the whole play was performed in such garish colours and with such violent movement that a strong impression of it will always remain with me.

CHAPTER EIGHTEEN

I WAS on my way up from the Signal School. The Heatstroke Express ambled along at its average ten miles per hour while four of us in one of the sizzling compartments discussed fights, murders, and massacres. Something special agitated the wires that day, but no one knew quite what. A battle had started at dawn at Dosalli, at Miranshah, at Chagmalai. We had lost twenty, one hundred, five hundred men. The tribesmen were using machineguns, artillery, gas. They had been very successful; they had been annihilated. It was my first experience of war's nervous, incessant gossip, of meeting the man with the working face, of listening over and over again to the same words—'Have you heard . . . ?'

I did not hear anything accurate until the train reached Bannu. The place was alive with the bustle of war. Droves of Frontier Constabulary filled the streets; the army depots were full of scurry as men loaded convoys to send up the road. No tribesmen were allowed inside the barbed wire that encircled the cantonment; at night guards were placed on the few wives and nurses who formed the colony of Englishwomen. I asked truck drivers coming down from the mountains what had happened. They shrugged their shoulders and said they had heard firing, but knew nothing more. The depots of some battalions had been ordered to send up all available reinforcements first thing next morning to replace casualties already suffered. The hospital had been alerted to receive a heavy load. Transport planes were on their way to fly the wounded out of Bannu back to the greater facilities of Rawalpindi.

Towards evening the official news was posted. There had been a big battle near Damdil, and it was still going on. We had had at least sixty casualties, and Peter Nicholson of the 6th Gurkhas was among the wounded. At sunset I went down to the hospital. A row of dusty ambulances stood in the drive, and hospital orderlies were carrying stretchers into the building. Men lay on them, wrapped in coarse, dark blankets soaked with blood. I sat in a bare waiting-room, strong with the smell of ether, until a sister came and told me I could see Peter for a few minutes. She said he had lost his leg from a dumdum bullet, and I went into the dark room.

He lay quiet, the bedclothes humped into a grotesque mound where a basket arch held them off his stump. His face, burned dark red by the sun, was tired in sleep. He must have dozed off the instant the sister left him. I stood and looked at him a moment. This was Peter Nicholson, twenty-two years of age, fair-haired, strong, brave, and shy, lately a junior under-officer of 'Lovely Five.' I don't remember thinking any thoughts about the injustice of the world, though it was unjust that the best should be taken first. We were soldiers, and infantrymen, and Gurkhas. I turned to go, and Peter opened his eyes. He could not have expected to see me, for the sister had not asked my name, but he smiled immediately, with his old fresh smile, and said, 'Hullo, Jack. Isn't this a bugger?'

I nodded—there was nothing to say to that—and smiled back at him. I asked him if there was anything I could do.

There wasn't. I wished him luck and went out. His eyes closed again as I left.

Next day I went up to the battalion in a supply truck. I sat tensed beside the driver all the way, a loaded revolver at my belt. Four riflemen stood in the back of the truck on top of the rice and meal, with their rifles ready. The convoy wound up the narrow road into tribal territory among the hot lower hills and gorges, but nothing happened. At Isha Corner the road forked, and the storm centre was fifteen miles up the left fork on the road to Razmak. We turned right and soon came out on the stony plain of Miranshah. The fort stood out in bright sunlight over fruit trees and an orchard. To the left were more trees and a village; to the right three aircraft shone silver in the middle of the plain. The windsock drooped on its pole, and white dust hung over the road.

I did not see the camp till we were right on it and stopped. I got out, stretched, and coughed, and walked away from the dust through a narrow gap in triple rows of barbed wire, then through another gap in a long, low wall. The brigade camp spread out in front of me on the plain, a field of brown tents and white tents. Soldiers sat on the ground and cleaned rifles; a marching fatigue party swung past to unload the rations. Irregularly along the walls sentries leaned silently beside the light automatics pointed out across the stony waste. A rifleman saluted with a grin and told me where the mess was.

Below the mess tent the ground had been dug out to a depth of four feet, and revetted with sandbags. Flies clustered thick round the entrance and buzzed in my ears as I walked down the steps. This arrival seemed familiar. The officers were having tea. James leaped to his feet and said, 'Good God, how did you get here? Where are your things? You're early.' He looked at his watch with a disbelieving expression, shook it, placed it to his ear, and began muttering under his breath, 'Christ—damned watch! Have some tea.'

James Sinclair Henry Fairweather, who had been

deputed to meet me, was off again. It was good to be back.

Two days later I went out on R.P.—road protection. This was the hardest task the Frontier offered, and we did it three times a week. The Damdil battle area was so close that we could not risk letting our convoys go along the roads under the doubtful protection of *khassadars* alone. The convoys ran every other day, and on those days the army protected the roads.

R.P. meant getting up very early and marching out along the road in battle formation. As we went we searched each place where an ambush might be lying in wait, and on every vantage point we dropped off one of the clusters of men called picquets. At the end of our sector we met troops from the next camp, who had been similarly working back towards us. Then signals were sent to higher authority that the road was clear, and at once the convoys set out from both terminals. R.P. was hard because every day we covered the same stretch of road, and every day it became more difficult to obey the cardinal Frontier principle of never doing the same thing in the same way twice running. We had to fight against fatigue and carelessness, because someone was watching. Someone was always watching—someone with an inborn tactical sense, someone who missed nothing.

The watcher might see that every day a picquet of half-platoon strength left the road at Milestone 27, and moved four hundred yards to the top of a hill. Every day two machine-guns waited among the boulders near the milestone, ready to support the moving men until they were in position. There was one little dip in the ground near the bottom of the hill, perhaps fifteen yards wide. The watcher never went near it, but his feel for country told him that the machine-gunners could not see into the dip.

The first four or five times the picquet went up, it split at that point. Half the men lay down on the near bank, ready to shoot, and half crossed the little dip. Then that half lay down on the far bank and covered the others while they crossed in their turn. Then they all went on together, again in view of the machine-guns. But the sixth time the soldiers got bored, because nothing ever happened and they couldn't see any Pathans, and they trailed across the dip in one tight bunch. They talked and laughed because it was such a small dip, they were out of sight of the machine-guns for only twenty seconds, and R.P. had become a peaceful monotony.

The next night twenty tribesmen arrived in the dip at 3 a.m., scattered among the rocks, and lay still. They were hard men and had full control of their bodies. No one of them coughed or cleared his throat, but all lay utterly still among the boulders. The nearest soldiers were four miles away but if an undisciplined young tribesman had moved a pebble the infinite, murderous patience of his elders would have withdrawn the whole ambush, just in case. They would have crept away, to return again three or five nights later—never the next night. Every man carried a straw so that, if he had to, he could urinate silently down the stem.

Around half-past six or seven in the morning the soldiers walked into the dip. One blinding volley—one rush, two seconds of stabbing and hacking, and it was done—six soldiers dead and six left for dead, twelve rifles and six hundred rounds of ammunition gone, one tribesman dead. Another typical Frontier incident.

It might have happened to us, to me, any and every day; but it didn't. The Second Fourth were not careless, not with M. L. watching through field glasses, and nothing ever exhausted the resources of his tactical ingenuity. We never did the same thing in quite the same way twice running. It might look the same to an untrained eye, but the watching tribesmen were not untrained. They noticed that the covering machine-guns were in a different position every day, so that no one could be sure on any particular day what they could or could not cover. Or the soldiers would not move on to the hill by going north-east from Milestone 27 but by going north-west from Milestone 27½. Or no one would go to the hill at all. But the next day the picquet would consist of a whole company—132 men. It is impossible to plan a safe and certain ambush in these conditions, and we were never ambushed. The tribesmen knew our hat badge and kept away. One tough old fellow told me as much the next month when we caught him on what appeared to be a genuinely innocent mission and gave him a cup of tea.

In the middle of the afternoon, when all the convoys were through, we got the signal to start pulling back to camp. This was the dangerous part of all Frontier operations. Except on the rare days of major battle the tribesmen knew that the army was strong enough to get forward and up the hill regardless of pinpricks. There would be no rifles or loot, because the troops would press on past their dead and wounded. At the end of the day's work, when we went back and down the hill, it was different.

From their eyries the tribesmen saw the last of the convoys go through, and knew we would soon be off. They gathered in creeping silence towards the ridges, and worked up snake-like into hidden positions near the picquets. If the picquet commander had been careless in his search of ground, or if he had sited his sentries badly, they would crawl up dangerously close. When the men of the picquet started down the hill the tribesmen would be on the crest before they had gone fifteen yards. The supporting guns open up but a man has been hit in the back and falls unseen in the scrub. A dozen tribesmen are inextricably mixed up with the picquet, shooting, yelling, hacking at the wounded man to get his rifle and ammunition. The whole picquet must turn back and recapture the hill-top—if it can—and then stay there for an hour, until the wounded have been carried down and away, safe from mutilation. Sometimes a reserve company has to be thrown into the battle before the hill-top can be retaken, and several more men are wounded and a couple killed in the process, and then the whole business of pulling down the picquet has to be gone through again, and it is dark before the brigade is once more on the move towards camp. The tribesmen follow hard on their heels in the night, and shots flash out, and more men are killed and wounded. . . . All this happened because one jemadar put one sentry one yard too far back, because one man walked when he should have run, because one machine-gunner pressed his thumbpieces one second later than he should have. War on the Frontier was not very dangerous, but it was exacting, personal, and merciless.

A resourceful commander like M. L. used many ruses to ensure that the Pathans treated his picquets with respect. Sometimes our men pretended to be careless. Sentries moved about instead of lying still; men walked idly and talked loudly. When the moment came to withdraw, the rear party got up and trotted back over the crest in no hurry. Fifteen seconds later, suddenly reverting to their true skill, they crept back up to the crest and met the confident, rushing tribesmen with a blast of fire at point-blank range. Sometimes a small picquet would seem too weak to hold the big feature to which it was allotted, but behind the hill was a concealed section of light tanks.

The country round the brigade's base camp at Miranshah was a stony plain split by low ridges and dry watercourses, all sparsely covered with sagebrush and scrub. This was perfect terrain for the most popular of all Pathan sports, night sniping. To protect us against this, the brigadier used the tanks. About 9 p.m. most nights, two or three of them would rumble out through the barbed wire, crouch hull down behind a ridge, and wait. In darkness or faint starlight it was difficult to tell exactly where they were, though they could be heard for miles. After twenty minutes they would suddenly switch on their searchlights, examine the ground all round them, switch off again, and rumble on through the darkness to another place. It worked; we were sniped only once. It was comforting after the long, menacing silences to see the flashes of light and hear the thunder of engines and the muted clank of treads. These tanks were old-fashioned things, useless for 'real' war, but we liked them. The Gurkhas made friends with the British tank crews and arranged tugs-of-war, a complete company of ours against one tank of theirs.

Every proper infantryman thinks that in the army only the infantry matters, but after he has been in a couple of engagements he will admit that other arms and services do exist, even that they can be quite important. Personally I found all of them interesting, and the Indian mountain batteries of the Royal Artillery positively frightening.

Standing beside the road among a crowd of men, I heard a faint and rapid sound, a rhythmic, pounding jingle. It came nearer and grew louder. A low cloud of dust rose over the hills. Two officers and two Sikh gunners, all mounted, big survey boards flapping on the gunners' backs, cantered past me. The leading officer yelled, 'Clear the way—*guns!*'

The battery pounded round the corner, two abreast, filling the whole road, the huge mules walking out at five miles an hour, the breeches, barrels, recoil mechanisms, wheels, and gun-shields swaying on their backs. Turbans, eyes, and white teeth bobbed up and down amid the flood of tossing steel. No one looked right or left or up or down, only straight ahead. If a man had fallen in the way the battery would have pounded straight over him and never noticed. A hundred yards past us they turned right and poured over the ditch beside the road and up a low rise, without check or slowing. Each gun team of eight mules formed a small circle, the pivot mule facing in, the rest facing out. Before they had stopped, the gunners hurled themselves at the loads. *Clang*, four sets of wheels and axles bounced on the ground. *Crash*, the pivots . . . cradle and slipper . . . trail . . . breech and chase . . . sights, traversing gear, gun-shield . . . A stream of orders poured from the subaltern at the flank—ammunition, angle of sight, range . . . At each gun a brown arm shot out parallel with the ground. Something like fifty seconds from the time they had reached the hill-top the guns stood ready to fire. The gunners relaxed. I shuddered and remembered.

I met engineers, very dark men of the Madras Sappers

214

and Miners, who wore khaki stovepipe hats, actually vestigial remnants of the old shako. Their British officers were preoccupied characters who mostly carried a slide rule in one trouser pocket and a slab of guncotton and a few detonators in the other. The Madrassis were the only people who could do rough work, like roadmaking or digging, at anything like the speed of the Gurkhas, and there were other times when we had to give way to their technical skill and stand admiring while they built a bridge or defused a booby-trap.

I met soldiers that I had never heard of or even imagined to exist—veterinary sections, supply-issue sections, men who knew what to do about Minnie's girth gall or could tell us what had happened to the canned milk ration. I met doctors—Irish or Scottish to an M.D.—who acted as if they were seldom completely sober but always seemed to be in tearing spirits, very comforting and fearless. I met a field post office under an Indian *babu* from the far south, who was a man of peace. (There was a lot of sniping one night, later on, and the staff captain told the *babu* this would entitle him to the Frontier Medal. *Babu-ji* replied, 'Oh, sir, only let humble body be spared. Let bloody medal go hang!')

My own first summons to action came at eleven o'clock at night. The brigadier ordered our battalion to move at once to cut off a large party of Pathans said to be escaping from the Damdil battle area. At midnight, after a cup of tea, I went out to find my company. The moon was well past full and the night cold. The company stood bunched and shivering, equipment creaking, bayonets gleaming in the faint green light. The Gurkha officers were explaining the orders to the N.C.O.s. B Company edged slowly past us in the dark. At the gate the sentries threw back the rolls of barbed wire, and I led A Company out behind B on to the metalled road. Our heavy, nailed sandals were in the haversacks slung high on our shoulders, but even the shuffle of our sneakers sounded very loud.

Once we were on the road the pace quickened, and we swung past the dark bulk of Miranshah Fort at four miles an hour. I saw no light and heard no sound from there, though inside the Scouts were getting ready to send a strong *barampta* across the river.

The miles passed and though the tension in the column never completely disappeared it eased appreciably after we had moved for an hour and had our first rest, sitting down in the drainage ditch beside the road and holding up our feet to let the blood flow away from the congested soles.

The advanced guard was strung out in double file a hundred yards ahead, rifles at the ready. The men moved fast and yet found time to search the little gullies beside the road and the narrow culverts that dived under it. Danger at night on the Frontier was great, but against an enemy who had no tripod-mounted weapons it was from close quarters. The risk we faced was from the silent group that might be right in the ditch, two yards away and unsuspected in the dirty light until they acted.

There was nothing. Twenty minutes before first light we were strung along the north bank of the Tochi River, crouched under a steep black bulk of hill. M. L. sent my company and the mountain battery up the hill and spread the others out to left and right on smaller features, or tucked them away in a ravine as reserve.

We started quickly on the climb of about six hundred feet as the light began to etch in the jagged skyline across the Tochi behind us. There was no path, and we worked our way up among boulders and scrub. I spread my leading platoon across the hill-side ahead, and kept two more close at my side. Two hundred yards down the hill behind me stones clattered and rolled as the artillery mules heaved their own bulk and their three-hundred-and-fifty-pound loads up the cliff. Kipling again—the words ran in my brain, though there was no snow:

> The eagles is screamin' around us, the river's a-moaning
> below,
> We're clear o' the pine an' the oak-scrub, we're out on the
> rocks an' the snow,

216

An' the wind is as thin as a whip-lash what carries away
    to the plains
The rattle an' stamp of the lead mules, the jinglety-jink o'
    the chains—'Tss! 'Tss!

We did not know whether there would be anyone waiting
for us on top. It was not likely, but it was possible, and we
never took avoidable risks. The leading platoon went
through the full battle drill of attack. In the hardening
steel light the men near the centre of it crouched for half a
minute below the last outcrop line of rock beneath the
crest, while the outer horns of the platoon curved on and
round the summit. There was a pause while all gathered
themselves together and carried out the professional check
—rifle, bayonet, ammunition pouches. On the extreme
right the light-automatic gunner and his No. 2 ran forward and dropped down, ready to fire across the front. A
hand waved, a voice whispered, 'Charge!' Each man drove
strongly from bunched thighs, and all across the slope the
bayonets flickered up and over the crest.

Silence.

Full dawn had hardly reached the valley when my glasses
picked up movement across the Tochi. For a moment I
found it difficult to focus in my sudden excitement. This
was the first enemy I had ever seen. Then I got them.
A group of nearly thirty men, less than a mile away,
were moving down to the river across the stony ridges on
the far bank. They came on unconcernedly, confident of
their own safety, confident that no one would be in this
place. They were already just within range of my light
automatics.

It is a strange feeling to open fire for the first time on a
living human being with intent to kill him. No one had
tried to kill me yet, and I had not seen anyone in the
moment of being killed or torn by bullets. The men down
there were armed tribesmen, and they had come from the
Damdil battle. Perhaps one of them had fired the dumdum
that blew off Peter Nicholson's leg. I had positive orders to

fire on such people. Yet they were human and unsuspecting. It is an emptiness in the stomach to kill. . . .

Perhaps they were Scouts coming back from a *barampta* no one had told us about! Such things happened. My hands were cold and my mouth dry. I looked again, hoping. They were not Scouts.

It seemed I had wasted half a day thinking, hesitating. In other circumstances that might have been true, and a fleeting opportunity would long since have gone. But this time, militarily, I should have waited even longer before I screwed up my will, broke loose from indecision, and said, 'Fire!' But perhaps if I had waited any longer I would never have given that order.

My company's light automatics stammered furiously, but it was really too soon. The tribesmen were nearly eight hundred yards away on the edge of the low cliffs across the Tochi. We did not know the exact range, and light automatics are not suitable for such a target. Over there the sudden bullets smacked around them. In a flash the group broke up; men darted to left and right, disappeared among the rocks; they were gone. Below on the road our machine-gunners picked up the target, and the steady, long-drawn hammering of the Vickers floated up the hill to make a tenor under the irregular staccato of my light automatics. A few riflemen who thought they saw someone and fancied their skill as marksmen joined in with single ictus taps. The heavy drumbeat of the screw guns thundered among the mountains.

Nothing else happened; no one else appeared; no one fired a shot in our direction. The ambush had been complete and, had I not sprung it too soon, might have been more successful. But then again a mule might have brayed and warned off the enemy before we had fired a shot. M. L. mildly reprimanded me for over-impatience—a form of correction that was at this time almost my staple food—and congratulated me on being so quick into position and so quick to spot the enemy at all.

We wound back to Miranshah late that afternoon more

cautiously than we had come out—but still nothing happened. The Political Agent's informers passed the word that between us we had killed eight of a party of twenty-seven tribesmen that morning. I did not believe it. Informers have to live, but I doubt if any Pathan got more than a severe fright—unless from the wonderful shooting of the mountain guns—in that unsung, exciting, and very minor engagement near Boya, where Lieutenant J. Masters first tried to kill someone.

I was getting the feel of the Frontier now. R.P., rifle inspections, R.P., laughter and singing in the mess, R.P., a hurried night march—long slow days, sudden, quick minutes. Near Boya I had tried for the first time to kill someone and had, in my opinion, failed. It was time for someone to try to kill me.

CHAPTER NINETEEN

FIFTY miles to the south the Mahsuds ambushed a truck convoy in a savage gorge called the Shahur Tangi. The escort of armoured cars got sandwiched on the narrow road so that they could use neither their weapons nor their mobility. Seventy-two officers and soldiers were killed or wounded. The government decided that the time had come to take the offensive. Our brigade, hovering in reserve off the north of the storm centre, was ordered into battle.

We marched on May 5th, 1937, and spent that night at Talin-Tochi. The camp site was on a bare ridge above the Tochi River, and no matter how carefully a commander sited his camp picquets it was impossible to prevent the enemy from sniping on to the face of the slope at night. The crawling-sweet smell of death pervaded the place when we arrived, and as I marched in I passed three mules rotting in open graves at the foot of the camp. It was late and we had not sufficient time to dig properly, but there were some shallow holes there already, and we used them.

At two minutes after eleven something exploded in the air over my head with a sharp *whip-crack* slap. A second later a dull thump sounded from the dark ridge to the west. Both sounds were rapidly repeated several times. At last I was hearing the real *crack-thump* I had imitated so often. At last I was under fire.

I was frightened. A dispassionate recognition of the

enormous odds against being hit, an ability to measure the distance of passing bullets, a degree of stoicism—all these came later with experience and after many bullets had passed without hitting me or anyone near me. The first time, in a six-inch pit on a stony hill-side, alone with the murderous whip in the darkness, afraid to speak for fear of being thought to be afraid, my only companion the cruel necessity of lying still and doing nothing, I was frightened. I stared up at the stars and waited, hardly able to control my trembling. I wondered whether it would be my neck, stomach, legs, or eyes—what it would feel like.

Unhurriedly the sniper searched the camp, firing twenty or thirty rounds. I heard men moving about near me and called to them to be still. A mule snickered; water splashed on the dim ashes of a cooking fire. Then away to my left a voice muttered a Scottish curse, and I heard a long whistling sound, continued for several seconds.

M. L.'s voice called, 'Hamish, are you hit?'

Major Hamish Mackay replied cautiously, 'No, sir. I just let the air out of my Lilo.'

The tension on the hill-side relaxed almost audibly, and all around there was subdued laughter. I was released from fear by the picture of our quiet, far-looking Scots major sinking lower into the friendly earth while the air hissed loudly from the vent of his inflatable mattress.

The sniper killed nine mules as they stood in their tethered lines just below us on the slope.

Next day we moved on up to the road to Damdil, and the day after, to Dosalli. All along I saw traces of battle. Dead mules lay in the ditch, their legs stuck out straight as children's toys. Bloodstains splashed the white stones; twigs and whole bushes lay broken in the road; and shell blasts pockmarked the ridges. On the right of the road just beyond Damdil camp stood a low knoll crowned with a *sangar*. We stopped and examined it with respect, for here on the night of March 20th–21st there had been a fight, small in scale but heroically great in courage. Here eight Gurkhas of the 2nd Battalion, 5th Royal Gurkha Rifles

(Frontier Force), had been left without support to fight all night against fifty crazed Wazirs. By dawn two of the eight were dead, and each of the other six had been wounded many times. They had fought with rifles, bayonets, *kukris*, stones, boots, and fists, and they had held their picquet until, at dawn, relief came.

We went straight into the fighting around Dosalli. Two brigades began to force their way slowly up the Sre Mela towards the centre of the enemy's resistance, the Sham Plains. I thought back to the sleet and snow of my first visit here, that February night with the Duke of Cornwall's Light Infantry. Now it was hot and the Sre Mela was only a trickle of cool water among the stones. At the head of the short stream the brigades faced giant precipices and steep ridges that swept up from the valley, and the tribesmen held their crest line in strength. The major-general decided to leave one brigade facing the ridges, to contain the enemy, and to outflank the position by moving the other brigade— ours—round behind the enemy's right. The operation was to be carried out at night over the Iblanke, a long, steep, and unreconnoitred mountain.

It sounded like a hazardous proposition. It was.

We went back to Dosalli and prepared in secret for the battle.

On May 11th, at 9 p.m., in full darkness, we moved off. Eight platoons of Tochi Scouts led the advance, wearing grass-soled sandals. At first the pace was painfully slow. I covered six hundred yards in the first two hours, while the Scouts, far ahead, picked their way across the Khaisora River and faced the black slopes leading up to the Iblanke, and the rest of the brigade struggled after them. Enough water flowed in the stream to wet me to the knees, so I started the night's work with wet feet—not cold, though. I was enjoying this, so far. All along it was start, stop, sit down, get up, move on a yard, stop, sit down again. The river valley was warm, and the air felt stuffy.

At last they got going in front. Soon we were all launched on the ridge. Movement became a steady grind of climbing, one foot after the other. I could see only a few yards off, a dim whiteness in front where the officer at the tail of the company ahead wore a white band on his hat. Fixed bayonets flashed faintly against the mountain-side, and I climbed in the strong mixed smell of sweat and the cardamom seeds the Gurkhas chewed.

We tried to be quiet, but our passage boomed indescribably loudly in the silence of the hills. Boots clashed on the stones; the harness of the mules creaked; their hooves struck sparks from the flints. There was no path on the knife-edged spine of the ridge, and men and animals floundered on up, panting, among the bushes and concealed rock outcrops. Sudden storms of louder noise burst over us as mules loaded with shovels or radio sets lost their balance and crashed down two hundred feet of mountain among us. Twenty times I dived for shelter and listened, appalled, pressed into a thick bush, while the heavy animals thundered down in the darkness, their loads rolling beside them. I thought any tribesman within five miles must have heard each one. As the night wore on and men and animals grew tired the falls became more frequent, more cataclysmic.

The ragged, disconnected column forced painfully on for eight hours. There were soldiers everywhere—on the ridge spine, lost along the sides, down in the dark gullies looking for fallen mules. I heard swearing in ten languages and saw soldiers cut mules' throats and manhandle the loads on up the mountain.

In the wind that blew before dawn there was a long check. No one moved in front. The clattering and banging behind, down the hill, came up and closer. I was in the middle of a lot of men, all waiting. Light began to silhouette the far hills, then to show grey on us. We were well up the ridge, but near at hand on both sides other ridges converged on ours, and at this point they were somewhat higher than ours. What if the enemy were on them? As far as the eye could see in both directions our ridge, the Iblanke, was dotted with men and animals. The trees and bushes had thinned out, and there was no cover. I took my binoculars from the case, hung them round my neck, and lay down. Shivering from exhaustion and nervous strain, I waited. There was nothing else to do.

Ahead shooting began, very loud and close-seeming in the dawn. The bullets came on over our heads—*cracrack*, *pause*, *thuthump*. Enemy's range, about six hundred yards. This was it. Here we were, strung along a knife crest with no power of manœuvre, about to be attacked on all sides. I remembered what had happened to the Guides when they were caught just like this, three years before, on another part of the Frontier. I braced myself for a long waterless day of slaughter.

A runner came down with a message. The Scouts had made contact and were in action. The tribesmen and the Scouts knew each other well—many by name. The tribesmen knew that the Scouts' only weapons were rifles. They were confident in their own strength and the strength of their position at the top of the Iblanke. They were confident that no one but the Scouts could have climbed that ridge at night under arms. They started shouting insults, and for a few minutes barrages of Pushtu invective and innuendo flew back and forth between the uniformed Pathans of the Scouts and their unreconstructed cousins on the crest. Both sides interspersed the shouts with shots, but the Scouts deliberately weakened their fire, and the tribesmen's taunts grew more pointed.

The two leading companies of the leading battalion, 2nd Royal Battalion, 11th Sikh Regiment (The Ludhiana Sikhs) deployed behind a roll in the crest. Back down the ridge the mountain guns clanged off the mules on to the ground. Machine-gunners dragged themselves forward on their sides, the heavy guns or tripods rested on their lower legs, until they were in position behind rocks and ledges.

In the full dawn shells rumbled through the air, machine-gun bullets rippled along the ridge crest, and Sikhs and Scouts went into the attack together. The tribesmen stayed only a moment in the face of this powerful, determined, and totally unexpected assault. Then we had taken the crest of the Iblanke. Ahead lay the Sham Plains. We were behind the enemy.

This day was May 12th, 1937. Back in England the Archbishop of Canterbury was crowning George VI King of England and Emperor of India, and we named our new camp Coronation Camp. Back in England they were firing rockets and roman candles and dancing in the streets. Out in Waziristan the event had also been celebrated with firing and fireworks; and we too rejoiced, because our night attack on the Iblanke had been the boldest stroke in the history of the Frontier, and it was a proud thing to share even a little in the achievement of the general who had the wit to think of it and the will to do it.

The general now decided to force his way farther into this part of the country and catch the Faqir of Ipi. Intelligence reported that the Faqir lived in a cave twelve miles east, at a place with the delightful name of Arsalkote. Trouble began at once, and we were soon in action on both sides of the valley—there was no road. It was a day of confused fighting, heroism, and humour. On the left Willie Weallens, our second-in-command, and Lance-Naik Dhansing of the buglers rescued a wounded rifleman from certain mutilation. Willie had a pistol and Dhansing nothing but a *kukri* —but then, the man who had singlehandedly attacked three hundred camels needed no other weapon, and Willie was an Edwardian to whom personal danger weighed nothing when put in the scale against good manners. They ran out under point-blank fire from forty Pathans and carried Kiruram to safety.

Also on the left Rifleman Tilbahadur was hit in the stomach and head and killed almost instantly. The tribesmen rushed his corpse. As it lay under our fire, they saved time by thrusting a knife into his stomach, ripped upward through his belt, and pulled off his equipment and ammunition pouches in one stroke. A counter-attack recovered the body, a torn and bloody sack that looked nothing like a man, shrunken, its hands rusty from dried blood. The

225

doctor put him into a *khajawa* with another dead man on the other side of the camel, and covered him with a blanket. These *khajawas* were camel stretchers, with headrests and raised sides. The dead or wounded swayed and rocked along in them to the camel's bouncing stride. This camel went back down the line past us, and Tilbahadur's hand fell out and trailed along over the side, swinging limp out of the stretcher. A rifleman standing near me lifted the blanket to see who it was, then shook the corpse warmly by its swaying hand as it passed on, laughing with a genuine and carefree laugh in which all his watching comrades joined. They all had been Tilbahadur's comrades too.

Over on the right B Company was startled by a hot volley from A Company while already under vicious fire from the enemy. B Company crouched lower, and the flags passed anxious questions and bad language—but it was only sport. An *oorial*, a species of mountain sheep, had become bewildered by the firing and trotted into the battle. Both companies forgot about the enemy, also about each other, and switched all available rifles and light automatics on to the fleeing animal. Subadar Dallu got it, when it was galloping all out, with a fine shot at a hundred yards.

This day was recorded the immortal remark made to James by a British soldier listless from too many years of manœuvres, too much Aldershot, too much make-believe with blank ammunition on the plains of India and in the more peaceful outposts of Empire. As the first bullets smacked into the rocks over his head he said in outraged astonishment, 'Look 'ere, sir! Them buggers is using ball!'

This day also I saw how it is possible to converse by thought transference, without interpreters, providing there is good will. M. L.'s orderly, Janaksing, squatted under a spiny thorn bush with the batman of the C.O. of the Argyll and Sutherland Highlanders. They sat there for an hour and talked. At first the Jock had of course demanded to see Janaksing's *kukri*. I saw it being brandished about, and Janaksing shaking his head vigorously. He was denying that he threw it like a boomerang. Then they just talked. I wondered what medium they were using for communication, since Rifleman Janaksing Thapa spoke no English and I doubted that Private Donald Campbell had much Gurkhali. I crept closer and stretched my ears. Each soldier was speaking his own language and using few gestures—it was too hot on the rocks for violent arm-waving. I could understand both sides of the conversation, the Gurkhali better than the 'English,' and it made sense. Questions were answered, points taken, opinions exchanged, heads nodded, and lips sagely pursed. When M. L. moved on, the two shook hands, and the Jock said 'Abyssinia, Johnny!' He had poor Janaksing there.

That night we established camp at Ghariom, half-way to the Faqir's cave, and waited for more troops to arrive. The wait was marked by a storm of appalling violence. In the afternoon the sky began to darken over, and dust devils hurried down the valley. A drizzle of rain set in, and after a few minutes changed to light hail. The hail quickly strengthened and was soon coming down like a barrage from a million machine-guns. I measured a hailstone 1·6 inches in diameter. The hail cracked tentpoles, tore canvas, and flattened every tent. It stunned five sepoys caught in the open, though they were wearing turbans, and maddened all our thousand animals so that they jerked up heel ropes and halters and crashed in snorting, frantic panic through the shattered camp, leaped the low walls, burst in tethered droves through the gates and scattered over the countryside. The hail changed to sleet, back to rain, and for an hour fell like Niagara. It became dark. Thunder volleyed across the low sky, and below our feet, under the earth, the mountains shook and grumbled. Lightning flashes sent searing shafts of ruin through the black rain. In one towering burst I saw four linked horses galloping abreast over fallen tents and broken boxes, their eyes rolling white, teeth bared, coats shining wet, a soldier in front of them. The riderless four of the Apocalypse vanished through the sudden wall of darkness.

The mess tent, dug down four feet against sniping, was awash to ground level with a dreadful soup of hailstones and grey mud, in which floated biscuits, chairs, newspapers, tablecloths, and hats. The tribesmen could have walked in anywhere while we grouted around in the soup for our rifles and machine-guns and, when we had found them, cleaned the mud from the barrels and locks and then set to work dredging up grenades and explosives of all kinds.

The rain stopped; the evening sun gleamed weakly for a moment before disappearing behind the ghostly hills. Shapeless grey lumps that had been tents covered half a square mile of the plain. Under the wall and in the ditches lay secret pits where men could—and did—disappear up to their necks. Around was a desolation of ropes, saddlery, arms, cooking-pots, bags of rice—all lying under a carpet of hailstones inches deep. We dazed soldiers stumbled about among the ruin, finding our belongings, looking like men just rescued from a fallen house. The stream outside the camp, which had been a clear trickle six inches deep and a few feet wide when we arrived, now thundered down in a heaving grey avalanche of porridge, a hundred yards across. It raced so quickly round the corner opposite the camp that the outer curve was twelve feet up the cliff, the inner only a few inches above the normal level. Carts and dead horses tossed in it like twigs until they disappeared. Twenty-ton boulders rolled and ground down, offering no more resistance than a rubber ball to the power of the flood.

I lifted up my eyes to the hills. For 360 degrees around the camp every summit was crowned with groups of mules and horses. They stood in statuesque attitudes and brayed and neighed to the evening sky. Just across the river our pet machine-gun mule, Minnie, trotted up and down, kicking out her heels. She had been born pale grey. M. L. had decided she was too conspicuous for battle, and we had painted her all over with iodine. She was now a brilliant orange, and in her disgust and shame brayed louder than any of the animals.

After a day of salvage and cleaning, we moved out at 1 a.m. towards Arsalkote, in the authentic atmosphere of night battle—heavy breathing, mysterious corners, a cold breath in the air, shuffling boots, and long bayonets sharp-pointed against the stars. Fighting began after the sun rose, and we found that the enemy's substitutes were in the field. The Wazirs had sent word over the border to the Afghans that the looting was good in this war, and hundreds of Afghans had swarmed across to join their cousins in the fight. The Wazirs had fought the Indian Army for a century and now knew as much about tanks, machine guns, and aircraft as we did. The Afghans were used to fighting only the ill-equipped and infrequently paid Afghan regulars. They now allowed themselves, blown up with an unfounded self-confidence, to be put in the forefront of the battle, where they suffered heavily.

Around noon our battalion headquarters came under fire from across the Shaktu. I saw a group of eight men appear in full view and run into an old *sangar* on the far side of the river. This was most unlike the Wazirs—but of course they were not Wazirs, they were Afghans. The machine-gunners looked interested but unbelieving. The rangetaker focused his two images and called 'Nine-fifty,' so two guns ranged at nine hundred yards, and two at a thousand yards.

The Number Ones bent down and peered through the sights, twisted the elevating wheels, and tapped lightly on the grips to traverse. Then they sat up straight to look at the target and observe the strike of the bullets. Each Number Two's left hand went out horizontally in the signal 'Ready!' The Afghans in the *sangar* began to fire at us. The machine-gun havildar dropped his hand; each Number Two tapped his Number One on the shoulder; the Number Ones pressed their thumbs on the triggers; the four guns rocked on their tripods; the quadruple stream of lead smashed into the *sangar*. The loose stones shattered, and the ramshackle old thing began to disintegrate. Inside, it must have been a hell of whining ricochets, smashing lead, and flying chips of stone. After each gun had fired a full belt of 250 rounds and was well into its second belt, the Afghans realized that they had trapped themselves, and decided to run. They ran out straight into the tide of bullets. In an instant all eight lay crumpled around the wrecked *sangar*. The bullets ripped on into them for a few seconds and then stopped.

The Faqir and his personal followers had left Arsalkote when we got there, but there were his caves, their mouths black with the smoke of his old cooking fires. Smoke still trickled out of one, and we knew that he could not have been gone long. A platoon of ours went up as close escort to the sappers who had been ordered to blow in the cave. The sappers stood well outside, rolled a grenade into the entrance, and waited for it to burst. Then they went in. There was no one there—only a few old rags, a blanket, and a smouldering pile of ashes.

The young sapper subaltern, who had gone in first with two of his men, soon bounded back again into the sunlight, cursing and slapping. From the waist down all three men were literally and absolutely black with fleas. The three victims went off for a kerosene bath, and other sappers burned a can of petrol inside the cave. In the evening they blew it up with three unexploded R.A.F. bombs they found near the entrance. A splinter of bomb hit one of our cooks in the back as he bent over his fire four hundred yards away, and all but killed him. It was the only casualty we had that day, but the sappers said cheerily, 'Accidents will happen!'

That night our mess tent was in an orchard near the lower wall of the camp. Outside, the stony bed of the Shaktu stretched away to low cliffs on the far bank. During the soup I heard a loud noise, a rattling and banging, as of a minor train accident. The leaves of the walnut tree over the tent whispered, and twigs fell down on the canvas. I peered out but could make nothing of it. Ten minutes later the noise was repeated.

M. L. began to laugh and said, 'Good God, a *jezail*!

Loaded with marbles and tintacks and nails and old boots! It's probably a hundred years old and has half a pound of gunpowder in the charge.' We agreed that a young boy, not yet allowed a rifle, had stolen his grandpa's *jezail* and come out to do his bit. (A *jezail* is an old-fashioned brass-bound musket.)

Someone went out and found that the sentry at the corner of the wall had seen the flash of the second shot. He said it was an unearthly glow, like a roman candle, lighting up hill and vale, about four hundred yards off in the bed of the Shaktu. The officer told him to lay his machine-gun on the site of the flash, and returned to the mess. A little later the *jezail* boomed again, and before the whirring collection of ironmongery had reached us the machine-gun was spitting back. The Pathan boy crept home with honour satisfied and no harm done to anybody—or so we thought.

About that time two rifle shots came into the camp. No one seemed to have been hit. A little later a new man went to relieve the sentry who had fired at the boy with the *jezail*. He found him hunched over his gun with a bullet through his neck. As he had aimed at the glare of the old musket, so the inevitable watcher had aimed at the flickering nozzle of his gun, and waited, and then put a bullet cleanly through the little hole in the wall where the muzzle poked through. The Frontier never relaxed.

Next day the brigade pulled back to Ghariom to prepare for fresh offensives elsewhere. The sun burned the rocks; the Afghans had gone home, grumbling; and the Wazirs had returned. Also, we were going back, not forward. All day the firing grew more vividly angry. I sat about in the thin shade of the holly-oak and waited. Prendergast, huge and fat and tough as old boots, dropped down the mountain among a rangy crowd of Scouts, drank five cans of our beer, and sprinted off again. Minden Scott, whose father had been in the regiment, was carried past on a stretcher, shot in the spine and dying. One of our picquets—two platoons, under James Fairweather—went up to a particularly dangerous ridge.

The actual withdrawal of picquets was made on the orders of the commander of the rearguard. Today he was Colonel Bruce of the 5th Gurkhas, a lean and imposing man with a lined face and shock of dead-white hair. M. L. went back to meet him and make special arrangements for James's picquet.

All our twelve machine-guns sighted on James's ridge. Two batteries of mountain artillery started ranging into the draw beyond and on the spur to the left. I 'talked' up to James by flag and told him what had been fixed. I made certain that I had communication to him by four different means—lamp, helio, flag, and telephone. I told him that when I sent up the word to go he'd better go like the wind, or M. L. would personally eat those parts of him the Wazirs had no use for.

M. L. ordered that when the orange flag of James's last man started to move from the crest all the guns and machine-guns should open up on that very crest. Two planes came over and searched the broken ground beyond the picquet. They told us they saw many of the enemy moving up, running among the bushes, and for half an hour they fired their guns and dropped their bombs. The already great tension increased when one of them dropped a bomb close in on the other flank, where there was no enemy, as far as we knew. This was a fine example of the fog of war, for we did not hear until much later that the bombing was an accident, and meantime Colonel Bruce, thinking that the pilot had been attacking a new group of Wazirs, made dispositions to guard against the imagined threat.

The real enemy kept closing in. Soon about two hundred tribesmen were hidden under the ridge held by James and his fifty men. Colonel Bruce came and ordered James's picquet to start thinning out. James himself moved halfway down the hill with one of his platoons. Theoretically he should have stayed till the last, being the commander, but in practice British officers usually went down with the main body rather than the rear party, because we were comparatively slow on the downhill and would have caused the Gurkhas needless casualties. As Sahabir once told me with one of his little chuckles, 'The trouble is, sahib, that you look where you're going.' So James left Sahabir on the ridge with one platoon, and himself stood ready, half-way down, to lead the counter-attack if Sahabir had trouble.

Shooting grew heavier all around. Suddenly I heard firing begin from Sahabir's platoon on the hill-top. They sent a message that they could see the tribesmen working towards them and had killed two. Colonel Bruce looked anxiously through his glasses to right and left—at the place where the aircraft bomb had made us think there was some enemy infiltration, at the position of the moving column that had to get round the next spur of hill before he could safely withdraw the last two vital picquets. He made up his mind and gave the order to call down the picquet on the right. His signaller sent up the RTR—code for 'Retire' —to them.

Then ours. M. L. was standing beside him, but Colonel Bruce whipped round directly on me, the signal officer, and said, 'Number Eleven Picquet, retire—and for God's sake get a move on.'

I flagged the order myself, and the firing increased as the picquet acknowledged it. The Wazirs had seen the signal. I raised my binoculars.

Subadar Sahabir and No. 8 Platoon of B Company had nearly six hundred feet of hill-side below them, very steep and creviced with fissures and cliffs up to eight feet high, with stones and scrub concealing the broken surface of the rock. After this murderous incline they had to cross the narrow, steep-sided stream bed, and finally run four hundred yards across the open plain to where we were. The attention of a thousand men concentrated on Sahabir's ridge, while the world seemed to stop.

As the signaller waved the last dot of his acknowledgment the picquet started to move. Sahabir picked up the orange screen in his hand—I could recognize his rotund

233

shape among the younger men—and the whole lot came down the cliff like falling boulders. They fell in great crashing bounds, twelve feet forward and six feet down at a time, leaning *forward* down the slope, their legs going as fast as in a sprint.

In half a minute—thirty or forty seconds from the moment they had acknowledged my signal—the platoon was out of sight in the stream bed. Often it took thirty seconds before a picquet even started to move.

Sahabir's feat was unbelievable, and for thirty seconds—the half-minute that mattered—no one did believe it. No one was ready—not the enemy, nor our gunners and machine-gunners, nor Colonel Bruce. He was still looking at the other picquet, which had just started. He turned on me in strained exasperation, for the responsibility was his, and snapped, 'Did you get that signal through? They ought to be moving by now——'

At this moment the startled artillery men got through the orders to fire. The massed machine-gunners opened up. The Wazirs rushed the crest. A torrent of shells and bullets made the earth boil along Sahabir's ridge. Colonel Bruce cried out in horror, thinking our picquet was still up there. With the deepest pride I had yet known I said ungrammatically but respectfully, 'Er—yes, sir, I think this is them.'

It is a joy to see anything done perfectly, when skill and luck and careless confident dash all work together, and I had seen it there. James and the leading men were well out of the stream now and running strongly towards us. There was nothing more to say. Colonel Bruce commanded a battalion of the 5th Royal Gurkha Rifles, the men who had provided the heroes of the Damdil picquet, a regiment that considered itself *the* expert on Frontier warfare. He let out a long whistle, shook his head, and smiled at M. L. Sahabir came into sight, shooing along his platoon as if they were a flock of geese, waving a thick stick and clucking. He wasn't so hot on the level and had fallen some way behind, but the grinning riflemen waited for the old man to sweat up to them; then they all closed up and trotted on along the track past us.

I turned back to look at the ridge crest, which was still seething under high explosives. Only a few tribesmen had been caught up there—the quickest among them, those who had run most boldly up the reverse slope. One was directly hit by a shell, and I saw the fluttering, ragged body tossed into the air.

I smiled at James and ran along with him. He was muttering under his breath, 'Christ . . . like some tea . . . damned Pathans . . .' Then he looked at his watch from sheer force of habit and held it to his ear as he ran. But he wasn't late that time.

There was no more fighting that day. There was no more Frontier fighting at all for me. My turn had come to command the party of clerks, reinforcements, and baggage at the base, and to have a little leave.

INTERLUDE IN KASHMIR

S RINAGAR, the capital of Kashmir, is a trade mart, and the bund is lined with tall ramshackle houses, their backs built up on stilts over the Jhelum River. Here lived the merchants with the exotic trade names—'Cheapjack Ahmed,' 'Suffering Moses,' 'Busy Bee Jack of Trades,' 'Butterfly.' Houseboats lined the narrow backwaters of the city, for Srinagar is called the Venice of the East, and in them the poor lived and thousands of prostitutes plied their trade. The Maharajah's new palace looked out over the river among a jumble of mean houses, a white elephant strayed into an automobile dump. Outside the city lay the lakes with the lotus, and there lived the pleasure-making English.

I see the lake, a mile across; the long, slow ripple on the water bends the reflection of mountains and bright clouds, a white boat with a gliding sail, three chenar trees on the bank, huge, dark, and round. A dozen houseboats are tied under the trees, and by the marshy edge of the lake are a wall and a fence, and behind them, a leper colony. I see a white road, an arrow across the level vale. It is raised above the spring floods on a six-foot bank, and lined on each side with a single rank of silver birch trees. They stand like a guard of honour, their shadows falling regularly across the road to the meeting of the perspective, and on the left a snow ridge shines through their branches. . . .

Among the wild flowers and the rush of cold water I embraced the lotus and the pale hands, pink-tipped and clinging—both. Perhaps there was something in the atmosphere here that led us singing along rosy paths, some aura lingering from the sensual delights of the Mogul emperors with their smooth-bellied concubines, for we were the heirs of the Moguls. Perhaps we had been made a little mad by the harsh glare of the Frontier sun on the Frontier rock and sand, and the remorseless crack of bullets by day and night. Here it was green and cool.

All day the gramophones played, and satyrs and girls swam in the water whose surface mirrored tree and ridge and far snow—and the leper asylum. Lunch parties under the awnings of the houseboats began with cocktails at eleven and ended in a drowsy repletion of brandy and ice soufflé at four. In the evening the Kashmiri gondolas slid every way along canal and lake, and men strained to women on the deep cushions, or trailed their fingers through the curtains into the rippling water, and thought they had found love.

The gondolas were called *Kiss Me Quick*, *Love Nest*, and the like, and the cheerful gondoliers paddled with long strokes to take us to the dance, to the dinner, to the midnight supper of champagne and strawberries at Shalimar— those pale hands again, and a million lotus flowers on the still water!

At the turn of the night it was quiet in the vale. Before the dawn the darkness again trembled to the *chunk* of paddles as the gondolas bore to their own beds the flushed and drowsy women, the men who smoked cigarettes, heads back, inhaling slow and deep.

'The grave's a fine and private place, but none I think do there embrace. . . .' '*Carpe diem* . . .' There are too many apt quotations. Let us instead reread 'The Miller's Tale,' smile, and return to work.

CHAPTER TWENTY

THE base depot was in Bannu. While I struggled there—at about 120 degrees in the shade heat becomes a physical blow in the face, and living a wrestling match—the battalion continued its pugnacious travels round Waziristan. I missed our most successful day of the campaign, a day when A Company went in with the bayonet. Two men of ours had been shot in the back by wounded tribesmen they had overrun and left for dead. This was quite legitimate, but the rest of the company saw red—which is not a figure of speech but a literal statement. When a Gurkha becomes really angry his eyes film over, and the whites flush to a pale pink.

When the killing was over Havildar Balbir still ran forward, sobbing in his fury and stumbling along the side of the slope with a dripping *kukri* in his right hand and five Pathan heads in his left, his fingers twined in their long matted hair. Headhunting is not customary or legal in modern war, but nothing could be done about it. Nothing could have stopped Balbir or his platoon in that mood.

At last the army broke the tribal will to fight, and though columns kept moving around the country and I rejoined the battalion, I saw no more action. Then M. L.

sent me back to Bakloh to command the battalion's main depot there. In the long journey I had time to think about the campaign, as two years before I had thought about Sandhurst. All the happenings and excitements formed a mosaic pattern in a general scene, and it was too early yet to assess the true value or importance of the scene as a whole. Only the sharp-edged incidents stuck in the eye and the memory; yet I was not the same young man who had gone to Bakloh two years before, nor even the one who had spoken to Peter Nicholson as he lay wounded in Bannu Hospital.

First, I belonged—not only by title and courtesy, but by right. I could now join in any conversation, understand any allusion. Before, men had said 'Do you remember . . . ?' and gone on to chuckle over manœuvres, personalities, and battles of the past. Now this campaign was, and would obviously continue to be, the staple of our reminiscence for many years to come—among the regular officers this remained true throughout the war—and I had been there. I had seen Bruce Douglas fall into a concealed trench under the hail at Ghariom. I was there when James Fairweather was caught on the thunderbox by a morning sniping attack. I had taken part in the crazy conversation, started by a slightly tight John Strickland, about what we would do if faced in Central Asia with an emergency obstetrical occasion and no other equipment than a dentist's tools and a copy of Regimental Standing Orders. I had made the draughty leaf-walled pub we called the Gurk Inn and heard a sunburned colonel intoning plaintively on opening night, 'All I want to be is fish-belly white all over.'

Every man in the battalion knew me as I wandered round with my signallers. They all knew I would slip away from the mess when I could, to have curried goat in their cookhouses. They knew I had learned to eat properly without knives or forks, using my right hand only—because they had taught me. They knew that I liked a marrow bone and a tin plate to bang it on to get the marrow out, and that for me tea must be, inexplicably, burning hot—they

liked it tepid. They knew that I always brought out a notebook and recorded the words and learned the tunes of the
songs they sang.

From the strictly military standpoint the campaign had
taught me much that was to be of value in the coming
world war. Many Aldershot-type officers maintained that
we learned only bad habits in this tribal warfare against
what they called 'ragged-arsed barnshoots.' It was not
true. From the Frontier itself we learned unwinking, un-
sleeping alertness. From the Pathans we learned more
about the tactical value of ground than any of our com-
petitors or future enemies knew. (In 1944 after a heavy
Japanese night attack on my brigade had failed, for the
reason that it was mounted across unfavourable ground,
Subadar Manjang shook his head and said to me with a
slightly disapproving cheerfulness, 'If these *Japani-haru*
were Pathans we'd have a very bad time.') I also learned
to respect the enemy—any enemy. Whoever he was, he
was only a man doing something that he believed right.

I had learned much about that subject which comprises
ninety per cent of an officer's ability and perhaps as much
of a civilian's—men, people, character, behaviour; it has
many names. The army had lately taken to giving it the
repulsive name of man-management, and some businesses
call it personnel management, which is worse. It has also
been defined as leadership, psychology, public relations,
and heaven knows what else. 'People' seems the best.

People were of many kinds, some senior to me, some
junior. Some had a call on me beyond any imposed or
accepted duty, some had not. There were little generals
who kept saying to Bill Mills, whose father was a big
general, 'How's your father, Bill?' There was the jemadar
who told me that a rifleman was dirty and unfit for promotion to lance-naik, but never that the rifleman was his son.
There was Major Willie, who seldom smiled and was never
satisfied—what did he want, for God's sake? I was doing
my best, and other people thought it was quite good.
Well, I *thought* I was doing my best, but I wasn't. I did

my best a few years later in Iraq, Syria, and Persia—for Willie. Then there was a lance-naik who showed great promise, but I had to keep spurring him on by dissatisfaction, as he was rather self-satisfied. (Ah, now, about Major Willie—I wonder?) And Havildar X, who was very, very slow, but never pretended to understand a thing till he really did, and if pointed in the right direction and given a smart shove would go through three brick walls. And Havildar-Major Y, fair, intelligent, honest-looking, as straight as a corkscrew; he had to be carefully watched. And Lance-Naik Z, dark, intelligent, sinister-looking, as straight as X and as quick as Y; it was safe to put any task in his hands, any responsibility on his head. And the two awful little signallers who picked their noses and behaved like urchins but knew more about electricity than I did and kept their nice dirty sense of humour through all tribulations. And the officer on whom the colonel reported accurately, 'This officer goes through life *pushing* doors marked *pull.*'

I had not proved any large, sweeping theories, such as 'Close-set eyes indicate a villainous nature.' I wished I had. It would have made everything much easier. But I had observed many people closely, for a long time, in conditions that thinned or dispelled the smokescreen most of us put up around ourselves. I had got better at 'people' and learned more about how to approach them and know them. Some men are born with the instinct for this; I was not, and I had tried to acquire it and made some progress.

To M. L. I was one of these 'people,' one of the reeds on which he had to lean. What sort of use had I become to him now? I had had two years with the battalion, three years of total service, and I had acquired the second star of a full lieutenant.

I thought it reasonable to assume that I was of at least average ability, or he would not have given me both A Company and the signal platoon to command, often divergent tasks that kept me rushing from one end of the battle to the other, now checking a picquet's sentries, now mending a telephone exchange, now panting up to take A Company into the attack. He said in his annual report on me that I was a very capable young officer, had done well in the war, and must learn not to be so impetuous. This was reasonable enough and I did my best to improve, for I was definitely of the battalion and the regiment, accepted and known everywhere as Jack Masters of the Second Fourth.

My dreams of the Staff now seemed foolish and mean. Service with troops was not just a stepping-stone to higher things, nor was the only purpose of an officer's stay with a battalion that he should there learn how to be a field marshal. I still wanted to be a field marshal one day and did not at all agree with M. L.'s ideas about the uselessness of the theoretical training Staff officers received. I was still determined to go to the Staff College as soon as I could, but I began to see that the true purpose of the Staff College was to train a man to become in all ways a better commander of troops, and not to enable him to get extra pay in a comfortable job, or even to fit him for the dizzy, impersonal heights above.

For here, with the fighting men, was the spirit. Higher up, troops become dots on a map; there are too many of them, too much mathematics, too many graphs and maps. But I had seen the brigadiers and the generals look at us, and I could not mistake the envy in their eyes. Perhaps it was only their lost youth that made them stand beside the track as we of the regiments went by in our long, steady columns, but I do not think so. It was the spirit of the regiments that they envied, for they could never again belong with us. That was the price they had paid for the patches of red flannel on the lapels of their shirts.

We seldom talked about these impersonal things, but once someone did ask how this spirit was to be made effective in a major war. The Frontier campaign had convinced me that our main responsibility in such a war would not be the work of staff duties, nor even the technically more difficult command of men, but the transmission of the spirit. It was only we who could pass it on to non-professional armies, and we would not be in one band of brothers, as here, but scattered everywhere in the expansion of war. There would be no conscription in India or Nepal, and we would not have to face quite the same thing as the regular officers of Britain and the United States. The men in our regiments would always be free volunteers. Yet an officer of the Indian Army would certainly deal at some time with formations containing conscripted British troops —that is, he would deal with the public, the hydra-headed, many-intentioned public. These men would come to us with three-quarters of their minds concentrated on their diverse handicaps, their late business problems, their deserted families, their immortal island-souls. They would be as brave as we, and as intelligent, wise, fit, and honest. Many of them would be better qualified than we were in all these respects. But they would be stamped, heavily or lightly, with the trade-mark of civilian life, the mark of trade: 'If I do this for you, what will you do for me?' They could not otherwise have survived in the civilian world, and their generosity they would reserve for people they liked. We, each alone among a score or a thousand of them, would have to show them that it did not matter, that they were no longer *ilands* embattled against the world, but a part of the *maine*. And they, who had been providing the money that gave us our sheltered life, might learn that in our seclusion we had grown a tree strong enough to shelter all of us against any storm.

It had been only a little war in which I had learned so much. In fact, from the point of view of the people in England it wasn't even war but only imperial policing. For us it was war and experience. The train rushed on and the raw Frontier mountains sank behind the plains of India. I was sunburned to the red of old Tudor bricks from hours of waiting in shadeless picquets, on treeless mountain tops, in arid valleys. The chinstrap mark stood out like a white scar around my face. My knees were nearly black where they showed between shorts and hosetops. The sound of bullets was familiar, and I awoke at night at each sudden crack of the old carriage frames, remembered where I was, and smiled at myself in the dark. My eyes ached from searching the hill-sides through binoculars. Half-healed cuts and scratches covered me, and I could sleep anywhere, any time, anyhow. My memory was bright with gallantry and sacrifice, harsh with pain and cruelty.

The business ahead lay at the extreme opposite end of a soldier's gamut. On Rawalpindi platform I bought three old copies of *The New Yorker* and wrapped its fallen day about me.

CHAPTER TWENTY-ONE

WHEN the battalion went up to the Frontier for war or down to the plains for collective training it left behind in Bakloh its recruits, the staff needed to train them, and all the Gurkha families. This mixed bag was collectively known as the depot. The colonel usually gave a newly-married officer command of it, so that he could have a year in one place to settle down to his married life, and so that his wife could be useful in helping to administer the families. Now M. L. had selected me for the post.

Being almost twenty-three, I was quite confident of my ability to train up into soldiers some sixty wild boys of sixteen or seventeen straight from the farthest hills of Nepal. I was happy about the hundred or so trained soldiers, storemen, clerks, instructors, and bandsmen who were also in the depot. The thought of all the buildings, stores, clothing, and equipment for which I would be held responsible did not worry me a bit. Being a bachelor, I was even fool enough to be calm about the two hundred women and four hundred children.

After three days of 'handing over,' my predecessor stepped into the truck that was to take him down the hill, the truck rolled off, and I was alone. The full weight of the new responsibilities settled on my shoulders so suddenly that I felt crushed. The battalion was three hundred miles away on the Frontier and liable to be called into action at any moment. M. L. could not send me detailed instructions even if he'd wanted to. He relied on me to run this complex organization well, for on its efficiency and happiness depended to a great extent the efficiency and happiness of his battalion. How could the battalion continue to fight well if my recruits joined it as ill-trained hobbledehoys? How could the men up there keep their minds on their duty if, back in Bakloh, their wives were being seduced and their children dying of neglect? Bowed and superhumanly serious I set to work and for a few weeks wore the mien of a very old and careworn banker.

The recruits were comparatively easy. In a fortnight, guided by the advice my predecessor had given me, I had made out a block syllabus for the whole of their eight-month training period and translated into detailed instructions the first week's work. Then I divided the boys into squads of eight or nine and settled down to the final checking. This meant cross-referencing all lessons with the proper page of the proper Army Manual for that subject; allotting rifle ranges, parade grounds, dummy rifles, aiming rests, schoolrooms, and football and basketball grounds so that two squads did not end up trying to do the same thing in the same place at the same time; and issuing books, clothes, and weapons. Soon the Gurkha officers and N.C.O.s were putting the complicated theory into orderly practice, so that it gave me a pleasant feeling of simple mechanical achievement to look at my chart and see that the curt symbols '1-A2: 2-RH5' had indeed ensured that Squad 1 was on the parade ground learning the second lesson in aiming and Squad 2 in the schoolhouse, listening openmouthed to the story of the 4th Gurkhas in Waziristan in 1895, their fifth lesson in regimental history.

Away on the Frontier the fighting men went short of food so that M. L. could wring back from the government a small monthly cash rebate on the battalion's ration allowance. He sent this to me, with other money he allotted from our funds, to buy extra milk for the recruits and provide them with games equipment and *nautch* clothes. Every week I weighed the recruits, since failure to gain weight was usually a sign that a boy was debilitated by hookworm or chronic malaria. The extra milk had its effect, though the recruits sometimes gave it to pet dogs or otherwise misused it. One dark, slow-witted boy was not gaining as he should, and, after weighing him, I ordered him to be given still more milk, using the idiomatic phrase, '*Aru dudh laga*'—literally, 'Put more milk (into him).' The boy got his extra milk, and 'put' it. Subadar Dallu found him alone in the barrack room, massaging it into his thighs.

A week or two before they arrived in Bakloh the recruits had been hill boys from the uttermost back of nowhere. Their hair was long and matted; they had never felt the bite of boots or the bonds of discipline; they had never seen a train, a motor car, or a road, let alone an aeroplane, a radio, or a telephone. To this cheerful, shaggy crowd of half-grown puppies we gave boots at once, and they tripped over their feet in them. They laughed when they should have stood sternly silent, chattered freely in the ranks, and when on parade suggested to the N.C.O.s that the sun was hot and they would like to rest under the trees—and of course they greeted each word of command with amused stares. Some of them did not even understand their own language, Gurkhali. These were boys from valleys on the Tibetan border so remote that the inhabitants spoke only an obscure local dialect, and I had to shift them to a squad whose instructor came from the same general area.

In those first days the recruits showed the basic qualities of the Gurkha—love of life, a warm and animal sense of humour, and fearless self-pride. I had one of them come into my office to give particulars of his home and family, and was lighting a cigarette as he entered. Dallu, standing behind him, nearly exploded when the lad too pulled out a cigarette, asked me for a light, and sat carelessly on the edge of my desk. I motioned the quivering subadar into silence and asked the recruit his name. He said, 'Puran-bahadur. What's yours?'

The N.C.O.s had the delicate task of superimposing on this confident self-respect, without injuring or diminishing it, the discipline that turns a brave man in uniform into a soldier. I watched Havildar Sarbdhan, only thirty-four but mannered like a grandfather, stand patient in front of his squad for weeks on end, slowly and tenderly bringing them to heel. Then one day he suddenly spoke to a recruit in the rear rank, the one who had in the dim past suggested they would all like a rest in the shade. 'Well, Birkha-bahadur, *now* what would you do if you felt hot on parade?'

Little Birkhe and the whole squad, appalled at the memory of their past misdeeds, stood blushingly silent—and then began working with the vicious all-out, all-together snap that later tore apart German panzers, Japanese Guards, and many evil theories.

Our results were of course not perfect. It annoyed me to find that the boys, who had understood my Gurkhali well when they first came, were now so thoroughly aware of the colossal gap between an officer and an unattested recruit that they could not understand a word I said. And they were so pleased to have mastered the etiquette of military life that in the early afternoons, when we sent them to lie down and get the rest their immature bodies required, I had to creep to my office by back ways and bridle paths because whenever I used the direct road past the barrack rooms some vigilant recruit would hear my step and ruin our efforts by bawling, 'Squad!' from a horizontal position on his bed, bringing the whole lot of them, in one motion, crashing delightedly to their feet out of deep sleep.

Dallu, now the senior Gurkha officer of the depot, was a model of punctilio, with finely pointed waxed moustaches sticking out a full eight inches on each side of his mouth, and he drove me mad every day exactly at noon. At that hour I was usually hurrying through a mass of paper work, darting up to look out of the window, rummaging about in drawers, raging to get on and get out. Then Dallu came in. For five minutes I could do nothing while he marched, *stamp-stamp-stamp*, through the door, carried out the eight drill motions of halting, putting his cane at his side, saluting, and starting his daily report. It was useless to say as he came in, 'Good morning, Subadar-sahib, what's the news?' or, 'Everything okay?' He only looked coldly at me and did not open his mouth until he had adopted the proper attitude for doing so. Then, ignoring anything I might have said, he started on a long report, detailing every minute mishap and occurrence of the past twenty-four hours—so many men here, so many there, so many in hospital, two slates loose on the schoolhouse roof— on and on and on, but invariably finishing with '*Baki sab thik chha*' ('Everything else is all right').

He might have had to report that five barracks had burned down, two women had been murdered, the treasure chest robbed, and all the recruits run away, but he would certainly have wound up with the confident statement that everything else was all right.

Again, it was useless to try to question him about his report until he had gone through another set of drill movements and stood at ease. Then we could talk, hampered only by the clash of his boots as he sprang to attention each time he opened his mouth. He spoke a peculiarly difficult and bitten-off kind of Gurkhali, and at this time I never quite understood what he was saying. I used to make sure nothing terrible had happened by casual-seeming conversation with his more intelligible juniors.

Somehow everything prospered. No recruit ran away; there was no fire; no equipment was lost; my accounts passed the audit board; no old soldier was caught in drunkenness or gambling. The weight on my shoulders began to feel less heavy.

I might have been lonely, but there was so much to do that loneliness or boredom never had a chance to creep up on me. The days were full of work, and in the evenings I read greedily and card-indexed the fine mess library. I took the opportunity to read some of the books people freely quote but seldom seem actually to have opened. With varying enjoyment but an unwavering sense of superiority I ploughed through Gibbon's *Decline and Fall*, Motley's *Dutch Republic*, Prescott's *Conquest of Mexico* and *Conquest of Peru*, Thomas Trollope's *History of Florence*, Frazer's *Golden Bough*, all of Mahan, Machiavelli's *Prince*, several of Hakluyt's *Voyages*, Froissart's *Chronicles*, Spinoza's *Ethics*, and *Battles and Leaders of the American Civil War*, besides a flood of adventure novels and all available books about exploration and mountaineering.

It was at this time that John Strickland came through Bakloh on a short visit. He found me one bitter January night, sitting alone in the large, bare room of my bungalow, reading Spinoza by the ghostly light of a single hurricane lantern. Paper lay scattered all over the uncarpeted stone floor, and I was wearing a dark-brown dressing-gown made of an army blanket. The wind howled in the chimney and rattled the windows; rats scurried on the ceiling cloth.

I said, 'John, I can't understand more than one sentence in three of this stuff.'

I must have had a mad look in my eyes. John said, 'What you need, Jack, is a damned great fat woman.' He shook his head and went back to Razmak.

In my spare time I made determined attempts to understand the theory of relativity, write a sonnet in Gurkhali, and extract some admission of affection out of a girl in Dalhousie. I was not bored.

A crowded but not untypical day of early 1938 might have gone something like this:

7–8 a.m.	On parade. Recruits' drill and physical training.
8–8.30	School. Children learning to read.
8.30–9.30	Mess. Breakfast.
9.30–11	Make monthly personal count of all arms and every round of ammunition in the depot.

11–11.30	Clinic. Weigh babies (and feel a great fool).
11.30–12.30 p.m.	Office. Routine work on reports, correspondence, and accounts—interrupted by Dallu.
12.30–12.45	Canteen. Supervise the unsealing and dilution, according to the proportions laid down in Standing Orders, of a forty-gallon cask of rum.
12.45–2	Mess. Lunch.
2–3	Attend Cantonment Board meeting. Inspect pensioner's new house for conformance to building laws. Arrange contract for repair of culvert and irrigation ditch. Argue fruitlessly about price of dog licences.
3–4	Rifle range. Supervise recruits' battle practices.
4–5	Office. Work out in detail next week's training schedule and instructions. Have tea sent up from the mess.
5–6	Watch recruits playing football and basketball.
6–6.30	Visit Gurkha officers' Club for drink and chat with Dallu and Sukdeo.
6.30–7.15	Bathe and change.
7.15–8.30	Mess. Continue cataloguing library, while drinking sybaritic glass of Bristol Cream sherry, alone.
8.30–9.15	Dinner, alone.
9.15–10.15	Study Jackson's Valley Campaign of '62 for my approaching promotion examination.
10.15–11.15	Bungalow. Read.
11.15	Bed, and very soon to sleep.

It is not surprising that after a time I began to feel the need of a break. It did not take much effort to persuade myself that the recruits, too, would be better off for a change. Our ridge, only four thousand five hundred feet above sea level, grew hotter as the hot weather approached, and my shirt toasted my back during the long hours on the open rifle range. I looked longingly at the high hills to the north, and in the end they gave me the idea.

I worked everyone a little harder, so that after a few weeks I had eight days in hand, the work allotted to them already done. Then I went in the bus to Dalhousie and asked the brigade major for a hundred rupees—about seven pounds—from the brigade training fund. It seemed like a lot of money to me then, and, knowing something of the wellnigh incredible parsimony of the Government of India, I was not optimistic—but I got it.

That was all I needed to take the recruits on a trek into the mountains. In a flurry of preparation we packed up food, medicines, and a book on first aid, and spent the hundred rupees to hire five pack ponies. We loaded them with the rations and blankets, and on a glorious May morning set off up the bridle path past Dalhousie, carrying packs and groundsheets on our backs.

The recruits sang with joy to be back in the mountains. By day we curved round the forested shoulders of great hills and climbed over bare spurs and toiled up steep valleys. At night we camped in clearings among the pines, beside running streams full of fish. At Jhot the little rivulet would not do for their fishing, and they insisted on taking me down to the Ravi, four thousand feet almost vertically below. In the morning we had marched twelve miles; all afternoon we ran up and down in the burning valley with our nets; by evening the recruits had to help me back up that gigantic slope from the river to the camp. They seemed surprised at my flabbiness—but they had to discover sometime that British officers were not demigods, and now they enjoyed their opportunity to be solicitous. When I reached my tent and flopped down I found a half-dead crab in the pocket of my shorts. Recruit Manparsad had put it there during the fishing.

In Chamba, the tiny capital of a small hill state, the Ravi was one hundred and fifty feet wide and a hundred feet deep and ran at ten or twelve knots, grey with melted snow. An icy breath blew on us out of its gorge as we walked with broken step across the jouncing suspension bridge into the town. The rajah was a slight, dark boy of fifteen, not yet invested with ruling powers. He gave us permission to camp on the miniature parade ground below his palace and that night invited me to dine with himself and his English tutor. After an unostentatious meal in a mid-Victorian room, they came out to our campfire. The young rajah laughed with pleasure and clapped his hands while the recruits danced the *jaunris* and sang the hill songs of Nepal.

When he had gone back to the palace with his tutor, and the recruits were asleep in the low bivouacs, I walked alone by the bank of the Ravi in the moonlight. Here and now a breath of relaxation and pure happiness came to me for perhaps the first time in my life—certainly it was the most strongly felt. Inside me my spirit sang: this is our life, you and I, the body and the spirit, the lonely mountains, running water, and friends. The Himalaya had breathed its breath into my nostrils while I lay asleep on the trail. The night was beautiful down by the river; the land was beautiful; but nothing was as beautiful as the feeling inside me. I wanted to share it and open my heart and love to a woman who would know without words what was in me, in whose nostrils too there was this mingled majesty and peace and excitement. But there was no such woman, not then, not there.

The next day, as we went back over a high pass into India, the strange feeling of utter content, yet with striving, came on me again, for now the main chain of the Himalaya stood up blindingly blue and white to the north beyond the Chamba valley, and we climbed in slow sweat through meadows blinking with the flowers of early summer.

After our return to Bakloh I knew I had caught two germs —in the low country, a second dose of malaria, and in the Himalaya, a passionate love of mountains.

The malaria struck harder than it had the year before in Razmak. As I walked out into the bright sunlight of the lawn on a Sunday morning my head quite suddenly began to split apart. My eyes hurt; my body trembled uncontrollably. I had to give in at last and creep back to my bungalow thirty yards away. I just reached the bed before my knees buckled. My head rocked and burned. The doctor came and said my temperature was 104. Later it grew higher, and my skin scorched the touch. That evening he gave me powders to bring on perspiration. I lay all night under four blankets in a room temperature of ninety degrees and sweated so much that Biniram had to change me like a baby—soaking sheets, pyjamas, and all—thrice in the short night. I was taken to hospital in Dalhousie next day, exhausted and faint, and slowly began to recover, though the fever returned with diminishing force every third day for over a week. An agile but agate blonde nurse helped me to convalesce, and at last, weak but officially well, I returned to Bakloh, accounts, and parades. This form of malaria is called 'benign tertiary' by the medical profession. It is a rough joke, since the disease is as benign as a cobra.

And all this time, while the recruits filled out into young soldiers and my other multitudinous responsibilities, real and imagined, became lighter and more formal, the two hundred women and four hundred children hung heavier around my neck.

I had three main worries—welfare, discipline, and morals. The government did nothing about family welfare, did not care whether the soldiers had families or not, and certainly was not going to spend a penny or lift a finger to look after them, so we did all this ourselves. Everyone in the regiment had subscribed to build, equip, and maintain a families' clinic. The Bakloh doctor, a British captain of the Indian Medical Service, gave up some of his spare time to work in it. Our funds paid the wages of a tiny staff and a *dhai*, or midwife, for each battalion.

It was always an uphill struggle. Gurkhas do not practise

infanticide, but some of them are not averse from letting an already ailing girl-child die from lack of attention. Again, though the women had no purdah taboos, they came from so sequestered and backward a country and were so steeped in traditional and semi-religious cures that they were unwilling to bring themselves or their children to the clinic except as a last resort. Last resorts, in war and peace, produce a high rate of mortality, and the clinic's occasional helpless failures made the Gurkhas even less willing to go to it. It once took me two hours of arguing to extract from a stubborn and frightened rifleman permission for the doctor to perform a cæsarean on his wife—the only hope of saving woman or child.

The 2nd Battalion *dhai*, a pleasant and educated widow of middle age, was addressed by all of us as Didi, a respectful term meaning 'elder sister.' Every day she went round the family quarters and reported to me, through Dallu, each domestic occurrence there—births, scratched knees, pink-eye, measles, miscarriages, everything. Then if the matter was not being properly dealt with I went into action. First I used the small guns of cajolery, flattery, and persuasion, usually acting through the Gurkha officers. If they failed I had a big gun. Once, as an example, in a particularly wilful case of child neglect that had ended in the death of a girl baby, I used it. I ordered the mother to be evicted from her quarters and sent back to Nepal. This was done next day. The woman cursed and cried, but the riflemen put her and her other children and all their little bundled belongings into a truck. The men's faces were quite wooden, and their minds, normally in close tune with mine, were now out of harmony and vaguely worried. If it had been a man-baby that had died . . . !

This power to allocate and take away quarters at a moment's notice was a brutal weapon, particularly in a case where my ideas of right and wrong did not completely tally with those of the men. But, poised on a delicate point of duty, with the soldiers far away and fighting in Waziristan relying on a general tone of happiness in the lines, I did it; and I would have done it again if there had been need.

Once a week I inspected fifty of the two hundred married quarters. I did this partly to see that they were in good repair and partly to award the cash prizes our funds gave to the woman with the best-cared-for establishment. The competition was open only to families of men receiving a rifleman's pay—that is, riflemen and unpaid lance-naiks— since those with more money would have had an intangible but unfair advantage. I allotted a maximum of ten marks each for the house, the children, and the place, used for cooking and washing up, that might euphemistically be called a scullery. A woman with many children had to be allowed an appropriate handicap, so I spent many hours, while inspecting snotty noses and unwashed necks, in attempting to equate the relative merits of Mrs A's unkempt brood against Mrs B's one well-scrubbed little Lord Fauntleroy.

Officers carrying out this duty were always chaperoned by a Gurkha officer—just in case. It was as well. One spring morning I walked round the corner of a hut into the full force of a deliberately hungry stare, sent burning into my eyes by a beautiful, passionate, and caged female animal. My stomach turned to water, and my masculinity tingled in my spine. The girl stared more longingly. I had only to whisper a day and a time. I looked cautiously round and saw my chaperon, Jemadar Sukdeo, a man of unusually humorous cynicism, interestedly examining the sky, the trees, the distant view, everything but me. I was in a cage too. I turned and walked away.

I wrestled with myself at night and after many nights managed to smother the memory of that open promise under the triple blankets of duty, example, and justice. She would have come to me at a word. The whole depot would have known, but such was the relationship between us in the regiment that, reading me like a book and believing I would not do what I was able to prevent myself from doing, the men would equally certainly have done all they could to keep anyone else from knowing—especially her husband and my colonel. Nor would blackmail have entered anyone's head, even if I had severely punished one of them for precisely the same sort of activity. It was just these considerations that enabled me to pull the blankets up under my chin and keep them there.

The reactions of the women to these visits of inspection were usually 'Oriental.' If there had been an Englishwoman with me, especially a wife, they would all have been smilingly natural and at ease. But in most of the East and even to some extent among Gurkhas it is unusual for a lone male to speak to a lone married female except on definitely furtive and amatory business—so unusual that though the women of Bakloh knew I was chaperoned, on duty, and intended no harm, all those who were still young enough to see themselves as likely targets for male libidinousness acted up in an alarmingly kittenish manner. Brown Chinese-looking dolls, they blushed and hid their heads, looked sideways at me, fluttered their eyelashes, and spoke to me but not at me in giggling whispers. The lined old grandmothers of thirty-five on the other hand, were frank, cheerful, and, where possible, Rabelaisian. I asked one such whether the roof was leaking badly. It had poured with rain the night before, and I could see the stains on the wall and the puddle on the floor. Puzzled by her denial, I repeated the question. She rocked with laughter, hands on hips, and cried, 'Oh, the roof! That leaks, all right. I thought you meant him'—pointing with her chin at the youngest of a gambolling platoon of infants.

Every Wednesday I weighed babies. In the early days this was a rough blend of torture and farce. I sat there, frozen with anxiety, among giggling women and howling children, while Didi deftly popped the babies in and out of the scale and I blindly wrote down the weights in a big book. As I had no idea what babies ought to weigh, or how the weights should increase, I muttered, 'Lovely baby,' to every third or fourth one and tickled its cheeks. This usually caused the infant to shriek in shocked surprise.

Then the more mischievous mothers, quite unencouraged, would press their human volcanoes into my hands and stand back to admire while I miserably clutched the squalling bundle like a football and prayed for deliverance. To cap all, my nervously roving eyes kept striking naked breasts, for the women suckled their children all round me. Gurkhas breast-feed children to the age of four or five and at any hour of the day or night. I was a silly young fool, still tied by one of the more prurient Western taboos, to be so disturbed by this pleasant display of an affectionate motherly duty.

I got to worrying because I found that no one, not even Didi, and least of all the mothers, knew enough about our children's diseases—green diarrhœa and conjunctivitis were the most common—to ensure their quick recognition and prompt cure. The 1st Battalion had just arrived back in Bakloh from the Malakand, so I sought out Barbara Hughes, the wife of their nicest major, and laid my problem before her. The Hugheses quickly became understanding friends to the forlorn commander of the 2nd Battalion depot. Barbara, who had two children of her own, came down to weigh babies with me and, when she had stopped laughing, gave me much practical advice. Then I went to the doctor, notebook in hand, and sat many evenings while he placed his fingers together and dictated notes on children's ailments in his powerful Scots burr. Finally I produced a forty-page pamphlet in Gurkhali on the care of Gurkha children in Bakloh, with one appendix on running a household and another on how to win the family cash prizes. It was a remarkable feat for a bachelor of twenty-three—far more remarkable than I thought at the time, though not in precisely the same way. Still, I meant well, and I dare say it was after all best to confront these responsibilities, the memory of which appals me, with an unhesitating, self-confident ignorance.

The discipline of the families, my second worry, turned out to be very good. In spite of formidable temptations and a natural rowdiness, only once did two of the women come to blows. These two became so incensed, or were enjoying their hair-pulling contest so much, that they threw stones at Dallu when he rushed along to stop the riot. It is a terrible thing to throw stones at a subadar of the 4th Gurkhas, and Dallu came back, his moustaches trembling at the indignity, with the two sulky wild-cats in tow. The women squatted on the office veranda and stridently shouted their stories at me through the open door, both together. A little farther along, the quarter-guard sentries, standing rigidly at ease, were shaking with laughter. It was a moment for which the army has a formula. (The army has a formula for every moment, and a good officer should know them all.) I jammed my hat on my head, said to Dallu, 'Carry on, Subadar-sahib,' and walked quickly down to the rifle range, which was a long way away.

The sexual problem was potentially the most serious of all. The East is not really fatalistic except about death and disease, and if a spark flies near its passion or pride there is an explosion. Gurkha men are very fond of rum, gambling, and women—especially, and sensibly, women. Gurkha women, on the whole, just like men best. Here there were two hundred women who had already been separated from their husbands for thirteen months—a parting that was to lengthen into twenty-five months before I left the depot. Not counting the recruits, who were not innocent but not forceful either, there were a hundred trained soldiers in my depot, and on the other side of the ridge the 1st Battalion, just back from four monastic years in the Malakand, contained another four hundred tough and tenacious bachelors.

What were my responsibilities, and what right did any of us have to interfere with the private lives of grown women? First, there were Regimental Standing Orders. Many years before, Gurkhas and British had combined to write them, and in matters of behaviour they conformed to the customs of the Gurkha in his own country. They covered an enormous field, military and social, but the most important clause affecting me was one that said no man might enter a married quarter other than his own unless on the invitation of the husband, the husband being present throughout. The men on the Frontier certainly expected me to enforce this clause, as they were not present to do it themselves. We doubled the guard over the married lines—but *quis custodiet ipsos custodes?* and, as Sukdeo said, 'Sahib, if a woman means to commit adultery you can chain her to the top of a thin tree, and she'll do it—with her knees and ankles roped,' he added wearily. But the East believes correctly that mankind is frail and should be protected against easy temptation, so we had to do our best.

Standing Orders also took cognizance of the Gurkhas' legal usages. In order to prevent fights, ill feeling, and personal revenge they laid down exactly how domestic tangles were to be dealt with. The case was to be tried by a *panchayat*, a court of five Gurkha officers. The *panchayat* had only to establish the facts and pronounce a verdict— guilty or not guilty. The commanding officer (in the depot, this was me) confirmed or rejected the findings. Then Standing Orders came back again with a fixed punishment. A Gurkha can undertake two kinds of marriage. In *biwahite* he has a wife, in *lehaite* a sort of legalized mistress. In either case the offending woman was sent back to Nepal. The offending man had to pay her fare—perhaps a pound—and a sum in damages to her husband. The damages were about twelve pounds for *biwahite* and seven pounds for *lehaite*. A rifleman's pay was twenty-three shillings a month.

Section 78.6 went on to state bluntly, 'The original husband of the woman will be the owner of the whole household property (i.e. ornaments, clothes, cooking utensils, etc.). No family allotment will be paid back to him.'

Nothing else special was likely to happen to the adulterer unless he was markedly superior in rank to the husband or had in some other way misused privilege or position. In these cases he would probably be told to go on pension.

There was no orgy of scandal in my depot. One case of

adultery was dealt with by a *panchayat*. Once the night patrol saw a dark figure slipping into a quarter. They ran up, to be met by a blank-faced girl, but were in time to see a man's legs disappearing through the high back window. They failed to catch him, possibly deliberately, but brought me a cap belonging to one of my senior N.C.O.s. After talking to the N.C.O. and Dallu, I returned the former to the Frontier without giving any public reason, and kept quiet, naming no names except privately to the colonel. A happy marriage, like California, is a state of mind.

My year with the depot did not pass without one exciting incident of the sort usually associated with India. A little after three o'clock in the afternoon of a cold and sunny February day 'Poppa' Donlea, who then shared a bungalow with me, came in and said that a grass-cutter had seen a leopard. We went out together to question the man. Oh, yes, he said, he'd seen a leopard, quite close. He pointed at Poppa's golden retriever and added, 'About that size, it was.' He had seen it first just below the squash-rackets court, and shouted at it. It had sneaked away through the long grass towards No. 8 Bungalow, which was unoccupied.

Leopards are not uncommon in Bakloh, so we had no reason to doubt his story. I went up to the lines to get a .303 service rifle and some beaters. Many men volunteered, and I selected five, including Naik Udiram and Lance-Naik Baliram. Turning back an eager mob of recruits, soldiers, small urchins, and the retriever, we set off to the squash court, where Poppa was waiting for us. He did not have a rifle, as we had agreed it would be safer in this crowded cantonment to keep down the number of weapons in action. The hunt began.

We spread into line across the narrow, shallow valley leading down from the squash court to No. 8 Bungalow, and moved slowly forward, throwing stones and beating the earth with sticks. Scrub and bushes dotted the valley floor, but Poppa and I moved along the right-hand slope, where it was clearer, and watched for the leopard to break cover ahead of the beaters.

We passed cautiously through the garden of No. 8. The empty servants' huts belonging to it were just down the hill in a dense thicket below us, ten yards or less away, when we heard a sudden coughing roar. An incoherent scream followed, then shouts, and the ugly crackling of leaves and twigs in the thicket. I could not get down the bank direct to the hut because it was so steep and overgrown. I ran forward and round and crept back into the thicket along a narrow, overhung path.

Nerves tensed, ears straining for the slightest sound in the scrub round me, rifle loaded, finger on the trigger, butt in my shoulder, I stepped steadily on, looking slowly right, left, up, down. On a flat ledge in front of the servants' huts I saw Lance-Naik Baliram, staggering about and muttering, '*Khayo!*' ('It's bitten me!')

I could see no damage to the right side of his face, which was towards me, but the corner of his mouth slowly dripped blood. I whispered urgently, 'What's happened? Where's the leopard? Speak up, man!' He swung blindly to face me, and the pit of my stomach turned over as the left side of his head came into view. A blow or bite had torn half of it away, so that it hung loosely outward, laying bare the inside of his head, the convolutions of the inner ear, and part of his brain. I saw no sign of the leopard, and Baliram could no longer speak. I shouted to Naik Udiram to come over from the other side of the valley and help, but no one came to me.

Silence hung heavy in the little clearing by the huts, and the bushes crowded in on me. Baliram looked through me with his dull eyes fixed on something miles away. The hanging flap of skin, muscle, and bone swayed with his slow movements, and the blood dripped soundlessly out from the corners of his mouth.

I leaned my rifle against the wall of the hut. I was trembling but managed to take off my thin tweed coat and knot the sleeves over Baliram's head to hold his face in one piece. While my arms were above his head, tying the awkward sleeves together, a huge blur of black and gold stripes streaked across the extreme corner of my vision. I turned and saw that a tiger was charging out of the cleft between the back of the hut and the slope of the hill, nine or ten feet away. A coughing, grunting roar shattered the nerves in my head. I jerked back and to the right; a steel-tipped forearm whistled past my face and blew the hat off my head. Baliram moaned wordlessly.

Seeing the way now clear for escape, the tiger ran on down the path by which I had entered the thicket.

Udiram had never liked the look of that place. As the beaters advanced he had shouted to Baliram not to go into it but to throw stones from the shelter of the huts. Baliram had not heard, or did not heed. At the first roar Udiram looked across the valley, saw the tiger, saw it stand up and bite through Baliram's head, saw it creep into the narrow cleft between the hut and the slope. From then on he had been shouting desperately to warn me, but I had tensed my ears and brain to hear some tiny animal noise, some leaf crackling, so that they had dismissed those loud human shouts as being irrelevant. I had heard nothing. So Udiram watched helplessly while I walked up to a cornered tiger and laid my rifle down within ten feet of it.

Action blew the uneasy, crawling fears out of me. Udiram and others came running. I left one man in charge of Baliram, sent another for the doctor, seized my rifle, and ran after the tiger. Behind Number 8 Bungalow, Poppa and an Indian bystander were sharing an emaciated tree, which stood about twelve feet high and gave the impression that it could not support a cat, let alone a robustly built officer. Poppa sat farther up the tree than the Indian, having won a sharp altercation with him as to who should go first. After charging me, the tiger had broken cover twenty yards from where they were and in full view of them. I believe a tiger can jump eighteen feet vertically, so they were not so safe as they thought.

The ground beyond Number 8 sloped down steeply in broken cliffs and ledges, lightly scattered with pine trees and underbrush, to a bridle trail and then to a rifle range below that. On the right were two-storied apartment buildings occupied by married soldiers and their children. Men were firing on the range; women and children were talking and playing in the afternoon sun; and a considerable crowd had attached itself to the tail of our own small party. It was like stalking a tiger through Green Park on Whit Sunday.

I stepped rather more cautiously over the brow of the hill and saw the tiger at once, bounding down just above the trail. I dropped flat, cuddled the rifle into my cheek, and waited till he leaped on to the path. There his stripes stood out clearly against the even yellow background, and his pace became a steady trot. I was above and behind him, and fifty yards distant. As he settled into his stride I opened fire with three rapid shots, aiming at the tip of his nose. The first bullet broke his near hind leg high up, smashing into the great bone with such force that it spun him across the trail as though he had been a cat kicked by a big boy. The second shot went through his off forepaw, and the third grazed his shoulders.

I jumped up and ran down the hill to get closer. As I ran, he dragged himself off the road into thin bushes below it. I came to the place, and the tiger roared. I backed off. I did not want to peer over the edge of the trail, where the ground fell steeply, at a wounded tiger that might be only a yard off. I moved along the trail for thirty yards and then went over the edge into thick thorn undergrowth. The invisible tiger watched me and accompanied each step with a sighing roar. I have never felt so anxious, keyed up, and angry, all at the same time.

I sat down with my back against a rock on the hill-side and waited for my breathing to settle. I brought the rifle into my shoulder and tried to see the tiger. Steady, rasping groans came from a patch of thin scrub thirty yards away. I stared and stared, trying to pick out his form, but could see nothing. Yet a very large black and gold animal lay stretched out there. It was an extraordinary demonstration of the art of camouflage.

Suddenly a streak of gold caught my eye and, following along it, a patch of white which I hoped was his ruff. Aiming at that, I fired. The whole animal leaped into prominent focus as he started convulsively, and lay still.

By now the hill seethed with people. The men on the rifle range had stopped firing when they heard the hunt approach, and streamed up toward the scene of action. All over Bakloh crowds of Gurkhas dropped what they were doing and came running. The women and children, at first frightened, now poured out, chattering and squawking like so many jays.

I climbed up the path and edged along it, meaning to look over above the tiger and make sure he was dead. I got to the place and raised my head slowly, the rifle pushed forward and every nerve quivering with tense alertness. Something tickled my back. A hot breath blew on the hairs at the nape of my neck. I whipped round in a convulsion and all but shot Dallu.

His hand trembled on my back; his long moustaches quivered on my neck; his breath blew gustily down the collar of my shirt. He was carrying a twelve-bore shotgun loaded with Number 8 shot, which is very useful for snipe. He asked me eagerly where the leopard was. I told him to take his moustache away, brought him up to date with the facts, and again nerved myself to look over the edge of the trail. The tiger lay stretched out twelve feet below, dead. My last shot had gone in just above the left eye and out behind the right ear, killing him instantly.

I left Udiram to guard the body, particularly to see that the whiskers and claws were not taken for use as aphrodisiacs, and went off with Poppa to the hospital. The doctor was in the middle of the long and delicate operation. We waited for nearly two hours while he put forty stitches into Baliram's head.

My excitement slackened and at last failed altogether. Who had stricken Baliram so that he lay near death—the tiger, or I? Should I not have allowed the beaters to take arms with them? As soon as I thought it I knew it was impossible. There could be only one rifle in such a hunt as ours. Had I made him come against his will? No, he had volunteered. He had not listened to Udiram's warning, so it was his fault. But neither had I, and my head was in one piece.

The doctor came out, his face drawn with the long effort. He said there was not much hope, and nothing else that anyone could do. Subadar Dallu came, looked at me, and said curtly, 'It's no one's fault, sahib. Come away.'

Bakloh had gone crazy while we waited in the ether stillness of the hospital. Men ran about, laughed, danced in the road, and slapped me on the back. Women kissed my knees; children brought flowers. Two hundred soldiers slung the tiger on poles and brought it up to the mess, singing as they came. Machhindra, with a touch of grim humour, put it in the guest room and surrounded it with a circle of kerosene to keep off the ants. By midnight Poppa and I were again mad drunk with excitement. We sat in my room, and drank, and played my seven variations of 'Tiger Rag' five times each on the portable gramophone. Gurkhas brought rum and growled hilariously in time with the rhythmic roars coming out of the gramophone.

Baliram had a good night and seemed to be recovering, but in the morning he died suddenly. Dallu said he was a good man, and a squad took him to the burning *ghat*.

The tiger was a young male, nine feet four inches between pegs, in perfect condition, with an empty stomach. No one knew what he had been doing in Bakloh, where no tigers had ever been heard of before, or where he was going. He became the Bakloh Tiger, and for the rest of my service, though I achieved rank and decoration, to the Gurkhas I was the Sahib Who Shot the Bakloh Tiger. They made a new song and sang it for me in Iraq, Syria, Persia, India, Burma, and on the seas between:

> *Urtis sale, February mahina,*
> *Bagh maryo Masteri-sahib le.*

In '38, in the month of February
Masters-sahib killed the tiger.

The officers, on the other hand, because they still remembered my snipe season, sent me a telegram. It read: 'First cease signing official correspondence quote Bahram Masters unquote. Second discard baffling disguise as *shikari* and do some work. Third re-count ammunition used in recent exploit and wire if stocks Bakloh short. We have one hundred seventy-eight thousand rounds available here if needed.'

CHAPTER TWENTY-TWO

WHENEVER we switched on the mess radio in those days we heard a raucous voice threatening dire things if its smallest wishes were not instantly fulfilled. Since the voice belonged to Adolf Hitler, and since his smallest wishes meant suicide for England, thoughts of war pressed more intimately upon us, and the better-informed of our seniors began to forecast dates for the outbreak.

My worry was not about the war itself, but about the possibility of its starting before I had had my first furlough. I was due to sail on September 29th, 1938, from Bombay, but instead of going directly to England I would go east to Hong Kong and Japan, thence to Hawaii, to Los Angeles, and across the United States by train, and then to England. By travelling in the humbler classes I could get round the world via America, and back to India, for only a few pounds more than the allowance the government gave us for a direct first-class return trip to England.

It is difficult to remember now exactly why I was so set on going to America, but I believe there were several reasons. First, I was convinced that a war was coming, and soon. I did not share my friends' generally low opinion of the United States Army and people, an opinion that was almost wholly due to America's tardy entry into the First World War. I believed that the United States would not be able to keep out of a war against Hitler, and that once it entered such a war it would dominate the alliance. I therefore proposed to spend four months of my leave attached to an American regiment, so that when the War came I would know how the regular army of the United States worked. No one seemed to show much interest in this plan, and finally I was told that there wasn't enough time to complete the arrangements and it was all off. However, I decided to go anyway, and see the American people if I couldn't see their army.

My second reason was a determination not to be put off again—an experience I had had in 1929. In that year I had had an American friend, a boy of my own age—fifteen—in Wiltshire. This boy's parents turned out to have enough money and generosity to invite me over to spend a summer with them all at their ranch in Utah. Their name was Odlum. To make the trip I would have had to give up part of a term at Wellington, since the English terms and holidays do not match the American ones. My parents and the tutor of my dormitory at Wellington decided it was unwise to do this, as I was hopeful of a university scholarship. So I did not go, but I never forgot Stanley's stories about Logan Canyon, and my head was filled with wonderful visions of New York, the Great Plains, and Buffalo Bill.

These specific desires had been strengthened by my occasional meetings with American tourists in India. I found them sociable, friendly, and interested, and I thought I would enjoy America and Americans.

On September 27th, 1938, I was on my way, buying a newspaper at every station, and listening to the radio whenever I could. Chamberlain had returned from Bad Godesberg. The armies of Europe stood by in a high state of tension—but our leave had not been stopped yet. The Frontier Mail ground on southward towards Bombay, and the ship waited for me at Ballard Pier.

When we reached Bombay nothing had yet been settled

in Europe. I got out of the train in a black frame of mind. Why couldn't they make up their minds, damn them? This was my first furlough, and the way they were messing up the world it might be my last. I walked slowly towards the ship; a military policeman was waiting at the gangplank with a list in his hand. Even before I reached him I heard a loud hailer calling my name. 'Lieutenant Masters, Fourth Gurkhas, report to the stationmaster's office . . .'

I stopped and glared at the M.P. So near—I could slip back into the city, buy a false beard, and hide myself on board until we were well at sea. The news of the Munich conference was already in the papers. There would be a war, but not this week. Why the hell wouldn't they let me go? We had surrendered—there might be a reason for it, but it hurt. We weren't going to fight this time.

It was no use. I walked to the edge of the dock and touched the ship's metal side, then returned wearily and told the M.P. who I was. He ticked my name off on his list—there were not many officers on that ship, eastbound— and directed me to the stationmaster's office. The stationmaster had a form: 'Leave cancelled. Return at once to your unit.' He gave me a travel warrant, and that night I was on my way back to Bakloh.

A week later, when we had eaten Munich humble pie, leave was reopened, and three weeks after that I was on my way again. The first stage was to Jullundur, where the 1st Battalion had arrived for cold-weather training. They helped me celebrate my twenty-fourth birthday and then, late that night, came in a gang to see me off at the station. The Frontier Mail drew in; I found a coupé and fell stertorously asleep.

I was armed, because every now and then bandits got on to the trains at night and robbed or murdered passengers in the upper classes, especially those in coupés. Indian trains do not have corridors, and a coupé is a compartment to sleep two. An upper berth swings down at night over the lower berth, which is by day a couch for both passengers. The year before, an officer had awakened to find two men with knives in his coupé. They had murdered the traveller in the lower bunk and seriously wounded the officer above before he managed to pull the communication cord. The murderers then jumped off the train. The officer was sent home to recover in England. A few weeks before my journey he had returned to India, his body fit but his nerve not yet normal after his horrible night of blood, and set off up-country from Bombay. He slept with a loaded revolver under his pillow. He awoke in the middle of the night and sensed a dark figure bending over him. He pulled out the revolver and shot the man dead—a brother officer in his own regiment, who had by coincidence boarded the train at a way station.

This story was all over India, and at first the padre who got into my coupé the next morning at Delhi was, I think, pleased to be travelling with me, especially as I had a revolver. The day wore on, and he became less sure of his good fortune as I sank into the worst kind of hangover and drank more whisky to get rid of it. By evening my companion was a very nervous padre indeed, for I kept losing things, stumbling about looking for them, and taking aim out of the window at passing deer and jackals, just for practice. He looked thoroughly happy when I scrambled on to the top bunk and went to sleep.

In the middle of the night I awoke suddenly to a terrible grinding, smashing noise. Lights flashed on and off and whirled past my head. Hard things hit me from different directions. It lasted only a short time, but in that time my thoughts were clear and consecutive: This is a train smash. I am being killed. It doesn't hurt much.

When it was over I felt no pain, could see nothing, hear nothing. All was black and still. The utter conviction of death lay on me. I *knew* I was either dead or at the portals of death, and it was all right. I have never since then felt the sudden paralysing fears of the nature of dying which used to come on me sometimes in the night—though plenty of fear of the means of death, the shells and diseases and drownings.

271

Under the silent darkness the sound of wheels, *taclacka-clack*, *taclacka-clack* over the rail joints, gradually hammered back into my senses. A light flashed below my feet. I saw the padre's anxious face, white and upside down, looking at me from a foot away. I knew then that I was not dead, but for a moment deliberately continued in my conviction. It is a noble and bizarre thing to slide feet first towards heaven's bright light under the personal escort of one of the church's ever-present pilots, who would, of course, travel right way up.

The eyebrows under the padre's eyes raised—lowered?—and I returned to reality. I was bunched on the floor in a corner of the compartment, standing on my shoulders with my head screwed under me. I had fallen out of bed.

The padre set his lips and said nothing. I climbed back to my bunk and lay like a man with paralysis, trying to restrain explosive laughter. I could think of nothing but the similarity of this ludicrous—but to me very real—facing of death with a recent experience of a man called, let's say, George.

He was the colonel of an Indian battalion, and after a celebration such as my birthday party his officers had been aroused in the early hours by cries of agony from his room. His second-in-command and dearest friend rushed to his room, along with others, and found him in bed, white but now calm, his forehead beaded with sweat. He had even forgotten his numerous affectations and said simply, 'Pete, you'll have to send for the doctor. Take over command of the battalion. I'm paralysed from the waist down.'

He sobbed a little. His officers went away, silent in the face of his affliction, to fetch the doctor. The doctor came and pulled back the bedclothes. He bowed his head for a moment while his face changed from its soothing professional calm to the rich, suffused purple of suppression—he was only a captain. Then he pointed down. George had both feet in one leg of his pyjamas.

In Bombay I was taken in tow by Reggie Sawnhy, a man of about my own age whom I had met in Poona. He had sold me a bullnosed Morris then, and, since the car had not broken down, we were friends.

This friendship with Reggie caused me for the first time to consider the political aspects of my position in India. Reggie's father was Indian and his mother English. This could have made him an Anglo-Indian if he had cared to claim the dubious privileges attaching to that station. But the Sawnhys regarded themselves as Indians. Reggie and the friends he introduced me to were nationalists. They told me clearly that they wanted the British to leave India at the earliest possible moment. I was astonished and hurt. They saw this and, being Indian, quickly added that they didn't mean *me*; I could stay as long as I liked, and welcome. But the British—they'd got to go.

It seemed to me that Reggie and people like him represented all that was best in India. Certainly they wanted us to go and I at once saw the justice of this, for I am by nature an iconoclast; but they were willing to give us at least as much credit as we deserved—and perhaps more—for what we had done in India, and they did not blame us for circumstances that were the fruits of history, not of a deliberate sowing. They avoided the twin pitfalls common to educated India—on the one hand, a dogmatic and cur-like snarling at everything the English did; on the other, a too ready acceptance of us and our position. They were for India, with no buts or maybes, yet they recognized that India's interests were often the same as England's, and that it is as important to steer a cart in the right direction as to fight over who holds the reins—important for the luckless passengers. They thought, on the whole, that the quickest and best way of getting independence for India was to prove that Indians would be capable of handling it when it came. This attitude was a notable contrast to that of most Indian politicians, particularly of the Congress party, who seemed set on proving only that they could never be trusted with anything more delicately adjusted than a crowbar.

Above all, Reggie retained that rarest quality in political India, a sense of humour. He was at his best with Indians and Anglo-Indians who spoke of England as 'Home.' One such announced that he had recently been Home for a holiday. Reggie asked politely, 'What happened to your face, old boy? Fall into the Black Sea on your way out?'

It would be unfair to leave Reggie without a reverent mention of his amazing gift for speech. Our Wilfred Oldham could talk the hind leg off a donkey and I'm not so bad myself, but we could have gagged Reggie and he would still have beaten both of us.

But I was twenty-four, and the good ship *Canton* waited on the tide, outward bound on her maiden voyage to Colombo, Penang, Singapore, Hong Kong, Shanghai, and Japan. I went on board with Reggie late in the evening after a fearsome ride through Bombay at eighty-five miles an hour in his red Bugatti. We stood awhile on the boat deck, looking out over the city and drinking a farewell glass of brandy. Then he left, and I went down to my cabin. When I awoke we were off the Malabar coast.

Nothing was missing for a tropic voyage—a soughing wind, phosphorescent seas, flying fish, good food, good wine, a stout ship, and a slim girl, with whom I promptly fell in love. Munich was past, but war galloped headlong towards us, and we danced and sang and drank our way to Hong Kong. As we docked at Kowloon the lights of the Peak rose in a fairy pyramid against the sky. I quickly packed my bags and set out on a ferryboat for the magic city.

Three days later I embarked on the *Empress of Japan* for Shanghai, Japan, and Honolulu. The Japanese, busy laying the foundations of the Greater East Asia Co-Prosperity Sphere, took every opportunity to make pale-skinned foreigners lose face. So it was that as soon as we left Shanghai every passenger was given a small cardboard box and a toothpick and ordered to provide a stool specimen for the Japanese health authorities. Some of the passengers duly felt degraded, but most of us could not help enjoying the situation created, for the ship's passages became full of blushing old ladies and furiously muttering tycoons, all creeping along to the doctor's cabin at the most unlikely hours, cardboard boxes concealed under unnecessary overcoats.

Then, when I went ashore at Kobe, the customs officer put his stamp on each individual cigarette of the seven or so in my case. My respect for the ruthless efficiency of the Japanese was complete and I eagerly awaited the next step, which any student of John Buchan can readily foresee.

From Kobe I intended to travel to Tokyo by train and rejoin the ship a couple of days later in Yokohama. It was a cold, rainy day and as soon as I got into the train I sat down next to an old peasant lady with rain on her hair and beautiful wrinkled hands and a large basket of food. I began to talk to her in sign language, and soon we were getting along famously. I began to wonder if I could have been mistaken in the Japanese. But after a while the train stopped at Osaka and two little men in business suits and homburg hats came up the aisle. Three or four seats were vacant around us, but they whispered rapidly to the little old lady. She got up, glancing fearfully at me, and went away. One of the men took her place. I decided that the secret service had been looking for me in the upper classes, and that was the cause of the delay.

I waited. After a time my companion's patience failed, and he addressed me in English, asking me where I was going. I told him. He asked me what I was. I told him. He was very polite, but he didn't have a basket of food. The conversation enlarged its scope, but only in certain directions. He was most interested in the Indian Army, and I gave him some interesting information about it. He told me of a British officer who had recently visited Japan and gone climbing on Fujiyama and there disappeared. He looked at me. I said it was very interesting and tried to help him guess what had happened to the poor chap. I said that our theory was that he had been murdered by the Japanese secret service, who were such fools that they didn't know that the officer was a leading proponent of friendship with the Japanese. None of this was true, but my companion's smug expression faltered, and he was silent for a long time.

Then he collected himself and asked me playfully how old I was. With equal coyness I said, 'Guess!' I was, as has been mentioned, twenty-four.

He said, 'Thirty?'

I said, 'No.'

'Forty?'

'No.'

'Fifty?'

'No.' My hair had receded from my forehead when I was nineteen, but this was really too much.

The Japanese said, 'You can't be sixty, and only a lieutenant?'

After a hectic thirty-six-hour stay in Tokyo I re-embarked on the *Empress of Japan* in Yokohama. We sailed out into the Pacific; Honolulu was our next port of call. I felt myself very much of an explorer. The seas of the western world had been the roadways of my family for several generations, and there was something almost routine for me even in a first passage of the Indian Ocean, the Mediterranean, or the Red Sea. The Pacific lay beyond our horizons, and was greater also than the seas we had known. Now it surged astern, hour after hour, unruffled but deeply massive in its breathing, and I gazed at it in a rapture of discovery. This sense of being an explorer sharpened every instinct of enquiry and appreciation, so that I stood late at night for hours on the extreme stern, leaning far over to watch the water boil up from the screws and trail behind like a knurled white scarf, embroidering the darkness with points of violet fire. I watched the sea birds hover on silent wings and keep pace with us, and the beasts of the sea plunge alongside us, and knew that these were not the birds and beasts of English or Indian seas. If I went to bed I don't remember when, for there were arguments to be held all night with men from China, girls from Manila, and Mormons returning to Utah, each one a beacon of unexpected light and new visions. I tried every cocktail on the list and invented several more that were even worse. I went into the bakery and baked a set of Dorset knobs. I went into the jail cell and imagined that I had been imprisoned there for baking bad knobs. I went into the engine rooms and the pantries and the laundry and the bridge.

In many of these enquiries my particular companion was a man some years older than myself, who shall be called Goldberg. Hymie's business was the importing of human hair from China to make into hairnets, and the head offices of his firm were in New York.

On November 22nd we crossed the international date line, so the next day was also November 22nd. This second day was called Meridian Day and since there was no place for it in diaries and the like it was a *dies non*, an extra day presented to us free by fate. Anything went, and that time I do distinctly remember going to bed, at 11.30 a.m.

In Honolulu I left the ship and stayed eight days. Since Hymie was also there it was a good week. The warnings of the taxi drivers to keep clear of the Waikiki Tavern, which they said was a haunt of fairies and tough beach boys, went unregarded. I didn't have enough money to bother myself much about looking after it, and I thought my moustache would protect me from other possible difficulties. I spent most of every day on the beach, learning to surf-ride; most of every night driving around Oahu with Hymie, my gramophone, a bottle of gin, and two girls from the *Empress*. We were not quite so depraved as we may have looked, because the girls had the distinctly American characteristics, here encountered by me for the first time, of being simultaneously as wild as coots and as virginal as— as wholesome American girls. We spent most of our time on lonely beaches in the north, where the moon poured down and the gigantic sea rolled endlessly in, its thunder so deep as to make even Paul Robeson's bass a thin fluting in the night.

And one night Hymie insisted that I go with him to a den of iniquity. It was a frustrating evening, because just after we had arrived and were creeping upstairs in pitch darkness a voice yelled, 'Police!' and I found myself dashing through thick shrubbery among an anonymous, heavy-breathing mob, and then we were in the car and tearing at breakneck speed through the back streets of the city, and I never did find out whether the house contained hashish, roulette wheels, or nekked wimmin.

And another day I put on my uniform and paid a formal call on the United States Army. It showed me great courtesy and allotted a lieutenant to show me round Scho-field Barracks. I felt a good deal older than my guide, who was actually my age. He was only a year or so out of West Point, for one thing, while I had been a company com-mander for three years, several months of them in action. Besides, he was married, which I couldn't understand, as he was in the infantry; and he had a child, which appalled me. Yet obviously he was a capable and zealous officer. I wanted to know how the thing worked in so different a fashion from ours and was more than ever sorry that my application for attachment to the United States Army had not gone through. Total ignorance would have been better than this brief glimpse, which showed divergences and alien-ness without giving me time to learn the reasons for them.

'*Aloha oe*,' the fat ladies sang on the pier, wiggling their behinds, and the garlands round my neck were called leis but they smelled much the same as the ones in India. I threw them into the sea off Diamond Head and watched carefully to see whether they would float back to land, but the *Lurline* was going too fast, and the dusk swallowed them. I went to bed.

An hour later, with the ship throbbing comfortably, the cabin dark, and my room-mates snoring, I awoke with a strong feeling that something was wrong. After an hour's thinking and searching I found out what it was. I had lost my wallet, containing all my tickets, travellers' cheques, and cash. I lay down again. This would have been terrible in England, or even in India. In America it didn't seem to matter so much. I considered the situation with dreamy satisfaction. A 4th Gurkha could do anything. I would work my way up to Canada and lumberjack for a while, until I had made enough money to get on my way. A captain in the regiment had done that in the twenties—something like that, anyway. Perhaps he had driven a taxi in Vancouver or been a fur-trapper in Alaska—something check-shirted and Canadian, it had been. But maybe America would suit me better. A docker in San Francisco; a railroad bum, riding the rods; a *tong* gunman—ah, that was a job I had better training for than most. In the whole of California there wouldn't be more than a handful of gunmen with degrees from a recognized small arms school. I fell contentedly asleep.

Next morning the purser sent for me and handed me my wallet. Everything was in it. Someone had found it on the dockside a minute before the gangplanks were pulled up.

The *Lurline* was a lively ship. The other men in my cabin told me it was always so at this time—early December—because the horde of beach boys, gigolos, and con men who spent the season working over the teachers and tourists in Honolulu were on their way back to the mainland, in many cases at the request of the Honolulu police. I soon located the trio who seemed to be the heart of this gang, for they had a large earthenware jug and a secret supply of whisky. We regarded each other with interest, for we might as well have come from different planets. They got into serious trouble only once, when they had been up all night drinking out of the jug and were still up, unshaven and villainous-looking, when the children began to appear on deck. The beach boys went down on hands and knees and gave the kids pickaback rides all round the deck, half-way up the masts, through the lifeboats under the canvas covers, and elsewhere. The mothers, snoring in bed, did not discover for a long time what was going on, and then suddenly the ship became full of screaming women and howling children and my friends were hauled off to spend a day in the brig.

On this ship, the first American vessel I had ever travelled on, I discovered the meaning of a classless society. On a British ship in those days, particularly a P. & O., everyone knew that I and others like me had to travel tourist because we were subalterns and could not afford the first class except on a normal Lee Commission passage, when the government paid our fare. But we were officers, and it would have been an unheard-of thing to turn us out of the first class, whose facilities we used more than our own, just because we hadn't paid first-class fare. The senior officers, who relied on us to marry their daughters, would have complained angrily if such an action had been suggested. Of course it was different for a *genuine* tourist passenger— one with a Cockney accent. Such as he could not be permitted into the first class so we were expected to make our visits without too much publicity in case these others decided that what was sauce for the subaltern was sauce for the plumber.

So, soon after boarding the *Lurline*, I wandered into the first class on a visit of inspection. In practically no time I was having a drink with a lady from San Francisco who was accompanied by her daughter, aged twenty-one. The daughter and I liked each other and next day I took her slumming in the tourist class and in turn spent several hours with her in first, while Mamma beamed on us. That night, though, while I was dancing with her in the first class, a ship's officer approached and asked me to go with him to the edge of the floor. I went cheerfully, thinking that perhaps the two of us were about to be invited to have a drink with the captain.

Once out of earshot of the girl, the officer brusquely asked me whether I was not a tourist passenger. I replied that of course I was, he must know that. He ordered me back to the kennel. I tried to explain to him that it was all right, that such as I were always allowed in first class, anywhere. He didn't seem to understand. He repeated his order with emphasis. The girl and Mamma arrived, listened, and told the officer I was their guest. The man repeated that it wasn't allowed. I shrugged and went.

I have seldom felt so humiliated and was very angry with the shipping company, the officer, and the American people. This annoyance, and a sense of being lost, were increased by my first introduction to the Old South. There were two ladies from Virginia at my table in tourist. They said 'bee-yoot' for 'boot,' made two syllables out of 'yes,' and pronounced 'about' as 'aboat.' I could hardly tear myself away from them, particularly as they seemed wonderfully impressed by my status as a King's Commissioned Officer of the Indian Army. Then came an evening of organized frolic in the tourist lounge. There was dancing and I taught several people the Lambeth Walk. There were foolish competitions, in which I joined wholeheartedly. And finally there was an event in which each contestant was given two crackers and, at the word 'Go,' had to eat them and then whistle a tune. The prize went to the whistler of the first recognizable tune. I won, with 'Alexander's Ragtime Band,' and returned, beaming and swallowing the remains of the crackers, to join the Virginian ladies.

The senior Virginian lady did not congratulate me. She asked me whether I did not think I was letting down my class, my background—I forget the word she used—by these antics. Wasn't it rather—degrading, for a King's Commissioned Officer of the Indian Army to stuff crackers into his mouth and try to whistle through them? I thought it over and said, 'No.' I saw little of the Virginian ladies for the rest of the trip; they avoided me.

I tried to shrug this incident off too, but it was much less explicable than my ejection from the first class, in terms of what little I understood of American ideals. It was no use trying to defend myself by saying that I had also played at cockfighting with the Gurkha officers in their club—two of us lying backs down on the floor and trying to overthrow each other with a thrust of the interlocked right legs raised high in the air. Or telling them about high-cockalorum, races over the mess roof in Bakloh, and dancing the *jaunris* while the firelight danced with us and the Gurkhas sang.

All this could only have made it worse. I might have justified myself, to the Virginian lady's way of thinking, on other grounds—by pointing out that the position of a King's Commissioned Officer in India was so unassailably high that it was unnecessary for him to give any thought to maintaining the appearance of it. And then she would have called me a British snob.

I decided that Americans were very strange people—thrown out of the first class for being tourist; upbraided in tourist for not behaving like Anthony Eden (but Eden was in the 60th Rifles, and I could have told them a thing or two about *that*!). Oh, well . .

*   *   *

Los Angeles of the Angels. I counted my money, decided I hadn't enough to cross the country by car, traded in my rail ticket, bought a 1932 Dodge, christened it Ol' Man Mose, bade Hymie good-bye, and set off eastward. My licence plates were 4R3431, California, 1938.

The road stretched as far as an Indian road—farther, straighter—but there was no dust; the people were white-skinned, and the road was full of cars. Yet it was very like parts of the Frontier—the light falling opalescent and cool over a vast landscape, the sky far and high, and mountains etched in pink and ochre against the horizon.

Barstow, California—my first auto camp. A strange experience, to sit there in the desert while the dry wind whistled through the cracks and my car bore traces of snow from the Cajon Pass. I got out my gramophone and the faithful, scratched records, and stuffed two pairs of socks into the amplifier. Robeson sang 'Ol' Man River' for me, and the deep voice shook the cabin; the wind sang low, and I was in America.

Boulder Dam—much gaping and gasping. These people can build with their hands! A long, long road—Kingman, Arizona, and it was raining. I found an auto camp that would take me and Ol' Man Mose in for seventy-five cents. The sheets were damp, and the roof dripped rain on to the floor beside my bed. Cockroaches made a loud noise underneath, and the gramophone gave no comfort. By God, afford it or not, I must get out of here and have a drink before I could try to go to sleep. I walked up and down the raised walk facing the Santa Fé tracks, where the saloons and the stores were. I remember it as a boardwalk, but perhaps it was of stone. It makes no difference; it was a boardwalk to me, the kind I had seen a hundred times and clanked along in a hundred dreams, my guns swinging low on my hips. There they were, in cowboy pants and shirts, leaning against the bars inside, drinking. I was limited to two dollars a day, plus petrol and oil. I swore and turned to go back to my miserable cabin. The twin lights on the grade crossing began to flash on and off, and a bell set up a steady tolling. A Santa Fé express came up out of California. I waited in the rain that was turning to sleet, until she had gone, then hurried back and went happily to sleep.

Phoenix, Tucson, Lordsburg, El Paso . . . I paid a formal call on the 7th U.S. Cavalry, taught *them* the Lambeth Walk, learned a square dance. In a bar where a cavalry-man took me were two tall old men, lean and white-haired, wearing high-heeled boots, drinking as quietly as you please; then, *wham!* one of them picked up a bar stool and flung it through the window. (Yippee, Texas, here I come!)

Pecos, Ranger, Fort Worth, Dallas, Longview, Baton Rouge and the river, the ferryboat's black smoke drooping over the wide water—U.S. 71, New Orleans!

Everyone asked me about Munich. Why had we crawled on our knees before the monster? I didn't know and could only reply with tart *tu quoques* about the League of Nations. Then everyone seemed to be reading a book called *With Malice Toward Some*, and I was teased about English plumbing, cooking, and stuffiness. I learned that the more I fought back the more people liked it, and I said to myself, 'Ah, *now* I understand Americans.' Ol' Man Mose broke down beside the road one evening, and I heard a boxing match on the radio, almost without interruption—not my radio, for I didn't have one, but the radios of the passing streams of cars, all tuned to the same fight. This was a great marvel to me, and it was not until the fight had ended that I walked down the road, chuckling delightedly, to find a mechanic.

I stayed in New Orleans longer than I had intended, because it was a friendly place; because in the Hotel Charles they had a small band, with an electric guitar, that would play 'That's A Plenty' for me as often as I asked for it; because of Anne Kilpatrick, Alice Westfeldt, and Mamoo and Papoo, and people who did not think it terrible that I should be in tearing high spirits when the sun was setting on Lake Pontchartrain, the wind filled the sails, and the boat heeled far into racing water. I danced a Gurkha *jaunri* on the deck and nearly fell off.

I saw the Sugar Bowl game, T.C.U. against Carnegie Tech.; can't remember the score—Davey O'Brien my hero for several days.

These people were Southerners, but I felt at home— except once, when I forgot where I was and whistled 'Marching Through Georgia' at a party. The New Orleans *Times Picayune* took a picture of me in full evening dress on my way to the Twelfth Night Revellers' Ball and paid me half a cent a line for an article on how the Gurkhas celebrated Dussehra—$8.95 into the kitty.

Too many good-byes, and on again. It was a sharp dawn, and I wore heavy corduroy trousers, tweed coat, and my *poshteen*, the clothes I would wear on a bitter morning in Jullundur or Bakloh. A *poshteen* is a Frontier garment, a coat reaching to the knees or lower, made of untanned goatskin, worn with the hair inmost; the yellow hide is decorated with strange patterns in red or black thread. The whole is strong-smelling as—a goat.

In Mobile I stopped for petrol and stepped out of the car for a stretch. Many attendants came out, until there were half a dozen of them there, industriously wiping the windshield, peering at the tyres, testing the oil, anything that would give them a close look at me. We exchanged generalities about the weather. I paid, got in, and started up. The owner, obviously unhinged by the accent, the clothes, and the smell of goat, approached and said, 'Excuse me, sir, but could you tell me, to settle a bet, what part of California you come from?'

Montgomery, Dahlonega, Asheville, Johnson City, Bristol, Lexington . . . Three days at V.M.I. as guest of the superintendent. I paid a call and told him I wanted to study Jackson's Valley Campaign on the spot. He had two Congressional Medals, but I did not know that. He offered me his hospitality and answered many questions. At his request I lectured the faculty on that same Valley campaign. Hell, it was no different from the Child Welfare Book really, and they did not know much about the war because it still hurt. The Europeans had started studying it much sooner than the Americans. It snowed hard, and I took Henderson's *Stonewall Jackson* out of the boot and lay down on my stomach with it in the blizzard at Port Republic, trying to find out where Tyler had put his guns and where was the forested path along which the Louisiana regiments had marched to turn the tide of battle.

I saw the mural in the V.M.I. chapel which shows the charge of the cadets at the Battle of Newmarket. I stood a long while by Stonewall's tomb in the cold churchyard at Lexington; and in the crypt of Washington and Lee's chapel I examined the sleeping hand of Lee, which would rest a long time on his marble sword there; and at last I left for the North with a strong feeling that I, who understood so little, yet understood the Confederacy. I drove up the Valley Pike, whose name had been foolishly changed to the Jackson and Lee Highway, and since I was an infantryman I could smell the sweat and the dust in the files and hear the bugles blow; and because I had suddenly fallen in love with America, the land, as tempestuously as with any woman, I marched in those long-dead ranks and knew why I did so and where I was going.

It was a very short distance, in this immense country, across the Potomac to Frederick, Maryland. ' "Shoot, if you must, this old grey head, But spare your country's flag," she said'—I knew that much; but it was hard to imagine the old lady's really disliking Stonewall, because they were both Americans, and surely she must have understood in her heart what made the grey infantry march on through the town. On, myself, into eastern Pennsylvania, and now it was another uniform that clothed the men standing in bronze and stone in the rainy squares of the ugly towns. But these men, bearing another flag—neither flag then mine—had also marched up and down the Valley Pike. I said to myself, 'The Union must be preserved,' tried to understand that, and went back to Washington to stand humbled before Lincoln's sadness in his marble palace.

Port Jervis, the Rip Van Winkle Bridge, on into New England—twenty-eight below zero and no heater in the car, or if there was no one had told me about such things. Also, I had been buying 'white gas' because it was cheaper, so icicles formed in the feed lines and at last I had to get a Vermont Yankee, who came, blew down them, poured hot water over the carburettor, and advised me to use better fuel; but he couldn't see into my pockets.

Manchester, Vermont, and a first meeting with old friends. This was a true Indian Army circumstance. In 1927 an American lady and her daughter had gone on a tour of India. December 24th of that year found them, owing to some slip in their arrangements, in Jullundur. Jullundur was not a tourist centre. All it boasted at Christmas time was the presence of the 1st and 4th Gurkhas, down from their mountain eyries at Dharmsala and Bakloh for cold-weather manœuvres. The colonel of the Second Fourth heard of the two stranded ladies and invited them to share in all the regiment's Christmas parties and dances. Before leaving Jullundur the mother urged anyone in the regiment who visited America not to fail to come to see them. Eleven years later I took up the invitation. In 1927 I was a boy of thirteen in England, but the continuity of the regiment took little heed of that. I knew all about the American ladies and there I was.

After a week of ski-ing and hospitality I set out for New

York, sold Ol' Man Mose at Poughkeepsie, and arrived at Grand Central by train on a bitter winter evening. I found Hymie, and he cashed my cheque for seventy-five dollars. We had a good time on Fifty-second Street, and then I managed to last out the week until the *Manhattan* sailed—mainly by spending hours on end sitting on a bench in Central Park, wrapped in my *poshteen* and with newspapers in my shoes, watching people walk up and down and pass in their cars. My diet—as throughout the trip, except when someone else was paying—was hot cakes and coffee for breakfast, hamburger and coffee for lunch, hamburger and coffee for dinner.

At midnight on February 9th, 1939, the *Manhattan* sailed down the North River. Lights twinkled in the towers of Manhattan and I was glad to be on my way. All the stewards on the ship seemed to be Germans. They said they were American citizens but as far as I could make out they kept their wives and families in Hamburg or Bremerhaven. I got into an argument with one about Hitler, whom he approved of, and was so rude that I received excellent service for the rest of the voyage. At my table were a bunch of college professors and their wives and at the next table a group of old men with beards, who wore their hats all the time. There were also many young men with pasty faces, scrubby beards, and hats too large for them. They had wild, deep eyes and an air of poetry, but we could not make one another out at all and my attempts at fraternization, founded on the bar, got nowhere. The passages smelled of cold pickled cabbage; I was broke; the wind was cold, the sea grey, the professors serious, the rabbis prophetic, and the young men absorbed in their books, beards, and hats. Again I felt like a visitor from another world.

On the last day I got up at 3 a.m., for I knew we would then be in the Western Approaches. A bright, high light shone on the sea from the darkness, revolved, and shone again. The sea came out of the west behind us, and rolled us forward. The dawn rose grey and bitter, and the white waves rode ahead of us past the loom of the great headland. It was the Lizard, and I was back again in the land of my fathers—but not of my birth.

Soon Hitler marched into Czechoslovakia and in the pubs I heard young men grumbling about conscription. I agreed with them, for conscription is a hateful idea. They were annoyed with Hitler, and so was I, but for rather different reasons. Soon enough I would be training a young man such as one of these to take over command of A Company of the 2nd Battalion, 4th Prince of Wales's Own Gurkha Rifles. In war it was doubtful whether he would understand the depth of his privilege before death caught up with him.

CHAPTER TWENTY-THREE

LATE in June of 1939 I rejoined the battalion at Loralai, in Baluchistan. Baluchistan lies on the Frontier, immediately to the south of Waziristan, but the two are very different. In Baluchistan there are wider, drier horizons and few trees. It is like New Mexico or Arizona—the same plains covered in sagebrush and stunted herbal-smelling scrub, ringed at a distance by the same jagged mountains sharp in the same opal-fired light, the same buttes and eroded gorges. The landscape is very large under the sky, not inimical to man but ignorant of him.

In place of Waziristan's thousands of armed and rambunctious tribesmen, here there was only one. In Baluchistan the word 'hostiles' was singular and meant one flea-ridden and variously brutal Robin Hood, who committed one outrage every year for the sake of his reputation but spent the rest of his time with his feet up, reading the newspaper or acting as informer to the Political Agents. The outlaw, and the grand sweep of desolation outside the tiny fort and tree-lined cantonment, made it clear we were not in Bakloh; yet it was a scene idyllically peaceful by contrast with the excitement of Waziristan.

But under the surface the deeper waters heaved with the increasingly urgent preparations for war. The training cycle chugged faster; the audit boards ran more confusedly in their quarterly courses; the rosters for furlough and the rolls for promotion began to tread on one another's heels. We set out on an endless series of cadres designed to fit every man for a rank two above that he now held. We checked and rechecked our mobilization stores, read and reread Mobilization Regulations, and prepared and filed away the telegrams that would be sent out to reservists and furlough men when the hour struck.

These military commotions brought on an odd but pleasing eruption of minor eccentricity. The great civilian world would soon be peering at us, as at rare animals in a zoo, and they would expect us to be excessively military, blunt, and matter-of-fact; so we behaved with an unnecessarily decadent preciosity and wore the green carnation while we could.

We took to drinking claret at late breakfast after route marches. Palmerston, the mess kitten, joined us at dinner for a small glass of sherry and a large bowl of peanuts, and wore a green silk ribbon when he followed me to my office. *Les Fleurs du Mal* became a bible and revealed to us that we were uncouth from being out of touch with that spirit which is always centred in France. To become more couth we talked only French in the mess on Fridays, and advocated art for art's sake. At a mess meeting the subalterns forced through a motion to decorate the bare walls with reproductions of the French Impressionists. This anæmic modernism was nevertheless rash enough to cause most of our seniors to think we had gone mad. They liked wild ducks, foxhounds, and stags at bay, in photographic detail. They finally decided that the sky in the Monet was an accurate representation of an anti-aircraft barrage, and were happy. Bill Mills arranged an exhibition of Surrealist art in which some unusual constructions, collages, and mobiles were unveiled over suitably baffling titles. At the preview we wore false beards and sandals and modestly explained to the colonel that unless he could without mirrors see both the back and the side of his own head at the same time he was, artistically speaking, a clod.

A new subaltern joined us; he had come through Cambridge, not the R.M.C. One morning the colonel and the adjutant were carrying out a routine inspection of barracks when they suddenly came upon this young man round a corner. The proper military action on his part would have been to salute, say, 'Good morning, sir,' and pass on his way. Instead, our Mr Hawkins gave the C.O. a friendly wave and cried genially, 'Morning, colonel! On the prowl again, I see.' Mr Hawkins was quickly told of his error—but we were delighted with him. This was the right spirit.

On the surface too there was much coming and going. Parta Sing had squawked his last 'oof-oof' and gone on pension. Sahabir wore the crowns now and did not have to imitate chickens. He was an old hen himself and gave every impression of being useless—until the bullets came close. The louder they smacked, the more Sahabir grew into a formidable old man, decisive, and not to be lightly crossed. Naik Dhansing of the buglers fell due for pension, and not much longer would he be with us to lie on ants' nests and play with the pretty things, or carry five men's rifles on route marches, or attack armed enemies with a knife, or bark like the colonel's dog when in the ranks of a most ceremonial parade, or pinch camels' testicles.

A piper came back ten months late from furlough. He had had syphilis. Havildar Shiblal did not come back at all. He had died of smallpox. Sukdeo became a subadar and still managed to be cynical while giving young soldiers the impression that life was real and earnest. Dallu was still stamping holes in the concrete at Bakloh, and after a few months the quarterguard bell could strike twelve without sending me into convulsions of nervous expectation. (Poor Dallu spent a lifetime of punctilious service trying to wipe out two things: the memory of the military crime recorded in his conduct sheet—Rifleman Dallu

Rana had dirty boots on April 4th, 1915; and the fact that Dallu was his baby nickname, not his real name.)

M. L. had finished his allotted span of command and was on long furlough in Scotland, awaiting the word as to whether he would be retired or promoted to brigadier. The new colonel spoke hand-hewn Gurkhali. One new subaltern was slight and handsome, and turned a delicate shade of green whenever the word 'work' was mentioned. Another was tall and thin, did not approve of any reading lighter than *Religio Medici*, and felt himself degraded because Beethoven could give him pleasure by ordering the hairs of horses to be drawn in a certain manner across the entrails of cats. He apologized, nearly in tears and scarlet with mortification, if any man in his company was found an inch out of line, and once every week he walked twenty miles by himself in the mountains and deserts.

James Fairweather was quartermaster and had difficulty in getting the colonel to sign a loss statement for two pennyworths of mislaid equipment. He kept secreting it in the middle of piles of papers but the colonel always discovered it as his pen was poised to sign, and told James to check up on one more regulation before he would commit himself. And I was the acting adjutant, soon to be confirmed in the appointment.

The adjutant of a battalion was the colonel's personal staff officer, like a private secretary, and was also responsible for the G and A sides of staff work. This meant that in war and manœuvres he prepared the operation orders that would convert the colonel's battle plans into exact detail—boundaries, objectives, tasks, fire support, troops allotted, and so on. (The colonel's other staff officer, the quartermaster, dealt with the logistical side—rations, ammunition, supplies, water, fuel, fodder.) In barracks the adjutant's principal concerns were dress, drill, discipline, military law, all forms of ceremonial, the functioning of the pipes, drums, and band. To fulfil his responsibilities an adjutant had to know everything, forget nothing, and forgive nothing. It was a most prized appointment and usually was held for four years—in peacetime.

There were many ways of being a good adjutant, but several factors were common to all of them, and the three first were that one must lose all sense of humour, all sense of proportion, and all desire to win or keep friends. A general could afford to pooh-pooh the importance of exact detail, but not an adjutant. The adjutant was the man whose eyes lit up when he discovered some tiny peccadillo, who poured on it the scorn and horror the colonel must reserve for great catastrophes. He was the man whose watch was right within one second, always, and who, when he said 0915 hours, meant 0915 hours and drove himself into a paroxysm of rage if someone else thought that ten seconds more or less did not matter. An adjutant saw nothing funny when Rifleman Gingabir Gurung slipped on a banana peel—only that the miserable fellow had upset the step, and someone must suffer for it. The adjutant knew all the correct abbreviations and forms and procedures and did not allow himself to think whether any of them were perhaps slightly ridiculous.

My predecessor, Bill Mills, was by nature a most lighthearted man, witty, kindhearted and with a keen sense of comedy. On his appointment as adjutant he set his lips into a misanthropic line, his expression into an agate stare, and his vocal chords to a curt and didactic harshness. He never relaxed them until I took over. In conversation his basilisk eyes wandered up and down one while his fingers involuntarily picked off specks of dust or turned one's crested buttons right way up. One of our newcomers, sitting alone in the mess with him at breakfast, was surprised to hear him call for the orderly and demand pencil and paper. When they were brought Bill wrote briefly and muttered a few inaudible words. The expressionless orderly carried the note five feet to Ben. It read in full: '2/Lieut Browne. Haircut, by 1000 hrs. A. W. M., Adj.'

But now it was I who glided around the parade ground, communing in silent scorn with a Gurkha deity who inhabited the middle air a hundred feet above my head. The young soldiers blinked in awe at my glassy boots and leggings, the beautiful sword at my waist, its leather wrist strap flapping long and loose to show that I was the adjutant. They were amazed to see that before my feet paths became smooth, doors opened, walls vanished, potholes were filled up; that I never looked down, round, or about, and I never tripped or stumbled. These things happened because I made cautious investigations from the corners of my eyes before trying out my supernatural powers and because my jemadar adjutant, Gumparsad Gurung, who could afford to be alert and bird-like, dogged my unseeing strides and coughed gently if there was anything in the way—also because it was Gumparsad's job to have holes filled in, paths made smooth, and doors opened.

Disaster strikes even adjutants sometimes, and our proficiency in French did not stave it off from me. I suspect it may have been a contributing cause. The catastrophe rode in on the shoulders of a French colonel from the interior of Afghanistan, who came through Loralai on his way back to Paris. What a French colonel was doing in Afghanistan was a different matter again—some piece of Quai d'Orsay intrigue, and very exciting.

Our Frenchman motored mysteriously out of the deserts —a slight, trim, English-looking type of about fifty-five, wearing khaki and a képi. We bowed jerkily until Rifleman Narbahadur, the mess orderly, asked me whether I had a stiff neck. We said, '*Bon jour, mon colonel*,' and, '*Veuillez boire un* pink gin, *mon colonel*,' and, '*Le lavabo est à droit, mon colonel*'; and somehow I managed to prevent myself from blurting out that I was *l'adjutant*, which in French means sergeant-major; and James kept muttering, 'Christ . . . *ooh là là, mon colonel . . . avez tu tay*;' until I trod on his foot. But on the whole all went well, until next morning.

Perhaps I was fazed by speaking a foreign language; perhaps I had carried too far my complimentary attitude to Gallic lightheartedness. Something went wrong with my arrangements for *mon colonel's* departure. The truck was not where it should have been; no one came to carry his kit into it; and he was delayed half an hour while I scurried round doing everything myself. It was bad that it should have happened, worse that it should have happened to a full colonel, worst of all that the full colonel was a foreigner. When he had finally left, an observer would have seen one of the most heartrending sights in the army, an adjutant conferring with his assistants over a calamity.

Gumparsad and I walked on the parade ground for an hour, heads down, with deliberate pace. Every ten minutes I shook my head and said it was a bad show—my fault for not writing it all down properly. Every other ten minutes Gumparsad shook his head and said no, it was his fault for not understanding what I had said; he was afraid he was no good and would have to think about asking to be relieved of his appointment. We walked on, while squads of drilling soldiers zinged past us and everyone left us to our melancholy pleasures. Finally we braced ourselves. 'The path of DUTY is the way to GLORY' had been written in stone over a gateway at Wellington.

I put on my belt and sword and marched in to make a formal apology to my colonel for the disgrace I had brought on the battalion. Gumparsad put on *his* belt and sword and marched off to mount the quarterguard. This he did with a ferocity beyond anything even he had used before, and his inspections were always rigorous. By the time he had finished with them that morning their havildar was in open arrest for daring to bring such a scrofulous collection of mendicants to guard-mounting at all; six riflemen were on charges; and the duty piper was in close arrest. He had blown a hole in the pipe bag from sheer nerves, and the instrument had made such uncannily impertinent noises that Gumparsad ordered him into arrest for 'Conduct prejudicial to good order and military discipline, in that he—etc., etc.— did play his bagpipe in an insolent manner.'

As adjutant dealing with the colonel's official correspondence, I met the *babu* mentality. The word *babu* is often used as a term of respect, in the form *babuji*, but the *babu* mentality is the universal attitude of junior civil servants, modified for India. It is impossible to reproduce in a few lines the beauties of *babus'* speech, but when you think of a *babu* think of his archetype—a middle-aged Bengali gentleman with thick spectacles and a small round hat pushed to the back of a nearly bald head. Think of him leaning back in a chair—the only man who can read and write among a crowd of unlettered farmers, workers, and peasants. Feel in him the immovable power of the only man who *knows*, the only man who can say, 'It is written.' His movements are slow to the point of caution, and he licks his pencil or dips his pen into the ink at each word. It is his aim to draw out the work, not to hasten it, because each moment he sits there, thumbing with snail-like deliberation through regulation after regulation, the waiting crowd becomes more keenly impressed with the vastness of his accomplishments. He may put 'B.A.' after his name, or he may put 'failed B.A.'—it makes little difference, because the *babu* is not a person but an outlook. No really large organization can function without many blinkered men of his type, who make references and cross-references, check and recheck, refer and confer, and willingly spend their human energy in inhuman exactitude.

The *babus* could of course be fooled in proportion as their knowledge of regulations had atrophied their knowledge of anything else. It was in this manner that the battalion escaped just censure for the loss of a steel crowbar. James reported the loss with an explanation as required, in triplicate, on the appropriate form. The *babus* above bickered for a couple of months about the way he had placed his commas but took no exception to the explanation given—which was that the crowbar had been eaten by termites.

The *babu* mentality in its finest flower, as in the Pursuit of Lieutenant Dishington (an imaginary name), had the eerie, simple beauty of *Alice in Wonderland*. Dishington, who was stationed in Multan, fell in love with a Eurasian girl of that unhealthy place and decided to elope. His first step was to burgle the battalion's treasure chest. Since he was the adjutant, and in charge of the chest, this was easy for him to do. Then he and the girl took a train to Lahore; but his flight was soon discovered, and a major followed them on the next train. In Lahore the major saw Dishington and his girl in a taxi outside Faletti's Hotel. He jumped into another taxi, crying, 'Follow that car!' The hunt led for miles around cantonments before Dishington was at last cornered, arrested, and pried loose from the weeping girl and the remains of the cash.

The major then wrote to the office of the Controller of Military Accounts, the very home and shrine of *babu*-ism, to reclaim the money he had spent in the pursuit. For a few months correspondence shuffled leisurely back and forth in the traditional way: 'Returned for favour of inserting comma after word "seven" by your goodself and oblige . . .' 'Reimbursement claims under authority Financial Regulations 108 (a) (iv) are renderable in quintuplicate. Kindly furnish extra copies and oblige . . .' 'Returned for favour of countersignature, please, by three witnesses vide F.R. 207 (b) as amended Amendment No. 18 of 1908, para 8 (cc).'

The money was in sight when the distant *babu* suddenly came to life and wrote, 'It is noticed that you are major, i.e. Field Officer. Field Officers are in entitlement to Government charger, vide F.R. 1097. Kindly state why Government charger was not used in apprehension of alleged culprit, and oblige.'

The major, breathing deeply, explained (a) that he had not taken his charger with him to Lahore because he did not have time to load it on the train, and anyway there had been no room for a horse in his compartment; (b) that he could not have caught Dishington on a charger because Dishington was in a taxi propelled by an internal combustion engine, which moved faster than a horse.

The *babu*, however, went to the root of the matter in his next. 'Ref your communication of 18th inst to hand. It is further noted that alleged culprit, i.e. Lieutenant Dishington, is Adjutant. Adjutants also are in entitlement to Government charger vide F.R. 1097. Kindly state why Government charger was not used by Lieutenant (and Adjutant) Dishington in alleged flight and oblige . . .'

In his capacity as the colonel's private secretary, personal confidant, and right-hand man, an adjutant had some unusual duties to carry out. Many years before in Bakloh an adjutant named, let us say, Harry, had spent a bad night ensuring that the colonel's children's Irish nursemaid was not frightened by tigers.

There is a phrase book for the use of English travellers in Norway which contains a translation of the following commonplace English sentence: 'See, our postilion has been struck by lightning.' Note that the Norwegian compilers did not regard the statement as vivid enough to merit an exclamation point. Ever since I came across that sentence I have searched for its Indian counterpart, which must surely exist somewhere in an English–Hindustani phrase book: 'Hark, our ostler is being eaten by tigers.' Actually it is uncommon in India to find a tiger in the stables, the bathroom, or anywhere else, without spending weeks looking for one. But each new arrival knows better, and the Irish girl was convinced that a tiger lurked in every rosebush. When the colonel and his wife wanted to go to Dalhousie for the night she absolutely refused to be left alone in the house with the children. (Everyone might not have laughed at her so cheerfully after February 28th, 1938, but this was many years before the Bakloh Tiger.) The colonel instructed Harry, the adjutant, an earnest and virginal type, to sleep in the bungalow that night.

Harry, however, was led into drinking too much at mess by two slightly older and much tougher young men. At about midnight these two thought it was time he went to his tiger-prophylaxis, and escorted him along the approximate line of the path, growling fiercely, while Harry whispered, 'Shhhh, be quiet!' The Irish girl lay on her bed and clutched the sheets, trembling as the roars and hisses moved closer; and she heard heavy bodies trampling in the b :shes. Then all noise stopped for a minute—Harry was taking off his shoes, creeping into the bungalow in his socks. Silence—the girl heard the cautious, menacing *pad-pad* approach, enter her room. Harry had lost his way in the unfamiliar house. The girl froze in mounting terror. Harry tiptoed, *pad-pad*, across the room to where the *ghuslkhana* should have been. He lifted the latch, opened the door, and stepped through.

The snick of the latch filled the girl's lungs with the piercing rhythmic screams of hysteria. The other two officers ran back up the path, yelling, 'We're here!' and, 'What's the matter?' and, 'It's only Harry'; but to the girl the shouts sounded like more roars.

Meantime, it was not the *ghuslkhana* into which Harry had stepped, but a tall wardrobe. He took a pace forward into hanging coats and dresses. Soft, enveloping things brushed across his face and smothered his nostrils. The pandemonium of roars and screams threw maniacal panic into his fight against the whispering, furry dark. He yelled —'*Bawp-gloff-yarrawarra*'—fought madly against the clothes until the wardrobe toppled over, doors down, with him inside it. There was a noise like the Fall of the House of Usher, the bungalow shook, half the ceiling fell, the two officers battered down the front door, and the girl fainted. Flashlights shone in the rescuers' trembling hands and played on an overturned wardrobe that jumped noisily about the floor while some fierce animal inside it bellowed in muffled and almost human rage, fright, and despair.

If tiger-watching was near the verge of an infantry adjutant's duties, horse-riding was unfortunately right in the middle of them. There were few chargers in a battalion, but of these one was allotted to the adjutant. As you know, I do not like horses. It was all very well for Paddy Massey, the adjutant of Hodson's Horse, to curvet past me, his monocle gleaming, on a polished chestnut mare with fiery eycs, scarlct nostrils, and twinkling toes. He sat there at ease like part of a dangerous two-headed animal; but that was his job, and he liked it. I wanted something that would not mistake my peaceable intentions, would not deposit dung between the ranks, and would keep step with my carefully drilled riflemen. I found a horse that satisfied me well. He was tall and old, with feet like soup plates and a Roman nose, and he would not move out of a walk unless I bounced about on his back and jabbed him furiously with my short spurs.

Personally I would not have dreamed of urging him beyond this sober gait but it was the custom, when the colonel arrived on parade, for the adjutant to gallop forward with the parade state. This meant that I galloped up to the colonel, stopped, saluted with the sword, reported the strength present, saluted again, turned my horse, and galloped back to my place. I had some narrow escapes from disaster. Once I leaped up and down so hard in the saddle to make my horse gallop that I lost my stirrups, nearly fell off, quite forgot the parade state, and when I reached the colonel could only stare at him as though mesmerized. Eventually I recovered myself sufficiently to give an imaginary set of figures.

I did manage, however, to avoid a realization of my recurring nightmare, an event I had seen take place in another battalion. That time the adjutant's horse, more fiery than befitted an infantryman, had actually refused to stop. The adjutant thundered up like someone in a scene from *Ben Hur*; his sword whizzed past his colonel's ear; and he disappeared off the parade in a pall of dust, bawling the state over his shoulder as he went, until his voice faded away among the barracks in agonized whimpers: 'Won't someone shoot this —— animal?'

Hodson's Horse was the cavalry regiment in Loralai with us. (A regiment of cavalry does exist; it is the equivalent of a battalion.) Indian cavalry in general we thought of as a government-subsidized polo club, but for Hodson's we developed a great respect. They had the genuine cavalry panache and yet were workmanlike, efficient, and unaffected. In some ways I wished we could have had the opportunity to meet one of the more outrageous regiments, such as the one nicknamed the Hindu Blues. The latter's young men wore their hair long, so that it floated to their shoulders and waved across their foreheads. They were accused of wearing scent and corsets. Their uniform tunics and ordinary sports coats alike hung wide-skirted to their knees and were split up the back to the shoulder blades, with sidepockets dashingly slanted. They liked to pretend they were not Indian cavalry at all but a regiment of the far more expensive British cavalry whose troopers had become a little sunburned. Their mess was like a ladies' drawing-room. They drawled and addressed the Indian servants as 'waiter.'

But we had Hodson's, and after we had worked off on them the joke about the cavalry subaltern—who was so stupid that all the others noticed it—we became friends. I found Paddy Massey had joined in a rather incredulous correspondence with the editor of *The Field* after my tiger exploit, and convinced him that I really had shot the tiger. He didn't seem to care. He was a very tall young man with a face like Punch, the lean nose and chin curving in ready to meet each other.

Later we gave a cocktail party in our mess and Paddy strode in wearing the monocle he occasionally affected, on a wide ribbon of black silk. The anteroom was crowded, and we began to discuss—well, let's say, Jones. Jones was an object of fascination, horror, and unwilling respect to everyone who came in contact with him. He weighed two hundred and ninety-five pounds, drooled round the stem of his pipe, steered his car by wobbling his belly, and was the second-best shot in India. He was notorious for his extravagances, the chief of which were rifles and orchids. They—and he—had been financed for many years by Indian moneylenders, to whom it was thought that he owed about thirty thousand rupees.

Jones arrived. We bid him 'Good evening,' as he waddled in, his little eyes sunk in rolls of fat. After a few introductions, and before I could stop him, he sat down heavily on the sofa. The mess kitten Palmerston's favourite resting place was among the springs inside, and when someone sat on the sofa he stuck his claws up through the covers. This time it was worse. He let out an unearthly shriek as the springs nipped him, and bounded out, bawling and spitting, into the middle of the floor from under Jones's very backside. Any man less generously constructed would have hit the ceiling, and Jones's start was sufficient to raise him several inches before his vast bulk crashed down once more on the tortured springs. Palmerston looked at him in a very marked manner and walked out with his fur up and his tail lashing. I apologized on his behalf, but Jones was chuckling wetly and already talking about something else.

And yet this was the man who one evening invited me round for drinks and started to talk, waddling up and down his study and dribbling as he waddled, about the origins of man. He told me how the site of one of the earliest civilizations had been traced to Baluchistan by the number of cross-breedings found in varieties of wild wheat. He talked about his own archæological explorations, and I was amazed to learn that he went out frequently with a pair of orderlies to dig in the desert for pottery—and found it. He showed me earthenware shards, two sets of pieces a thousand years apart in time. He showed me how the black frieze of realistic bulls on the earlier pottery had after a thousand years become stylized ornamentation. At first glance they had looked to be quite different patterns, but as his thick fingers caressed the shard the lines fell into place and showed the continuity of this desert civilization.

What does a young man make of an old man who was once the Rugby football equivalent of an All-American, whose dreams are of tigers, orchids, larceny, nubile girls, and archæology—a man both ruthless and delicate, sensual and insensitive? Jones should have been a Medici or a Sforza. Whenever I felt repelled by him I put imagined gauntlets on my wrists and a bell'd falcon on one gauntlet. I gave him a velvet hat with jewels and saw him with courtiers, riding a high horse in the morning of the Renaissance, trampling the lilies in an age when all creation was wonderful—all lust, all cruelty, all bravery; the hawk and the dove alike; the swelling breasts of the barefoot peasant girl, the face of the 'Smyler with the Knyf.' . . .

The cocktail party wore to its smoky and desultory end. The seniors went away, and Hodson's subalterns stayed with us for supper. Our respect for them increased when, after we had eaten, we decided that we must for a moment lay down the heavy burden of sophistication and have some horseplay, for they beat us at our own game of mess-mountaineering.

There were two forms of this sport. The first was to race over the roof of the building. After starting at the front door one climbed a tree, leaped from a swaying branch on to the veranda roof, shinned up that, climbed a four-foot vertical stretch of wall to the roof of the mess proper, went over the gable, slid down the other side, jumped the last ten feet to the ground, raced through the building, and touched the front door again.

In the second form the contestants had to get round the walls of the anteroom without touching the floor. This meant a jump from the corner of the mantelpiece to the curtain rod over the door; a difficult pull up to the picture rail; a finger-numbing, arm-breaking grind along that; an easy stretch across the back of the sofa and over a couple of tables; then up to the picture rail again; and so on all round and back to the mantelpiece.

We beat them only at high-cockalorum. In this violent game the first act is to remove spurs. One team then forms up in a row, the leading man's head pushed into a sofa or armchair against the wall, the rest behind him in Indian file, each man bent over, pushing forward into the buttocks of the man in front, with arms clasped round his hips. The attackers line up one behind another, as far away as they can get in the room—or out on the lawn if there is a clear run-in. They then start running forward, all together, to leap in the air and crash down in succession on the defenders. The purpose is to break the human chain, so the

first man of the attackers selects a weak-looking spot—
say, where No. 3 is shoving against No. 2. Clearing Nos.
4, 5, 6, and so on, he crashes down on No. 3's neck. All
the rest of his team lands on top of him. Something is
bound to give; either the chain breaks or the attackers get
topheavy as they pile up on each other, and at last topple
over to the floor.

We and Hodson's bruised one another severely, and we
liked them. It was they who were the chief organizers of
Loralai Week, 1939. In most small cantonments in India
the year consisted of fifty-one weeks and one Week. During
the fifty-one weeks life ran in its normal rut, but into the
Week were compressed many kinds of party and celebration. The average English population of Loralai might be,
perhaps, eight married couples, three grown-up daughters,
six children, and sixteen bachelors or grass widowers. These
proportions, not unusual for a small station, did not give
the bachelors much choice of female company. A committee was formed to make up a programme that would
induce the girls of Quetta, two hundred miles away, to
accept our invitations. The committee deliberated and
came up with a schedule that included a club dance at the
beginning, and a 4th Gurkhas ball at the end, and, in
between, a dog show, a horse show, a crazy gymkhana, two
more dances, a treasure hunt, a ceremonial beating of
'Retreat,' a ladies-versus-gentlemen cricket match, and
several other less highly organized picnics, tea, cocktail, and
dinner parties. Paddy Massey was instructed to produce
girls and went off to Quetta to lay his snares. My colonel
appointed me—naturally, as I was the adjutant—to
organize our ball.

I decided that it should be a fancy-dress ball, and that a
theme should be given. With no great originality, but
because I liked girls in grass skirts, I chose the theme of 'a
lotus-eating Pacific island.' The colonel approved, and we
all set to work.

At this moment Hitler invaded Poland, and England
declared war on Germany. For a moment there was a

pause while we looked at one another and listened. Nothing happened—nothing at all, except that the brigadier told us a German heavy bomber had taken off from Siam in an attempt to fly direct to Persia, and might cross our part of the Frontier. We lay out with rifles for several hours, staring up at the sky and fulfilling a function about as useful as sitting up for a tiger with a peashooter. For the rest there was nothing we could do except wait for orders. It had all been done weeks and months ago. We were ready.

But the brigadier and the Political Agent conferred together to decide whether our Week should be abandoned. Everyone of us expected England to be plunged into a hail of bombs within a matter of hours. The senior generals in Quetta were rumoured to think that the Week should be cancelled as it would give civilians a bad impression of military heartlessness. I think the generals were wrong. We were regulars, and it would have been hypocrisy to pretend we were not happy that hate had at last come into the open, where we could deal with it on the terms that were the basis of our profession. We did not want a war, for we would be the first to die in battle in it, and many of us would die only because the weapons our country gave us were inadequate and out of date. We did not complain unduly at this—it was part of being one of a people who did not plan war but waited to defend themselves until war was at the gate. But now war had come, and now we could justify our existence. So I think the brigadier was right in ignoring the wishes of his superiors and allowing the Week to go on as planned. A wave of relaxation swept over us when we heard of his decision. We had perfect confidence in ourselves, in England, and in the Gurkhas with whom we would have the honour to serve freedom. Hitler could howl and fret. Sooner or later he would come to his reckoning. Meantime, we would finish our game of bowls.

I co-opted the battalion into the preparations for the ball. I had no right to do this but, as I hope this book makes clear, a regular soldier ought not to think over-much of 'rights.' If he does he will serve his country ill and his men worse. The key words are 'duty' and 'self-respect,' and perhaps the latter includes the former.

A couple of days before the ball I showed a puzzled but interested group of Gurkha officers what a lei was, and explained its points of difference from an Indian garland. They went off and explained to the riflemen, who got the idea at once—too well. That night they invaded the officers' gardens and pulled up every flower in Loralai. The owners sent me sharp notes, and I bugled the pack to heel. There still were not enough leis, so one of the havildars suggested they make them out of coloured paper. I agreed; Gumparsad went out to buy the paper; and four hundred men at once set to work, producing several thousand leis in time for the ball.

That time came at last. The guests were bidden for 9.30 p.m. We, as hosts, were ready by nine with quarts of a special cocktail called the Bakloh Bombshell, gallons of champagne cup (six parts of champagne to six of champagne-cider to two of brandy, the whole iced), and scores of records for the club gramophone. In my other capacity as the last flower of the jazz age I had brought along my best Nichols, Moles, Teagardens, and Langs, and a unique collection of Beiderbeckes. Our officers were all on duty as disc jockeys, butlers, barmen, and receptionists. The room was banked with flowers. A platoon of C Company had spent the afternoon rolling french chalk into the floor with beer bottles, which, naturally, became empty. Each of us wore so many leis that only our noses showed, and hundreds more were ready for the guests. Half the battalion, including every one of my 1938 recruits, was crowded round the back of the club, grinning, laughing, and pointing through the windows. I winked at them, for they had plenty to laugh at. Their officers, in torn trousers, flowered shirts, ramshackle topis, and big, neat moustaches, were a crew of hoodlums who bore little resemblance to the beachcombers of Tahiti or anywhere else but looked cheerful and very, very odd.

306

By half-past ten no guests had arrived, we had drunk much of the Bombshell, and I, as master of ceremonies, had started to chew my fingernails. Then miraculously, from a score of dinner parties, they all came in a bunch. The Bombshell spoke—once was enough—and within half an hour the collection of embarrassed English became a carnival riot. Paddy was riding a bicycle round the floor because we wouldn't let him bring in his horse; the Sailor had cut off most of the girls' grass skirts so that they were in panties or wearing curtains borrowed from the tall windows; Ted Royds was hanging upside down by his knees from a tree on the lawn, a position he often assumed in times of stress; James Fairweather, the Lord be merciful, was singing. And so on, and on, and on, till nine-thirty in the morning.

When that hour struck four girls were having coffee in my room, and Bix was attacking the 'Royal Garden Blues' for the twentieth time. We were dishevelled, but none of us was tired and none was drunk. James was not with us. He had stolen a bullock cart from a Pathan and was galloping in a one-man chariot race round cantonments. We saw him flash by, his bright Hawaiian shirt and curly fair hair whipping in the wind as he stood up, shouting, in the rocking cart, while the owner ran cursing and laughing behind. Then we saw my colonel's wife, wearing a nightdress and a coat and riding a bicycle, join James in his chariot race. She pedalled hard beside him, and we wondered vaguely what she was doing. It was an eerie scene in the long shadows of the desert morning—the maddened bullocks, the flapping nightie, the running Pathan, the aloha shirt.

We soon found out that the colonel's wife was asking James what had happened to one of the girls, whom she was chaperoning. The girl was with me. The colonel's wife burst in on us a moment later like a prophetess robbed of a vestal, her young-grey hair and flowing robe adding a proper touch of doom. Perhaps some disappointment was visible in her face, mixed with relief, when she found the girl was not snuggled in my bed and unconscious from drink; but she quickly recovered her temper and joined us in coffee.

Loralai Week was over. Our game of bowls was ended. England had not been bombed. Ben had had a telegram about his brother in the Royal Air Force. I dressed and buckled on my spurs, belt, and sword. I drew the sword to have another look at the inscriptions I knew so well—on one side of the blade: *Capt. A. Masters, 34th Sikh Pioneers, killed in action, Festubert, 23rd Nov., 1914*; and on the other: *Prize for Military History, R.M.C. July, 1934, G.C., J. Masters.* Then I went down to mount the quarterguard.

CHAPTER TWENTY-FOUR

Soon Dewali came, the November holy day and the most beautiful of the Hindu year. Across the stony waste the fort was outlined in lights. Hundreds of little earthenware saucers stood in ranks on each side of the road leading to the big double gates of steel. Each was full of oil, and in each a flaming wick floated on the surface of the oil. Hundreds more twinkled on the walls and on the ground outside the barrack rooms. There was none on the quarter-guard veranda but there were some close enough, by the armoury, to illumine the bronze triptych and bell of the regimental war memorial.

The sentries were at their night posts and dressed in fighting order, for we were on the Frontier, and it was war. They stood half hidden in the shadows, moving little. Their webbing pouches bulged with ammunition, and their swords were fixed. Both of them had been my recruits—Manparsad, who had put the crab in my pocket, and Birkhabahadur, who liked resting in the shade. They half smiled as I walked past them; then their eyes returned to their duty of watching.

The thousands of tiny lights flickered on the faces of men

walking about between the barracks and made them a redder bronze. They burnished with a warm glow each detail of dress, each hard edge of the fort, each crawling loop of barbed wire outside. There was a smell of smoke in the cold air, and the lamps guttered as the men passed them. And groups of men sat on their barrack steps, ringed by the phantom lights, and sang softly. Debsing was playing his accordion among the signallers when I went in, and we hummed together for a little while.

The air thinned and sharpened; a halo grew around each light as the night deepened. Gumparsad came smiling out of the irregular dark, saluted, and walked slowly beside me. He was a man whose honesty of purpose shone through his speech and his silence alike. I loved him and could have hugged him then as we passed together among the singing and the lights.

In the Gurkha officers' club they were drinking rum and talking lazily about the war. They had just bought a radio set and Sahabir was twiddling and pulling at the knobs. His juniors winced in disciplined silence at the cacophonies he called forth.

In the N.C.O.s' club they were playing cards with a muted noisiness, hurling each card on to the table with all possible force in the Gurkhas' customary way.

I walked back alone to the mess. An arc of light glowed in the sky behind me, a fullness of love glowed inside me. Out there in the open a small, edged wind blew on me across the desert. The mountains were hidden by the night.

My fellow officers had all been asked out to dinner. By old custom, when an officer dines alone he is entitled to a free bottle of champagne. A log fire burned high in the anteroom, and it was warm there. Narbahadur and Biniram set a table in front of the fire for me, and I ate my dinner. Then I sent them off to enjoy Dewali and the lights in the fort, and I was quite alone.

There were lights in the Pissarro over the mantel—not our simple patterns but a blurred night sheen on wet pavements in Paris. There were lights in my glass—the ascending, never-ending stream of sparks in the golden wine. The logs burned slowly, dark shifting red, pale red, and static grey. It was warm, and I stretched out my legs. The spurs jingled as I put my feet up on the fender seat. I half closed my eyes.

Palmerston peered out at me from under the sofa, his small head hanging upside down. He slid out, jumped to my lap, and began to play with the looped black cords swirling over the front of my jacket, and batted with his paw at my onc medal. 'N.W. Frontier 1936–37,' the inscription read. He purred in loud fitful gusts. He was a little cat with big lungs and an independent spirit. The wood crackled in the hearth, the champagne fizzed, Palmerston throbbed. I closed my eyes. . . .

On a hot day in those wide, hard places there were mirages—not big or clear ones, just blurred lakes, wavering villages, far mountains brought nearer. The roads led east through the mirages, came at last to the edge of the desert plateaus of Baluchistan, and wound down to the Indus. Standing on the extreme western rim of the country, I looked across the river and across India.

Eastward, past the burning grey scrub of the Sind deserts and the Rajputana deserts, the country grew more fertile. There were the fields and woods of the United Provinces and the steaming fertility of Bengal and Assam. Southward it was the same—desert, then the stony jungles and dwarf teak of the Central Provinces, Deccan trap rock, scattered villages in the clearings, and again lush greenness in Madras. It was a long way from Jiwani to Ledo, or from Travancore to Gilgit, farther in spirit than from Tomsk to Cincinnati, immeasurably farther than from Boston to San Francisco. Were we British the only people who felt the oneness of the land, and that only because all its people shared a common subjection to us?

The line dividing service from dominion is thin and wavering. Some forced their service to the point of domination, and some who thought to be lords of creation ended by sacrificing themselves for their servants. In whatever spirit the tilling, the land was irrigated with English blood. We were none of us quite strangers, nor ever would be. Nor were we at home, as in our own homes. If we loved and served, we were the heralds of some truer service yet to come in the world, running our blind courses in the darkness of our time and throwing a little light in a few places. We were intruders, yet there are illogical necessities in history, which India understands, because India sees no truth in logic. We were imperialists, and perhaps it was for empire that my Uncle Dandy died at Festubert and the Sikhs died across his feet; but the word their bodies formed as they lay in the pattern of death was not 'lead' or 'obey,' but 'give.'

It was five years since I had returned to India—not long, but I could look at India and know what I saw, and know that I did not see one thing but a composition of contrasts in the way that the brain, seeing white, yet realizes that it is looking at a rotated spectrum.

India was matt, grey-green, motionless, flecked here and there with white and red. It was a silence with an undertone of creaking—crackling leaves, whispering grass in the jungle, distant bullock carts—something always moving somewhere, a long way off. It was a smell of hot dust, mixed strongly with wood smoke and faintly with ordure. It was a feel of grit in the teeth, of needing a manicure and a haircut. It was a man of medium height, dark-skinned and with very thin legs, patient, unsmiling, yet ready to smile. It was a building of brick and mud, two-storied, with patches of cow dung on the lower walls and a balcony on the upper story; the building was about to fall down.

At a railroad station were clamour and bustle. People fought to get on and fought to get off; all shouted and gesticulated. It took time to realize that other hundreds sat or lay about, rolled up in sheets, passed around a hookah, and muttered low or did not speak at all. When their train came they too would jump up and rush to and fro.

So I heard at one and the same time the roar of the bazaar and the vast evening silence of the Himalaya. Yet there were corners of silence in the shouting, and across the snowfields the wind bore the distant voices of men and rivers.

The summits of the mountains were blinding white; the sands of the Coromandel Coast were blinding white; the hills dark green, the crops rich green, the jungles hot yellow and brown. But over all, the country was matt and motionless. In all the space there was no aloneness. Try to find it, and a man came out of nowhere with a greeting. But there was loneliness, even in crowds, because each man carried it around with him like a portable tent.

The body tautened in the exhilaration of Punjab cold weather and drooped sullenly in the flaccid pre-monsoon heat. There were wild excitements, pressing dangers, nights of crawling depression. For the unfocused memory there was a feeling almost neutral—but gritty. When the memory focused it had to fix on something definite, and the neutrality faded.

The diverse peoples did not war against one another any more than the mountains warred against the seashore. They lived on different planes. All the people were poor, but all travelled, and each took his loneliness with him. They went to Kashi or the Kumbh Mela or the Pabbi horse fair, and they saw, but they were not interested in what they saw. They saw faqirs and beggars, who were familiar; and aeroplanes and factories, which were not; and they encountered strange religions and fantastic customs, and went home to report that the cows in the Central Provinces were on the whole a few pounds lighter than the cows in the United Provinces. Wars and riots were not usually the result of a striving between men pushing to go somewhere but rhythmic collisions between men doing what they had always done and as regularly crossing the orbit of others doing what they had always done. This was so unless fear was injected. Fear is very powerful when men observe so little that they can believe so much.

I sat up and stirred the fire with my toe. If there was a justification for my family's long guestship here, for my making so free with the Indian wood in the fire, and sitting here with champagne at my elbow, this was it. We removed many fears—for instance, fear of blue-eyed, white-skinned men in ships. Before they had done so, I knew that Indians could now beat Germans.

To hell with justification. Let someone else worry about that. I was in love with India, and she'd have the hell of a job getting rid of me. I was the adjutant of the 2nd Battalion, 4th Prince of Wales's Own Gurkha Rifles, and I had been formed by my blood, my country, my profession, my regiment, and India. There had been mess kit and silver and tradition. I had hunted the wild duck and moved laughing through the corn stubble on winter manœuvres. I had seen that rusty hand, and could see now, my eyes fixed on the fire, the black and gold tiger running close to my left side, the hanging flap of Baliram's face, entrails spewed out over the Frontier's scorching rocks, the breasts of women, and the lotus flowers of Kashmir. A mountain wind drove snow flurries across my memory so that I was back on the little hill-top with the British soldiers. Then there were only Naru and me, climbing the Bakloh ridge, and Christmas lights above in the mess.

Men everywhere—kind men and cruel men. Some women—the Gurkha girl, faces and fingers, caressings and scoldings. The regiment, a part of whose honour I held in my hand. India, which was not my mother but my lusty, disinterested mistress. They had formed me—for what? War was the obvious answer, this war that had begun, for which we were even then making our last rehearsals, standing in the wings ready to take the stage. It was true; but they had also made me a man appreciative of peace, love, friendship, and space.

We were on our way. When we went from Loralai the life we had led would die, never to exist again. Only once more would I move across the mountain with James on my right and John on my left, Naule beside me, Amarsing,

Debsing, Ranbahadur, Balbir, Sahabir, Mangalsing, Bhimsing in their places, with little Dhansing and tall Lalbahadur. This last time was going to be an experience of perfection, for the battalion was on the crest of technical efficiency and spiritual unity. We were fast, flexible, and fit. We were a delicate instrument that reacted to the rustle of a feather. Nothing ever had to be said twice, and no word could be recalled, for with the breathing of it action was completed. The discipline of skill was so ingrained that in the field there appeared to be no discipline. There were no stiff ranks, only carelessly grouped men, but all in the best places for doing whatever they had to do. Every man nourished in himself part of the single, driving confidence of the regiment, which would not brook delay or incompetence, which tore into obstacles and pushed aside difficulties.

The subdued strength, the feeling of power suppressed, was very strong when that last night came. We had joined other battalions from Fort Sandeman and gone north to the borders of Waziristan. Officially it was a routine column, so we were officially playing at make-believe, but on the borders of Waziristan nothing is make-believe. It was not blank ammunition but ball that filled the men's pouches, the magazines of the light automatics, and the long belts of the machine-guns. And it was not the excitement of manœuvres that moved us in quick silence through the night, but the cold tension of war.

We were moving to surround an outlaw's fortress tower. We marched three miles along the road in the darkness, behind a battalion of Indian infantry. A steep-sided gorge, very narrow, came into the road here from the right. Both battalions were to work up this, one behind the other. The Indians were to put up picquets on the mountains on the left of the gorge as they went. We were then to pass through them, turn left, and sweep round in a half-circle back to the road, so completing the cordon. All troops were to be in position by first light, 6 a.m. If all went according to schedule we would pass through the Indians at 2 a.m., which would leave us four hours to cover three miles. We had seen nothing of the country except by study of maps. It was very dark.

We reached the mouth of the gorge at 11 p.m. in bitter cold. I cannoned into a yielding bulk just beside the road and peered a moment before recognizing the vastness of Jones. He chuckled hoarsely and said, 'You'd better not barge into Goering like that, Jack,' and chuckled again.

I whispered apologies and turned right up the gorge. The pace became very slow, and in two hours of shuffling we made a quarter of a mile. At the bottom the gorge was only twenty feet wide, the floor covered in large, loose stones. The sides swept up sheer into the darkness.

At 1 a.m. we stopped. A dense mass of men blocked the gorge in front; we could not move. We stayed there till 3 a.m. Bill Mills, acting as C.O., grew restive. The sharp, cold stones bit through my boots, and my bones stiffened. I made an attempt to force my way forward to find out what was happening, but gave up after half an hour's struggling and cursing among the interlocked bayonets and men. I came back, reported, and said that no one knew what had caused the block.

At about four I made another attempt, taking two orderlies with me. This time we got through. Some stars had come out and I saw that the gorge narrowed still more until the sides were only twelve feet apart. In front of the leading men of the Indian battalion the starlight reflected faintly from black water filling the gorge from side to side. I lay down to look from that level. The water seemed to have no end, and at my feet the stones dropped away very steeply into it.

I stepped in. Sepoys round me cried, 'It is too deep, sahib! We have tried.' I went in to my waist and gasped with shock, for the water was numbing cold. Another two steps and I was in to my armpits. Another two, and the water grew no deeper. Three more; I was out of the pit and splashing knee deep. The water stretched on for a hundred feet, and I quickly floundered through to the far end. It could be done, though I am six feet and the average rifleman just over five feet.

Coming back I hugged one side, thinking to have a handhold in the deep part, but there was a pothole there and I went in over my head. I struggled out at last, shivering and retching, and sent the orderlies with a message to Bill to say the way was clear and to keep to the middle of the water.

Below the numbed surface the driving force in the battalion surged into action. Down the gorge I heard a crescendo of clinking, crashing, and cursing. Soon the Gurkhas began to arrive. Some trotted down the middle of the gorge, treading heedlessly on feet, faces, and stomachs, and, when they reached me, crashed like porpoises into the water, drove on, and surged out at the far end. Others traversed the cliff faces, twenty to fifty feet up on each side. I heard the quick, irregular *clink-clink* of their boot nails on the rock and could just make out their backs as they scrambled along. I couldn't have done it—nor could our sub-assistant surgeon, two hundred pounds of Indian plainsman, but the Gurkhas picked him up by main force, passed him from hand to hand along the cliff, and at the end dumped him like a huge sack of potatoes at my feet.

Nothing could stop them. Men fell from the cliff into the water or on to the rocks. Men slipped and broke their ankles. Men came near to drowning—but still they went forward, and faster still, in silence, water streaming from them, and blood running from long flint slashes.

Precisely at 5 a.m. all company commanders had reported to me that they had arrived. Hurriedly Bill talked over the situation with me. We turned our minds back two and a half years to the night march to Boya. He decided that the only thing to do was go all out for our objective, and to hell with form, formation, and orders. He himself would keep his proper place with battalion headquarters, just behind the leading company. As adjutant, I should have been with him, but I asked him to let me lead with the compass. He nodded. Now we had fifty-five minutes, not four hours, to cover three miles of big country at night.

At five minutes past five I started up the first hill, the luminous compass in my hand, my mind counting the short paces I was taking and roughly estimating them in yards. When I topped the ridge, into a wind that knifed through my wet clothes, I could see by the spacing of the men immediately about me that the battalion must be badly spread out. But I could not afford to worry about that. I switched to a compass bearing of 320 degrees magnetic and moved down the slope as fast as I could in the starlight. Far ahead I could see nothing, but under my boots I felt the ground was loose shale, a perfect surface for glissading if it was steep enough. I jumped out over the black slope, turned sideways, and slid down forty feet at a time in a continual flurry of stones.

It was not fast enough for the Second Fourth Gurkhas. To right and left the men caught up their distance from far behind, and black groups of them swished past in cataracts of stone so that the whole hillside moved and quaked. When I reached the bottom most of the battalion were waiting for me, eddying about in a tangle of men, eyes, and gleaming teeth, breathing a little hard. I trotted off again, still at 320 degrees, over a stony valley and two low, rolling ridges. Up again, down another steep shale slope, again the runaway herd of madmen, at the bottom a worse tangle than ever, utter confusion. I ran on.

A few minutes before six o'clock I was running due west along the back of a broad ridge. It might be the right one, or it might not. My compass reading had been rough, and though the map had given me a good idea of the ground I had had no time in this furious scramble to stop and make any checks. We were all running now, a big marathon field under paling stars, and then I thought we were there.

Bill came forward. Without orders or warning, company commanders came forward. Out of chaos their companies suddenly materialized with them. Miraculously grouped, they ran on or swung off the ridge crest into reserve in the

318

hollows. It was just light enough to see that their faces were covered with a light sheen of sweat, and their clothes dark with wetness, but that they were not tired. They were hard, concentrated, and utterly confident. The Number Ones of the light-automatic teams, each carrying a gun and two hundred and ten rounds of ammunition, sixty-five pounds in all, trotted past, bowed under the weight but steady and unconcerned. Everyone knew where he was, where he was going, and why.

The running figures dropped out of sight, and suddenly there was no sound, no movement. Below in the valley the tower began to loom out of a low ground mist, and it was forty seconds to six o'clock. I fumbled awkwardly at my haversack. Naik Dhansing of the buglers was laughing and fondling a leveret he'd caught during our crazy stampede. He tucked it gently into his shirtfront, undid my haversack with strong, sure fingers, and handed me the Very pistol. It was ready loaded with one red cartridge, the success signal. I cocked it. I looked at Bill, and he nodded. (Close to the north, close back in time but far in the journey of the spirit lay the first blizzard, the first hill-top, the young man from Sandhurst.)

I waited with the exact insolence that was the regiment's pride until our synchronized watches pointed to sixty seconds past 5.59 a.m., and fired the pistol. The leveret's wide eyes dulled with fear, but Dhansing whispered comfort to it, and the light flashed with a whoosh up into the pale sky, a trailing ball of red fire, to tell the brigadier, India, and the world that nothing had stopped us, nothing could stop us. We were ready.